CONSPIRACY
OF
GRACE

CONSPIRACY OF GRACE

A *wild* TALE OF TRANSFORMATION

DALE FIEGLAND
WITH ROBBI CARY

HILLTOP
HOUSE PUBLISHING

Conspiracy of Grace: A Wild Tale of Transformation
Dale Fiegland, with Robbi Cary

Hilltop House Publishing

Copyright © 2020 by Dale Fiegland and Robbi Cary

Printed in the United States of America

ISBN 978-0-9893754-3-6 (softcover)
ISBN 978-0-9893754-2-9 (eBook)

All rights reserved solely by the author. The author guarantees all contents are original and do not infringe on the legal rights of any other person or work. No part of this book may be reproduced in any form without the permission of the author.

All Scripture quotations, unless otherwise indicated, are taken from the Holy Bible, New International Version®, NIV®. Copyright ©1973, 1978, 1984, 2011 by Biblica, Inc.™ Used by permission of Zondervan. All rights reserved worldwide. The "NIV" and "New International Version" are trademarks registered in the United States Patent and Trademark Office by Biblica, Inc.™

Scripture quotations marked (CEV) are from the Contemporary English Version. Copyright © 1991, 1992, 1995 by American Bible Society. Used by permission.

Scripture quotations marked (ESV) are from The Holy Bible, English Standard Version® (ESV®), copyright © 2001 by Crossway, a publishing ministry of Good News Publishers. Used by permission. All rights reserved.

Scripture quotations marked (GNT) are from the Good News Translation in Today's English Version- Second edition. Copyright © 1992 by American Bible Society. Used by permission.

Scripture quotations marked (MSG) are taken from THE MESSAGE, copyright © 1993, 1994, 1995, 1996, 2000, 2001, 2002 by Eugene H. Peterson. Used by permission of NavPress. All rights reserved. Represented by Tyndale House Publishers, Inc.

Scripture quotations marked (NHEB) are from the New Heart English Bible. Edited by Wayne A. Mitchell. Public domain.

Scripture quotations marked (NLT) are taken from the Holy Bible, New Living Translation, copyright ©1996, 2004, 2015 by Tyndale House Foundation. Used by permission of Tyndale House Publishers, Inc., Carol Stream, Illinois 60188. All rights reserved.

Scripture quotations marked (Phillips) are taken from The New Testament in Modern English by J. B. Phillips, copyright © 1960, 1972 J. B. Phillips. Administered by The Archbishops' Council of the Church of England. Used by permission.

Scripture quotations marked (Voice) are taken from The Voice™. Copyright © 2012 by Ecclesia Bible Society. Used by permission. All rights reserved.

Author's Notes:

To protect the privacy of individuals, some names have been changed.
These include counseling clients, friends in Romania, and Mafia connections.
I give special acknowledgment to Alcoholics Anonymous (AA).
Their teachings, which are all based on Scripture, have influenced my life
and this book and come through years of meetings, sponsors,
the AA Big Book, other reading materials, and its sayings.
I have tried to attribute credit in numerous places that resonate with AA's materials.

This book is dedicated with endearing tenderness to my wonderful wife, Karen, who has given me love and grace in generous measures—pressed down, shaken together, and running over.

In addition, this book is dedicated to my children, their spouses, and my grandchildren—all of whom I dearly love. May you be blessed in knowing more of my story, God's grace, and all that He has done for me.

Finally, I dedicate these pages to many friends and counselees who have blessed my life and have asked for my story.

Contents

Foreword ix
Preface... xi

Section One: BEGINNING YEARS

Introduction: A Rocky Path................................... 2
Chapter 1: Shaped by Pain 4
Chapter 2: Snapshot Memories................................. 9
Chapter 3: Mountain of a Man................................ 13
Chapter 4: The Wrong Crowd.................................. 19

Section Two: MOVING ON

Chapter 5: Trains & Trouble................................. 28
Chapter 6: College Daze..................................... 33
Chapter 7: The Teacher Learns 46
Chapter 8: Transitions & Family Memories 55

Section Three: STARTING OVER

Chapter 9: I Surrender...................................... 66
Chapter 10: A Flophouse & a Feather 76
Chapter 11: Marriage Mess................................... 84

Section Four: NEEDING GRACE

Chapter 12: A Messy Baby Christian 90
Chapter 13: Grace Gifts Everywhere.......................... 98
Chapter 14: Steps on the Road of Grace 108

Section Five: GOD'S PLAN FOR GOOD GIFTS

Chapter 15: Smoking Surprises & Everything's New!.......... 128
Chapter 16: God's Crazy Pastor Plan........................ 138

Chapter 17: God Wants Me to Love Him............................147
Chapter 18: Potatoes & Grace 154

Section Six: HEALING GRACE

Chapter 19: What's Low Worth Got to Do with It?..................168
Chapter 20: Jesus, Prayer Miracles & Peace......................179
Chapter 21: God's Crazy, Relentless Instructions 192

Section Seven: RELENTLESS GRACE & MORE MIRACLES

Chapter 22: People, Bumps & Bruises 206
Chapter 23: A Love that Transforms 211

Section Eight: ALWAYS MORE OF GOD

Chapter 24: Good to Go!...226
Chapter 25: God's Not Done......................................236
Acknowledgments...245

Appendix

Appendix A: Cleveland & Hopping Trains 248
Appendix B: The 12 Steps of AA 250
Appendix C: 12 Step & Counseling Resources.....................251
Appendix D: Thoughts on Enjoyable Living & AA 253
Appendix E: Scripture on Being Fully Loved, Forgiven,
    Accepted & Complete in Christ.............................258
Appendix F: Scripture on the Blessings of Being Humble
    & Confessing...260
Appendix G: Scripture on Being Conformed to & Transformed
    by Jesus 262
Appendix H: Scripture on God's Proof & Evidence 264
Appendix I: Scripture on End Times & Good Things to Come........266
Topical Index 269

Foreword

Years ago, when I pastored Riverside Church at its Tarpon Street location, I met Dale Fiegland, a Christian at this point for several years. Normally quiet and unassuming and frequently around church, I watched him lovingly care for people. If someone needed a ride, groceries, or a place to stay, he would stop what he was doing, offer help and give encouragement. Dale ministered to a wide range of hurting souls, including addicts, widows, parents who buried children because of their drug addiction, and children who lost addicted parents.

While his care and ability to assist in tangible ways was remarkable in any setting, it became even more surprising after Dale shared a few stories with me about his past life: his rough early years and abuse, how he grew up on the mean streets of Cleveland and ended up as a Mafia runner and enforcer. Not only did one man from those years declare Dale to be the meanest man he ever knew, but statistics today state that, given his harsh experiences, he should have been dead or in jail. As you will see God had different plans for this alcoholic brawler that came with more than one miracle.

During my time as pastor, Dale stood out as a servant-leader, especially in our culture of self-important, glory-seeking personalities. He never seemed to need a title, status, or recognition, but simply served God and others, whatever the task. While I was at Riverside our property included several houses, which were primarily used for Sunday school classes. Because they sat empty during the week, the staff began letting Alcoholics Anonymous and Alateen use them. As you can imagine, proper church folks quickly grew upset at the sight of recovering addicts smoking outside "on church property!" I often gave a sharp rebuke such as, "Well, it's either smoking for now, or they spend an eternity in hell if we don't help them find God." Meanwhile, Dale would be picking up cigarette butts and talking with the addicts.

Thanks in part to our location in the older, more run-down part of town, Riverside attracted many people who hadn't grown up in church; they had known only a harsh life and had the rough edges to prove it. But no one surprised or flustered Dale. He is a Clint Eastwood-type counselor—not shocked, frightened, or put off by anyone. I sent many troubled, hurting individuals his way when they needed special care. In Africa, the Maasai tribe describes their bravest warriors as being able to "run to the roar." That describes Dale perfectly.

He personally helped me years ago when a bedraggled man, Bob T., showed up off the streets, claiming to be my father (in actuality, stepfather). Growing up, I had lived in at least six foster homes and had about as many stepfathers. Numerous men and women blew into my life, blew it up, and then blew back out. Bob T. was one of these—quiet as a lamb when sober, violent and abusive when drinking. As a teenager, more than once I stood between him and my mother, Louisville slugger in hand as I hollered, "No more of that!" I was none too pleased when Bob showed up out of nowhere one day, mired in one of his needy phases and begging for help.

Knowing the inner struggle I faced, especially because God tells us to honor our parents, Dale said, "Jay, let me help." He took it on himself to love, care for, and minister to my stepfather even when he was old, crippled, and broke. Dale took him into his home for several years and cared for him as much as he could until Bob died on an obscure side street. Since I was away conducting a crusade, Dale concluded by giving Bob an honorable funeral service.

Dale has never forgotten what it's like to be alone, abandoned, and abused. With kindness and love, he is quick to help others and weep with those who weep. Yet he also loves a good laugh. Dale lives and shares God's grace and truth.

—**Dr. Jay Strack**
Author, Speaker, and Pastor
President and Founder of Student Leadership University

Preface

Pastor Dale is a counseling pastor and—among those who know him—a unique and almost indescribable figure. He has experienced more in his lifetime than have several people added together. When you combine his wild experiences and God-given wisdom, you end up with this book.

It has been a blessing to help Pastor Dale tell his story, because he made a profound difference in my life and, consequently, the lives of my family members. When life dealt our family a series of difficult blows, I wanted to fix the problems or spiritualize them down to a more manageable size. Because I had no idea how to deal with my feelings, the stress affected me physically. Pastor Dale helped me slow down, acknowledge my pain and fear, and then seek God. As I did these things, I was able to know God and His help—in very real ways—in the difficulties. For this, I am forever grateful.

Besides being thankful to again work with Pastor Dale, listen to him share, and take in more of Jesus's grace and truth, it is my fervent hope that many others will be blessed through these pages. Some of the details of his life may sound like a fantasy or a movie but, I assure you, they are true.

Those who seek Dale's help already know, or quickly discover, that he isn't your typical pastor. Carol, one of his counselees, said it well. When her friends gave her a hard time for talking with a pastor, she told them, "Dale's sort of different. He's not like any pastor you've met before. Well, he's not like any Christian you've met before. Come to think of it, he's not like anybody you've ever met before."

When a doctor, Pete Daws, came to him for help, Pastor Dale asked him the reason for his visit. Dr. Daws replied, "The word on the street is that you understand, and you shoot straight with people."

In these pages, you will see these aspects for yourself. Dale's sort of different, but always shoots straight. He is God's Word on the streets of life. Along with this, he is down-to-earth, real, salty, and always full of Jesus. He is honest about his foibles, shortcomings, and sins, while his love for God shines bright. Through Dale's story, we can clearly see God's forgiveness, love, and new life that He wants to give each of us.

Sometimes, when I walk away after another uplifting chat, I smile and think, "What a difference a Dale makes!" I pray that Dale's story will make a life-changing, very real Jesus-difference in your life, too.

—**Robbi Deborah Cary**

Section One

BEGINNING YEARS

Introduction

A ROCKY PATH

I'm always surprised by how much God loves me, how much He wants to bless me, and how much He wants me to know Him. But it's not because I have lived an easy life or a good life. My life was a wreck—filled with painful and sordid problems—some caused by others and some I caused myself. Still, throughout my life, I felt God pursuing me while I ran from Him.

God in His grace thankfully placed enough roadblocks and difficulties in my path that enabled me to surrender and call on Him. When I surrendered, He rescued me and brought about miraculous changes to me and my life! Then, He used every pain and problem for good purposes.

I'm astounded when I think about what God has accomplished in me and my life. For years I have called it *a conspiracy of grace*. While a conspiracy normally is a plot to bring someone down, God conspires amazing plans for our good.

One day, I looked up *conspiracy* in my old dictionary and found something like this: a covert plan and agenda, concerning a person and situation, in order to promote a selfish interest. This thought—that God has a selfish interest in me—caught my attention.

In fact, the Lord keeps showing me this. His love is very real, active, and personal for each of us. It's not generic and bland; rather, it is a dynamic, daily love. God's Word explains that He has such a passionate interest in us, He is jealous for us (Exodus 34:14 and James 4:5). God loves us, desires to give us great blessings through Jesus, and wants us to know Him and love Him back.

There is a problem, though. This world is incredibly broken, with all sorts of chaos, conflict, sin, and ugliness, which seem to be increasing the deeper we walk into the twenty-first century. These broken, fearful things make God's love seem difficult to comprehend and sometimes nearly impossible to receive, which is why we need Scripture to explain everything to us.

The word *conspiracy* also brings to mind intrigue, pursuit, collusion, and danger, which are all part of my story, too. While I ran from and resisted God as He pursued me, besides roadblocks, He kept putting Jesus people in my path. He seemed to love to do this, even though Jesus people weren't to my liking at all.

So this is my story. It's one of fighting God and losing, and then surrendering to the Lord and winning. It's a story about how much God personally loves each of us and how He wants to do the impossible in us and for us—but first, we have to call on Him. Then we are to grow in knowing and loving Him.

While I share my story, there are things I have done that I'm not proud of, but I include them, so that you may know the truth about my life and just how much God has done for me. I hope you see God's deep love for you, too, and His mighty power to help.

In the New Testament, we are told about a man named Paul. Although he was an elite member of the ruling Jewish followers of God, his life was messy. He thought he was living for and pleasing God by persecuting the strange new sect known as Christians, but the Lord captured his attention, caused him to fall to the ground, and told Paul it was Jesus he was persecuting. Once Paul recognized who Jesus is, and the plans God had for Paul's life, then, God used him greatly (Acts 9).

I agree with Paul, who, as his ministry grew, said something like, "Whatever I am now, it's because God has poured out much grace on me. I still need a lot of grace, and I know God will continue to provide this, too" (1 Corinthians 15:9–10, my paraphrase).

I pray that through my story, you will experience Jesus's presence, grace, and truth, and when you're finished reading, you will seek to know Him more and live for Him.

Chapter 1

SHAPED BY PAIN

Dad's favorite method of punishment for me was beatings, often down in the basement, with a leather strap. Both my parents also hit me with coat hangers, two-by-fours, or anything else they happened to have in their hands. I bear scars from the physical abuse. In addition, I endured put-downs and belittling names from them, which were as emotionally painful as the beatings were physically.

Even though Dad was smart, witty, and enjoyable to be around when he wasn't angry or drinking, he was a raging alcoholic. Every night, starting with dinner, he drank a case of beer—twenty-four beers in all—while his rage became more violent and unpredictable. He needed only about four hours of sleep a night, which gave him plenty of drinking time. This was his pattern from as far back as I can remember—work hard all day, drink hard at night. People outside of our family thought Mom was a mild-mannered sweetheart, but she, too, had a violent streak.

So I lived with emotional and physical pain, as well as an ever-present tension and fear from either the latest violent episode with my parents, or dreaded anticipation about what might happen next. All of these—Dad's drinking, my parents' abuse, screaming, anger, and the feeling that I didn't matter—were always with me. My brother, Larry, who was four years older than I was, and my much younger sisters, Judy and Linda, would all be products of this crazy-making environment.

Because of my parents' unpredictable rages, I gravitated to my favorite uncle. I loved Mom's brother dearly; he made me feel important and valued, told me funny and wonderful stories, and regularly brought me gifts. Then, when I was five, his supposed love turned dark, and he sexually abused me. After several incidents, I told my mother what he had done. Bursting into a rage, she began beating me until I was black-and-blue. The whole time, she cussed, yelled, and said I was lying.

While the sexual abuse stopped after I told Mom, the combination of that abuse, and Mom's not believing me, calling me a liar, and beating me added to my pain. I felt shameful, damaged, and dirty; unloved and unprotected; alone and crippled with despair.

My desire to defend and protect myself and my longings for relief from the pain became driving forces in my life. I was five and couldn't literally run away, but I sought every way possible to fight for myself and escape my hurt. Besides fighting every way I could, I discovered that daydreaming brought relief from my pain. As I grew, so did my fighting and daydreaming.

A HERITAGE OF PAIN

My family was filled with brokenness. There were probably numerous reasons for Dad. Like many of us, he experienced his share of pain while growing up, which he tried to stuff down. Struggles in the U.S. Army, which I'll share more about later, and an affinity for beer sparked his descent into cigarettes and booze.

Both Mom and Dad's parents all emigrated from Germany to America in their midtwenties, though each arrived separately. (I heard much German spoken during my childhood, with Grandma Keen throwing in some Yiddish.)

Dad's father, Gustav Fiegland, went by Gus. Gus's parents both died by the time he reached six, leaving him an orphan. Family members frequently shared tales of how he had no shoes and ragged clothes, and grew up wandering from farm to farm, begging and working for food. They said that it was a wonder he survived at all. He managed to come to America, arriving with twenty-five dollars in his pocket. Once here, he began working long, hard, backbreaking hours shoveling coal for fifty cents an hour. Gus met an attractive girl, Ottilie (pronounced "O-tee-lia") Lau, through relatives at their German church. "Grandma Tillie" was gentle and spiritual, although she struggled with worry. Despite a brood of five children, Gus and Tillie scrimped and saved to buy a sixty-acre farm. My father had fond childhood memories of walking to the barn at sunrise and asking his father for a squirt of fresh milk into his little cup from Daisy, their dairy cow. However, the dire economic collapse of the Great Depression ripped the farm from their grasp. Gus had always struggled with the loss of his parents; now he had to deal with another great loss and start over again. To survive, he moved the family to the big city of Cleveland, where they settled into a two-room shack near Schaaf Road,[1] doing all they could to eke out a living. My siblings and I repeatedly heard the story of Grandpa Gus running home one day to get Dad and his little Red Flyer wagon to retrieve a discarded cast-iron bathtub on a rubbish pile about a mile away in a rich neighborhood. After loading the tub onto the red wagon, they excitedly hauled it home and refurbished it, thrilled to have a bathtub.

Years later, Tom Brokaw's best-selling book, *The Greatest Generation*,[2] helped shed more light on my father's life. He was part of the generation of Americans who were deeply affected and shaped by the difficulties and sacrifices needed to survive the Great Depression and then World War II. Members of Dad's generation not only survived—they thrived through hard work, perseverance, ingenuity, courage, and great patriotism. In turn, they helped forge America into a great nation.

Dad never shirked responsibility. He worked long, hard days, never complaining. He wasn't afraid to get dirty and could outwork just about anyone. When he had his own employees, he was strict and demanding, yet worked alongside them so that many would return over the years to visit him as a friend. He made do, resourcefully sacrificing and scrimping to not merely survive and provide for his family, but to conserve resources for emergencies, get ahead, and save for the future. Dad was certainly a mixture of good and bad.

---

1 Cleveland, by the early 1900s, was known as the Greenhouse and Tomato Capital of the United States. The business started on Schaaf Road, in the village of Brooklyn Heights, when Martin Luther Ruetenik grew five acres under glass. The industry grew, ultimately to four hundred acres. A fleet of Ford Model Ts distributed the tomatoes to places as far away as Indiana and Pennsylvania.

2 Tom Brokaw, *The Greatest Generation* (New York: Random House, 2001).

A VARIETY OF INFLUENCES

My mother's parents, Gottlieb and Emma Keen, met in their homeland. When his parents didn't approve of Emma and tried to end the relationship, Grandpa decided to follow his dream and come to America. However, he kept thinking about Emma. After writing a letter home, inquiring about her, he was surprised to discover that she was living in Waterbury, Connecticut! That sparked many letters between them and a courtship by mail before she moved to Cleveland. A wedding soon followed.

Grandpa Keen's last name had been Keühn, with German umlauts over the letter *u* and pronounced "Cue-in." Because Americans always pronounced it "coon," he changed it to "Keen." His first name, Gottlieb, means "God's love." It fit him well.

Grandpa Keen was the preacher for our small German congregation at the Daisy Avenue Church of God. A bivocational pastor, he worked in the White Sewing Machine factory during the week, preached every Sunday, and handled church business matters at night and on the weekends.

While Grandpa was a positive influence during my troubled childhood, our small church where I first learned about religion leaned toward legalism, which didn't leave much room for gentleness and grace. I constantly heard rules: "Do this," and lots of "Don't do that." Besides no smoking or drinking, we were not allowed to dance, bowl, or go to movies (not even *Lassie*). Legalism demands harsh conformity to rigid rules that seem to breed more rules. It is a lifeless, joyless form of religion that rarely attracts others. While trying hard to be spiritual and righteous, in truth, legalism kills the spirit of grace and people's spirits.

One time, when I was very young, I sat next to Mom during a church business meeting when the men were trying to decide where to hang a clock so Grandpa would know when it was time to stop preaching. People were arguing from all sorts of viewpoints, including whether or not it was too worldly to hang a clock in the sanctuary. The disagreement grew so heated that two men broke out into a brawling fistfight right next to the pulpit. Mom yanked me up by my arm, started cussing up a storm, and dragged me out of the pew, down the aisle, and out the door.

We didn't attend church for a long time after that incident, partly because Mom felt people didn't treat her father kindly. Although most people liked Gottlieb, many complained—both to him and among themselves—about his wife's rudeness, his children's excessive drinking, and that he wasn't doing enough to control his family.

Still, I know that God's conspiracy of grace included Grandpa Keen in my life. A humble man of God, he brought a refreshing breeze of comfort, compassion, and love to me. He never gave me a stern lecture about what I should or shouldn't do, or reminders of my many destructive choices. Eventually, he would offer me a choice and a way out of the ruins of my life.

But first, a long, bumpy, painful journey stretched out before me.

Chapter 2

SNAPSHOT MEMORIES

A postwar baby born in 1947, I grew up in Cleveland, Ohio, in the fifties—a great time to be a kid. Despite my chaotic home and the many troubles that plagued me, my childhood included fun memories.

Until I turned five, our milk still arrived by horse and wagon. Barney was our milkman. Max, his horse, pulled the wooden, creaky wagon for Producers Milk down our block on Colburn Avenue. Everyone in our neighborhood loved Barney and Max. Barney would park Max and the wagon, grab a metal milk container in each hand—each with eight bottles of milk—and deposit the correct number of bottles into the galvanized box on each customer's porch. When he had emptied his containers, Barney would whistle for Max, who trotted down the street to him. They would repeat this process for the next set of houses.

On hot summer days, my friends and I followed them down the street, stealing ice chips. In winter, the clip-clop of Max going down the street would often wake me. Later, I would go to the front porch, brimming with anticipation. If it had been cold enough to snow during the night, the cream on top of the milk would freeze and make the cardboard lids pop open, having made nature's version of ice cream—a tasty and tempting treat. As a young lad of three or four, I remember giving in to temptation, even knowing it would mean a beating.

The first day that Barney had to drive his new truck instead of driving Max and his wagon, he was not happy. Now after delivering the bottles, he had to walk back every few houses to get his truck. Learning some new words from Barney that day, I went home and shared with Mom, "That damn truck is ruining my life." Mom washed my mouth out with Lifebuoy soap for that one.

BALONEY SANDWICHES AND TRICYCLES

We loved our neighbors and our neighborhood, where everyone knew one another and there was a warm sense of community. We lived in the downstairs portion of a two-story duplex. Our landlords, Mr. and Mrs. Dorner, lived above us. The spaces were so close and the walls were so thin, it seemed if they sneezed, we could say, "Gesundheit."

One day, while hurriedly riding my tricycle home for my lunch of fried baloney, I cut right through Mrs. Goldberg's flower bed. My double back wheels cut a wide path of destruction. Mrs. Dryer, our neighbor, saw me, grabbed me off my tricycle, and spanked me for trampling her friend's flowers.

Our telephones were the old-fashioned, candlestick model that was common until the 1940s. You spoke into the transmitter at the top and held the receiver to your ear. They featured a party line, which meant several families had to share and wait their turn for time on the phone, but news could still travel quickly on them. Having already heard about my dastardly deed when I limped in the house, Mom spanked me again and made me go apologize to both Mrs. Goldberg and Mrs. Dryer, who first spanked me.

FEATHER BLANKETS & FUTURE SNAPSHOTS

One of my favorite experiences as a little boy was staying at Grandpa and Grandma Keen's house. I loved waking up to the smell of bacon and eggs frying and the smell of their wood-burning stove. Nothing tasted better than Grandma's cooking on that stove.

Their house, like everyone else's, had no air-conditioning or central heat. Instead, in the winter, they used a wood-burning stove in the kitchen, a potbelly stove in the parlor, and cozy feather blankets in the bedroom to keep warm. One cold night, after brushing my teeth, I came out of the kitchen and saw a scary-looking witch with no teeth and long gray hair down to her ankles, standing there. I froze on the spot, and then started screaming and running all the way to my grandfather's bedroom and jumped under the feather blanket. Shaking, I told him about the horrible, long-haired witch with no teeth in the parlor. I can still hear Grandpa roaring with laughter. Grandma never believed in cutting her hair, and I had seen her only with it up in a bun. Until then, I hadn't known about false teeth, either.

Saturday nights were bath nights and not to my liking at all. The old metal washtub was brought into the kitchen, and then Grandma would stick me in it. I shivered in the cold metal until she took nearly boiling water from the reservoir on the side of the wood-burning stove and poured it in. If that didn't almost take my skin off, the scratchy Fels-Naptha soap and hard-bristle brush seemed to finish the task.

When I was four and Larry was eight, Dad and Mom bought fifty acres in the country, near the Cleveland suburb of Parma. Dad was designing the house that he would build for us. On the weekends, my parents loaded Larry and me into our 1939 Chevy Coupe and headed to the property to clear the land. They returned to the car one time and found me lying on the running board, unable to stand up; I had found an open bottle of beer and polished it off. My parents laughed at their cute four-year-old drunk and snapped a picture, which they loved to show everyone.

Still, more often than not, this feeling of fighting for survival followed me everywhere. I was determined to stand up for myself and prove I wasn't small and weak. Even in kindergarten. During recess one wintry day, we had a great time playing in one of northern Ohio's frequent snows. After coming in from the fun and frolic, I was first to get in front of the radiator to dry off my cold, very wet corduroys. Just then, a classmate, George, stepped in front of me, blocking the heat. Determined to show him, I shoved him hard. He went sprawling, hit his head on the radiator, then lay motionless on the floor in a puddle of blood.

Our teacher, Miss Scott, came back to investigate the commotion, saw all the blood and George lying motionless, and fainted. The next thing I remember, the principal was standing in the doorway, while the whole class shouted, "Dale did it!" I thought I had killed two people and was going to jail.

I didn't go to jail, but I quickly earned a reputation. The next year, on the first day of first grade, my teacher greeted me with a big smile as I entered the room. When she asked my name, I told her, "Dale Fiegland." Her smile turned to disgust as she snapped, "Your desk is right here next to mine, so I can keep an eye on you. I've heard you're a troublemaker. Sit down. I don't want to hear a peep out of you."

I couldn't help it. From somewhere inside of me, I had to say, "Peep!"

Once again I was off and running, trying to prove that I could stand up for myself, while at the same time living up to others' low expectations. George and I did end up becoming friends, though. Years later, I would rub the scar on his head and say, "You know, George, you helped start my career as a troublemaker."

It seemed I couldn't stay out of trouble, whether at school or at home. Even my father's example and instructions to be hardworking and industrious could send me in the wrong direction. He was always giving us jobs and responsibility as soon as he thought we could handle them. Every other day, Dad bought two cases of beer and turned in the old bottles. When I was six, he showed me how to retrieve twenty-four beers from the garage and put them in the inside refrigerator to chill for his evening binge. During my eight trips, I carried the empties out to the case in the garage.

Shortly after this, in addition to stocking his beer, Dad gave me another job. He showed me how to get firewood from the garage and keep the wood bins filled for each of our four fireplaces, which roared throughout the winter. The large woodpile in our spacious, two-and-a-half-car garage ran its entire length and was stacked six feet high. While doing my jobs one day, I wondered what would happen if I hid a bottle of beer in the woodpile. I was surprised—Dad never missed it!

That inspired another idea: I could sell beer to my older brother's friends. Prior to this, they considered me to be a pest, but now I achieved newfound popularity. Whether hanging out or camping in the woods on our property, they would frequently ask, "Hey, little shit, want to come along?" For years this seemed to be my name.

Chapter 3

MOUNTAIN OF A MAN

My father, Reinhold Arthur Fiegland, stood six feet, four inches tall. On the job, he liked to be addressed as R. A. He was the owner-operator of the Brooklyn Excavating Company, which designed and built parks for cities in the Greater Cleveland area. Dad had a small fleet of heavy equipment and a large workshop, where he and his men worked on the machines or various projects. Late at night, Dad was often the one repairing bulldozers or dump trucks, so his crew could be on the job early the next day. In fact, Dad began his business when he put together a bulldozer after buying it in several large wire-wooden crates on a skid-equipment trailer. His brother-in-law thought he had lost his mind and the money, but later he said, "I can't believe it. Reiny made it work and started making money from it right away!"

Intelligent, witty, and a perfectionist, Dad was also an avid reader who studied subjects that interested him. He was always busy building, repairing, or designing something. He could lay foundations, do finish carpentry, electric work, lead his own band—and more.

It took him a year to build our house on the fifty acres in the country. We moved in when I was five. The year was 1952. Our house was beautiful, unique, and filled with Dad's craftsmanship, containing such special touches as outlets under the eaves with switches on the inside of the house, so that we could turn on our Christmas lights without going outside. He transformed the property as well, turning a rubbish-filled ravine in front of our home into a large, beautiful lake with an island in the middle. In winter, all the neighborhood kids came over to ice-skate and play hockey on it, although they eventually insisted Larry and I be on opposite teams to keep the games fair.

Thanks to its picturesque qualities and being featured in Cleveland's home section of the newspaper, our home was visited regularly by folks who snapped pictures of our front yard, the lake, and our three swans: Gus, Matilda, and Hilda. That is until Hilda was run over by a car. While not a religious man, Dad thought it was a sin to waste anything so, in second grade, I took swan sandwiches to school for lunch. (If you're wondering how they tasted, pretty tough is what I recall.) After that, Dad added a nice wooden fence to protect Gus and Matilda from the same fate.

All the parks that Dad built gave him the inspiration to turn our property into a recreational park. We would offer swimming and picnicking for an entrance fee or annual membership, and rent out the park for special events. We designated five acres around the house for our yard, which left forty-five acres for the park, a spring-fed lake, and parking. Because we lived on Pleasant Valley Road, we named the park Pleasant Valley Lake.

Dad surveyed the property and found a small, wet depression indicating a fresh spring. He tied a red bandana to a nearby tree, saying, "This will be the top surface of the lake." It was taller than I was! The lake was about five acres in size and ten-to-twelve-feet deep. He even engineered a dam, so the lake could be drained every year and refilled with fresh water. This meant that he could change the lake's depth or the placement of the lifeguard docks, diving platform, and slide.

Dad's men, with bulldozers and dump trucks, worked hard to clear the land. Massive trees were transformed into things like eight-foot-long parking bumpers or picnic tables so big they took four grown men to move. To cut the wood, Dad fashioned a homemade sawmill, made from a diesel engine and leather straps. Once the workers skinned the bark off the logs, many were soaked in large homemade vats filled with creosote to prevent the wood from rotting. The vats were made from galvanized sheet metal, salvaged from somewhere.

After two years of preparing the lake and buildings, we opened the park in 1956. Every year, we were open from Memorial Day in May through Labor Day in September. Seven days a week. Saturday and

Sunday, we opened at 9:00 a.m. Weekdays we opened at noon. Every night we closed at 9:00 p.m.

The Cuyahoga River, which runs through Cleveland and into Lake Erie, was known for years as a fire hazard. Industries dumped their wastewater into it and people (even in the 1950s) would boat out onto the lake, take their garbage with them, and simply dump it there. It's no surprise, then, that our clean, clear, spring-fed lake proved very popular with families and young people. Dad had the entrance-gate employees track cars with manual clicker-counters and was thrilled every time we had one-thousand-car days!

WORK & PLAY

As a hard worker, Dad expected a lot from us. Whenever he was working on anything and Larry or I was around, he expected us to pay attention, anticipate what tool he needed next, and hand it to him. He didn't want to have to say, "Hand me the socket wrench." It didn't matter how many different wrenches were on the cart; we had better know which one he needed.

When it came to the park, Larry and I were the janitors and cleaning crew. Every morning before it opened, either before school or before we could play on the weekends, Larry and I had to pick up trash and clean the park. We quickly learned that whether on cleaning detail or not, we had better never step over a piece of trash. Mom taught us how to clean the combination restroom-bathhouses to Dad's specifications. For some reason, cleaning the bathrooms became my responsibility. On the days the Red Cross held swimming lessons at our lake, I had to clean them twice. By age nine, I was an expert and in charge of them.

Our concession stand sold soda, pizza, ice cream, candy, and cigarettes, all for a healthy profit. Employees, including my brother and me (once we were old enough to work at the stand), were allowed three free items a day. No one better take a fourth, because Dad always knew.

Dad was a good musician. He skillfully played the saxophone, clarinet, piano, and organ. He formed his own polka band and built a bandstand at the park, occasionally playing there with his band. They also performed at many weddings around the Parma and Greater Cleveland area. Indeed, this was how Dad made his living in the winter. Though a self-taught keyboard player, he hired the owner of a music store, Norm, to give him saxophone lessons. Poor ol' Norm always seemed to get attacked by our swans on his way up to our front door.

Besides these interests, Dad loved gardening, which he took up a notch or two. He tended two greenhouses, a large one out back and a smaller one near our kitchen door; composted his own soil; and experimented with plants, later selling them wholesale to our local Kmart and Topps stores. He loved growing corn on the cob but, once again, was a fanatic. We had to have the water boiling and be ready to sit down to eat dinner before we went and picked the corn because: "Every minute the corn is off the stalk, it is losing flavor!" We all gave Dad a hard time for this one.

TALENTED & TORMENTED

Hardworking, intelligent, creative, driven, and a tormented man. Dad wasn't always that way. His sisters—Betty, Thelma, Elsie, and Frieda—all had only good memories to share about their brother.[3] As a young man, he was charismatic, outgoing, and thoughtful, as well as tall, slender, dark-haired, and handsome. Everyone looked up to him. He was also known for being able to easily start a crowd laughing with his sense of humor.

Alcohol didn't enter his life until the army. Grandpa Keen once told me, "Before the army, your dad never drank or smoked, but after he got out, he drank like a sailor and smoked like a chimney."

Although he never experienced combat, the military affected Dad in several ways. Drafted right before the end of World War II, he was older than most other recruits were, and sadly had to leave behind his wife and a young son. Then, being older than the other men, he was the one they picked on. When his platoon was marching or on field maneuvers and took a break, every man smoked, except Dad. The men gave

---

[3] All dad's sisters were younger than he was and, at the writing of this book, Betty, Thelma, and Elsie are doing well. They range in age from their late eighties to midnineties.

him such a relentlessly hard time about it that he gave up fighting them and started smoking. On top of this, the army's odd ways frustrated Dad. Once, when his company was on a snowy, wet overnight field-training exercise—sleeping in pup tents—an officer strongly reprimanded Dad for stuffing newspapers in his uniform and sleeping bag to keep warm and dry. It made no sense to him why such resourcefulness would be scorned.

Finally, another incident proved quite unsettling. Because he was of German descent and spoke German, several superiors brought him in for intense questioning over several days: Did he have any allegiance to Germany? Would he mind going over there and killing Germans? What if they were family members? On and on it went for days.

Ultimately, Dad experienced some type of a nervous breakdown. The military gave him a medical, honorable discharge and sent him home. Over the years, we saw some letters from his friends that mentioned how it was a shame he received such a raw deal.

After World War II, Dad couldn't really talk about his inner demons and hurts, which included his desperate attempts to escape the poverty and hopelessness he had experienced as a child. While he relentlessly pursued success and achieved it, becoming successful in the world's eyes, he fell victim to the grip of alcohol. It was sad, watching an otherwise-talented man drink himself into hysteria and be robbed of his good nature. Gentle and fun during the day, he was rage-filled and uncontrollable at night.

I still remember the time as a boy when he forced me to throw my teddy bear into the coal furnace and made me watch it burn. Another time, he killed and cooked my pet rabbit for us to eat for dinner one night, even though he raised rabbits and we had a few hundred. (Years later, he told me, "I thought I needed to help you learn to be a man.") Added to all of this, my siblings and I were only disciplined in anger. Certainly whippings are traumatizing; but even when you're little and screamed at by adults, you are flat-out terrified.

Years later, when Larry was the first to achieve sobriety, we tried to help Dad realize that he was an alcoholic, but he replied, "That's impossible. I go to work every day, and I'm successful. You have to be on skid row to be an alcoholic." (I would learn later that just 3 percent are skid-row types; 97 percent of alcoholics function at various levels.)

Dad tried to be stoic and deny his feelings, but once he started drinking, there was no telling what would catapult him into a rage. Mortal fear was our constant companion. My sister Judy told me there were times she thought Dad was killing me in the basement during those beatings. Some nights she crawled into bed with me as a young child, trembling with fear. She became a perfect, good kid, which is better than getting into trouble all the time, yet it brings its own problems. People freeze up and shut down emotionally for fear of messing up.

Dad delivered harsh treatment to Mom, as well, although she never bore any bruises from it. Once, I came into the living room looking for her, and found her hiding behind the couch. She called the police on Dad a couple of times, but he had a friend who was a cop. When that friend showed up on a call, it didn't go well for her. My parents always seemed to be caught up in conflict and anger that boiled over into harsh yelling and screaming, which affected everyone. Sometimes it would simmer for weeks, with no direct communication between them, but lots of sulking, and pouting, and taking out their anger on us kids.

My parents never apologized for their unpredictable, excessive behavior. Mom's ego seemed too fragile to admit any wrongdoing and say she was sorry. Plus, the church doctrine she learned as a girl taught that once you're saved and a Christian, you're sanctified, sinless, and you can't do wrong. This attitude is certainly not helpful in relationships. When we were older, we tried pointing out her flaws, but she denied everything. Dad seemed to feel remorse, but he handled topics indirectly, saying things such as, "Oh, I guess you had a bad time last night." I wanted to say, "Yeah, because you beat the crap out of me," but knew better.

While Larry was passive, lay low, and stuffed his feelings, more often than not I had the tendency to say what was on my mind and fight back, which got me into more trouble. In fact, standing up for myself would eventually be what caused me to move out at the age of fifteen.

Chapter 4

THE WRONG CROWD

Because tension, fear, and feeling that I never belonged were always with me, I longed to find peace and acceptance somewhere. The place I felt accepted was the gym—a boxing club for boys and men, amateurs and professionals. It was located on Cleveland's West 25th Street in an old, yellow-beige brick firehouse.

Larry took lessons at this gym, and his buddies pestered me to start taking lessons, too. By the time Larry was in high school, after training diligently, and honing his skills, he won the state division of the Golden Gloves and qualified for a tournament in Chicago. While I was scrappy, ran track, and took gymnastics, which made me more agile, I never advanced to Larry's level. Instead, I excelled at street fighting—because there were no rules.

Johnny Avon, known as Avon, was our well-known and well-liked trainer-manager, whom I liked also. After I trained and fought for a while, Avon would tell me, "Dale, you don't go into a fight fully engaged until they bang you around a bit, and then you get angry and are out for blood. A lot of guys don't think well when they get angry in a fight, but you do."

Because Larry and his friends were older than I was; because of my training and fighting at the boxing club; and because of my self-protective, rebellious streak, by the time I was twelve, I was hanging out with a gang of rowdy older boys from the gym. These kids came from rough families and tougher neighborhoods. One day they broke into homes and told me to be the lookout. When they were done they divided up the loot among us, which was mostly random, dumb items and liquor.

A few days later, while I was sick at home watching TV, a knock sounded at the door. When I answered, two plainclothes detectives with badges stood there and started asking me questions. Knowing this wasn't going to go well and wanting to put it all behind me as fast as I could, I immediately confessed and offered to get the loot from my bedroom. The deputies found out that my dad was in his workshop, and one went to get him. He returned with my father, who was beyond irate, as he yelled and stomped around the room.

Sitting in court before the sentencing, with my heart pounding, I cried out to God under my breath: "Please God, help me. I'll be a good boy, if You help me." It wasn't the first or the last time I prayed this and God granted my request. The judge, after sentencing each of the three boys to reform school, had them whisked out of the courtroom and on to their destination. When he got to me, he said, "Six months of probation," released me into the custody of my parents, and the gavel sounded.

Needless to say, my parents were deeply ashamed of having a troublemaker for a son. When it hit the paper, they hated it even more, telling me, "We can't face our neighbors." As a youngster, this made no sense to me because they hadn't seemed to be overly fond of their neighbors. Because I felt I was a burden to them and in the way, I preferred being anywhere but home.

GOOD LESSONS

Besides our connection with the Church of God, our community brought exposure to other faiths, particularly Catholicism. Numerous parishes, including Irish, Italian, and Polish Catholics dotted our area. The Holy Family Catholic Church was nearby and, though not a member, I participated in its Catholic Youth Organization (CYO), which hosted fun activities for neighborhood children. These events included swimming at the quarry, watching movies in the theater (like *Gone with the Wind*), going to the music hall for concerts, and attending a few carnivals they hosted. I liked all the pretty Catholic girls who were in the group, but every time I would ask one out, after asking her parents, she would come back and tell me, "I can't date you. You're not Catholic."

Complaining to a priest one day, I inquired flippantly, "What does it take to be Catholic?" He told me about a six-month catechism class that I could take and then be confirmed in the Catholic faith. It didn't sound too hard, so I signed up. Taking it seriously, I asked questions in class, read the assignments, and completed the homework. When I told my mother what I was doing, she wasn't happy and said, "You can't become Catholic—they don't even read the same Bible we do."[4]

Well, I had to see this for myself! I read through the Bible twice—reading a book at a time—first from the Protestant Bible, and then, from the Catholic version to compare. Since this happened around the same time as my arrest, Mom let the issue drop—at least I was reading the Bible!

I finished the class and was confirmed. While my life didn't profoundly change, God planted spiritual seeds of truth in me. These truths from the class made an impact on me:

- I gained a reverent respect for God and His church.
- I began to understand some about our shortcomings and sins before God, as well as the need to confess them and receive forgiveness.
- I came to understand that God provides proof and evidence, so we might know Jesus is God's Son; He is who He claims to be; and He is the way of salvation.
- Proof includes many amazing predictions about Jesus, His miraculous birth, and His life and death. Precise facts were incredibly proclaimed centuries before His birth and seemed impossible to come true, but were fulfilled just as God declared they would be.
- Much proof can also be found by examining the miracles Jesus performed and what He said and claimed, along with the events of His life, death, and resurrection.[5]

---

4 We'll see that the key issue we face is grander and more important than Catholic, Protestant, or which denomination we follow.
5 For a few verses regarding God's proof and evidence, see Appendix H.

ON THE RUN AT FIFTEEN

Still, these truths and head knowledge weren't enough to keep me from a downward spiral, which picked up momentum in my teenage years. One day at home, things boiled over when I arrived after a long, intense boxing workout at the gym. Famished, hot, and worn to the bone, I barely made it in the door when Dad, in a rage, came charging at me—yelling and calling me names because I had left some of his tools out, instead of putting them away. He shoved me backward and slammed me hard into the wall.

Instincts and three years of boxing training took over. Without thinking, I jabbed him with two lefts to his nose, followed by a hard, right uppercut to his chin.

Even though I stand only five-foot-seven, all six feet and four inches of Dad caved to the floor; his nose was broken and bleeding profusely. Mom was screaming. I knew this wasn't going to go well, and I needed to leave.

Quickly throwing some clothes into a duffel bag, I caught a bus back to the gym. That night, after the gym closed, I climbed in through a locker-room window. The accommodations weren't too bad—I could stack up mats for a bed and even shower. After a few nights, I tried staying with Larry, but that didn't last long; he had just gotten married, and his couch wasn't all that comfortable. I went back to the gym.

Avon came in early one morning, caught me, and was not happy, but he listened to my story and predicament. He responded, saying, "Well, you can't stay here, but I know a place you can." With that, he drove me to The Bird Cage Lounge, a bar and strip club. The manager of the nightclub, Antonio, frequented the gym, so we had met occasionally. He had a spare room upstairs at the club and agreed I could stay there if I cleaned the place every night and kept the upstairs, where the girls stayed between shows, clean. No problem. I was good at cleaning bathrooms and messes.

Some men I knew from the gym also frequented this joint. They were part of the Cleveland Mafia and liked this young boxer they saw with a chip on his shoulder, who handled himself fairly well in fights—both inside and outside the ring. Before long, they started asking me to run errands for them and pick up and deliver packages. Not only did they pay well, but I felt important hanging around them. Plus, it was exciting going to places with names like the Blue Angel, the Thunderbird, and Pete's Wayside Inn. I even saw famous people (such as Frank Sinatra in the back room). The stories seemed like scenes out of a movie. For instance, one of my Mafia bosses lost a leg in the war at Iwo Jima. Now he had a hollow wooden leg and kept his gun there.

At first, I enjoyed the acceptance and camaraderie I felt with these men, who seemed like a special group to me. Additionally, in this environment with the skills I was gaining, I was looked on as a young man of worth and this, too, felt good.

WHICH FAMILY?

While Dad and I hadn't spoken since our fight, Larry and I saw each other often. He started asking me to come to Thanksgiving dinner. I knew the invitation was coming from our parents, which reflects our family's broken, indirect method of communication. Hopeful, though, I began stopping by Dad's shop to work on my car. As he and I talked about vehicles and mechanics, the ice slowly thawed between us.

Thanksgiving! What an exciting day as I anticipated a reunion with my family and a delicious dinner! Everything went well until we sat down at the table—and I asked somebody to "pass the butter," adding a foul expletive. Dad stood up and declared, "You need to leave." He walked me to the door, and before closing it behind me, tersely said, "Don't come back."

As I walked outside, sadness and anger at my own stupidity overwhelmed me. I kicked myself over and over, saying, "What a dumbass I am." Hanging around shady characters all the time, I had no idea how crude even my everyday language had become.

Although I was filled with disappointment regarding my family and the separation, my Mafia bosses kept taking me under their wing. One day my boss said to me, "You know, son, a man is judged by his clothes, his shoes, and his handshake." Handing me a one-hundred-dollar bill, he told me to go to his tailor on nearby Short Vincent Street, buy some new clothes, and tell him, "Antonio sent me."

Short Vincent Street was a unique experience in itself—a slice of now-vanished Americana history. While officially named Vincent Avenue,

Short Vincent Street was known by this legendary, descriptive nickname because it was only one block long. As the hub of downtown Cleveland's nightlife, it acquired a romanticized image, thanks to the restaurants, bars, and nightclubs jammed into its few hundred feet and the people who were seen there. The street was famous and attracted citizens and tourists, as well as numerous mob bosses, underworld figures, and gamblers. More respectable establishments were on the north side of the street, while more randy burlesque venues were on the south side. We called the Gay 90s a "high-class joint." The Roxy, a famed vaudeville theater, was nearby and where many well-known singers (such as Judy Garland and Dean Martin) performed. Famous people were seen in the audience, as well. I always entered the Roxy by going down the alley to the back door and waiting until someone came out. The street bustled at night with people and activity, while large neon signs practically filled the evening sky, blinking their welcome and the attractions they offered.

The tailor, after outfitting me with new pants and a new shirt, told me to go next door to the shoe shop and, after that, the hat store. When this whirlwind fashion tour was complete, the outside of me had been transformed.

I stepped out onto the sidewalk in black, shiny Florsheim shoes; black pleated trousers; a white-on-white, short-sleeved shirt; and a black fedora-style hat. Snazzy, the picture of prosperity, and ready for my life and activities on Short Vincent Street! This became the outfit I wore everywhere. Later, in the winter, I would add a white silk scarf and a jacket, which I always kept unbuttoned.

At my home, which was now The Bird Cage Lounge, I had only a hot plate for cooking. Fortunately, I landed a side job at the nearby Pearl Ridge Tavern—cleaning up the kitchen and bar, and polishing the beautiful, but extensive, woodwork with Murphy's Oil Soap. The owners, Stan and Rosa, took a

Granddaughter Kayla Nipper's drawing of her Grandpa with his fedora and a suit and tie liking to me and allowed me to cook my meals there. Sometimes, I cooked dinner for them, along with their friends, making them tasty feasts—like corned beef, onions, and potatoes.

One night at The Bird Cage, a drunk was trying to pick a fight with everyone. I ended up taking him on, when he pulled a knife on me. I did all right for myself, but later one of my bosses came to me and said, "Next time, son, here's what you do." He showed me how to hyperextend and quickly break someone's arm. After this night, "bouncer" was added to my list of duties at the bar.

During that first year, one of my bosses gave me a gun, casually remarking, "Here, just in case you need it." From then on, somewhere on me, I always carried both a knife and a gun. After a while, they decided I would make a good "enforcer." So, I began collecting money for loan sharks and bookies. Sometimes, the bosses would arbitrarily levy taxes on businesses, such as telling the owners of high-rises that they needed to pay a "window tax" on every window in their building. My job was to convince the owner it was a good idea to pay it.

Like everything I tried, it all started out with a sense of excitement and potential, but only left me feeling emptier and dirtier than before. With an increasing roster of duties, I was continuing to be drawn deeper into this criminal lifestyle of immoral and illegal activities. Pursuing what I thought were the pleasures of life and trying to receive a pat on the back had me on a slippery slide, feeling worse, but what could I do? There seemed to be no hope for this mess I was in. How could I possibly get off this runaway train that I was on? And where was it taking me?

Section Two

MOVING ON

Chapter 5

TRAINS & TROUBLE

The year after leaving my parents' house, I landed in trouble again, while out drinking with my buddies. We had let some air out of my tires so we could get my car, a 1955 Ford Fairlane Crown Victoria, a fifties-style, boat-size sedan, onto the train tracks to play "chicken" with a locomotive. A freight train was now speeding toward us, but we had let too much air out of the tires. I was trying, with all my might, to pull my tire-size steering wheel (with no power steering) hard enough to get my car to jump the tracks, but it wasn't happening as we anticipated it would.

Why I risked my life and my car to do something so stupid is still beyond me. Especially because I loved my car. It was the debut model of the Ford Fairlane, the behemoth style so common in those post–World War II years. My sweet thing was painted Mustang burgundy and had a tachometer, which let me wind smoothly through all three gears. I covered the steel dashboard with a genuine black bearskin (from a bear shot by my Uncle Bob), and installed extra gauges and cherry-colored ambient lights under the dashboard. She was a beauty.

1955 Ford Fairlane Crown Victoria

As the mammoth monster of a train steamed closer, my buddies bailed out of the car. I never saw "Tank" move so fast. We called him that because he was a big hulk of a guy. He was sure running fast that day. My friends told me years later that I looked like Evel Knievel, the famous motorcycle and stunt-car performer, as I sped up faster toward the freight train to gain traction to pull off the tracks.

The truth was—I was sick with fear. Some people who have lived through near-death experiences describe seeing a bright light at the end of a tunnel. I saw a bright light all right, but it had a freight train attached to it, with an abundance of sparks spewing from its wheels and an eerie screeching sound coming from its brakes. My grandpa's familiar warning rang in my head: "Your life is a train wreck waiting to happen."

I think I gave myself my first hernia by pulling the wheel so hard to the left with every ounce of strength I could muster from my hands, arms, and stomach. Just when I thought for sure I was dead, the Ford jumped and jostled free of the tracks and slammed into a pile of nearby railroad ties. I felt the whoosh of the train as it half-roared, half-screeched past, with horn blaring and cries of "Idiot!" echoing from it.

Heart pounding, I sat there dazed and fuzzy-headed, trying to get my bearings, when I realized my nose was broken, and I was bleeding all over myself. Managing to push my bent door open, I got out and proceeded to get sick as I listened to the sirens getting closer.

Standing there, wobbly-kneed, I'm sure I was a sight to behold when the cops arrested me.

THE GAVEL SOUNDS

Once again, standing before a judge, I was pleading with God, "Please help me," and promising Him that I would be good if He did. First, the judge ordered me to pay for new wheels for the train because the other wheels were flattened from the engineer applying the brakes, for so hard and long, to try and stop the train and avoid a collision. The new wheels cost a thousand dollars—a sum that felt as if it would take me forever to pay off![6]

For the second part of my sentence, the judge gave me a choice—sixty days in juvenile detention, or six months of Alcoholics Anonymous

---

6   For a few short, interesting stories about trains and Cleveland's train station, see Appendix A: "Cleveland & Hopping Trains."

meetings. Wow! This was easy. I was excited thinking, *AA can teach me how to drink and not get so drunk!*

Later, sitting in my first meeting, listening to others share their stories, I thought, *I'm so glad the judge let me come to AA. This proves I'm not an alcoholic; these people are sick and need help. Thank goodness, I'm not as bad as they are.*

It isn't surprising I felt this way. I had erected numerous defense mechanisms to protect myself from rejection and emotional pain. Smoke screens of denial, dishonesty, and rationalization kept me blaming others and from accepting the truth about myself. Sadly, this state of denial would be my residence for years to come. While the Bible tells us that we're blessed when we know our true condition and how much we need God (Matthew 5:3; Psalm 34:18), I wasn't anywhere close to this. Unable to admit my brokenness, fear, and shame, I tried to cover them up by wearing a tough-guy façade—all in an effort to display to everyone and myself, "I'm fine."

After six months of court-mandated AA meetings, I hadn't changed. Not a lick. My thoughts were still, *I'm glad I'm not as bad as they are. Those people need help.* Consequently, I couldn't get away from AA fast enough. Because I couldn't see or admit that I had a problem and, because I didn't even attempt to work any of the program's steps, I continued traveling on my bumpy road of ruin.

This bumpy road stretched far back into my life. Though it seemed funny at the time, there was my drunken encounter at the age of four. By the age of eight, I was drinking regularly; by twelve, I had added pot to my repertoire. By fourteen, I rarely showed up at home on the weekends, drank heavily, and was suffering from a bleeding ulcer. I tried drinking scotch mixed with milk to ease the pain, but it didn't help. When I started throwing up blood and stripped the varnish off the floor at our house, Mom took me to see Dr. McGill. He put me on baby food for six months and gave me a pill that I had to take hourly, around the clock. (Yes, you read that right.) Fortunately, following this regimen for six months, coupled with God's grace, brought me a miraculous healing. The ulcer never returned—which is especially amazing, considering that one of my uncles would die from a perforated, bleeding ulcer.

A SICK PERSON

Now eighteen, and in my senior year of high school, the question was—would I graduate? My grades weren't the real problem. I was making mostly Cs and Ds, although I could earn an A when I liked a class. It was my life that was pulling me down—working as a Cleveland Mafia enforcer, frequenting joints and back rooms, and living on my own.

The excitement had long since worn off. My tasks on the weekends had grown increasingly gruesome and exacted a physical and emotional toll on me. By Mondays, I was so sick, drained, and unable to function that I usually couldn't make it to school. My attendance record was spotty, to say the least.

Even though the things I was doing turned my stomach, I didn't know how to break free from this life. My intense sense of shame competed with my great longing for acceptance. These conflicting values drove me into convoluted loops, creating a crazy-making cycle and a confused mind-set that left me unsure about what was right and what was wrong. I had a driving need to prove I was right, even when everything about my life was wrong. Determined to prove my worth, I kept on the same track, even though what my Mafia bosses asked me to do repulsed me. Additionally, my shame grew every time I accepted money, gifts, and praise for doing these terrible things. This merry-go-round of people-pleasing and activities to numb my shame—money, success, sex, and food—were all driving forces in my life. They were entrenched idols, to which I clung, despite their negative consequences. Though now a full-blown addict, I was blind to the reality. I now know, like many survivors of abuse, I tended to stay in relationships and situations in which I could use my survival skills, instead of risking further hurt and abandonment by leaving or changing directions.

My perception of life was faulty, broken, and based on lies. I believed my approval and worth depended on my performance. Additionally, my screwy thought process and life experiences made it more difficult to trust others, including God. This was the God whom I heard so much about while growing up and who was the focus of these AA meetings. How could anyone ever love and accept me, especially God?

GRADUATION DRAWS NEAR

With graduation fast approaching and my attendance record full of a mountain of unexcused absences, my teachers formed a committee to determine if they would allow me to graduate. Strangely, I saw a number of them at the same hangouts where I worked and I think they knew I was on my own. Taking a vote, they all agreed I could graduate. This was certainly grace because shortly after I graduated, the Ohio legislature passed a law mandating the number of classes that students must attend to receive their high-school diplomas.

In the midst of this, I faced a serious choice: attend college or be drafted and most likely go to Vietnam. Some of my friends had already gone to Vietnam and returned home in body bags. I decided to try the college route. However, when I shared this with my school counselor, she laughed and replied, "You need to be a bricklayer and join the union." Her condemnation flashed like a neon sign: "You're not good enough. You're not worthy." But it fired up my anger. I would show her! She was wrong. This was certainly more evidence of God's conspiracy of grace; for once, a negative event gave me momentum in the right direction.

Surprisingly, I did end up laying bricks in college as one of many side jobs. Every time I thought of my teacher's stinging rebuke, I resolved all over again to prove my worth and succeed at college.

Chapter 6

COLLEGE DAZE

Somehow I scored well enough on my college-entrance exams to earn admission to Kent State University, located less than an hour southeast of Cleveland. My plans seemed to be in place—until I received a message from Mom that Grandpa wanted to see me about something important.

When I arrived at Grandpa's house, he told me he missed me and was happy to see me, as he poured us both a glass of Kool-Aid, which he always kept in his sparsely stocked refrigerator. Then we headed to the parlor with the potbelly stove, chatting about what I had been up to lately and my college plans. Along the way he slipped in the question, "Are you still hanging around with that bad crowd?" Ignoring his pointed inquiry, I shared that I had been accepted to Kent State.

"I'm proud of you," he replied. "I'm really happy that you're going to college. I always wanted to go. Besides your dad's sister, Aunt Thelma, who's a nurse and we're all proud of her, you will be the first in our family to graduate from a four-year college. You've already proven yourself, making it through high school on your own. I know you will do well." Inwardly I beamed at Grandpa's confidence in me and his compliment that I was smart.

After a pause, he asked, "Would you consider going to a different college? I've been praying about this and want to help you financially." Now, I loved Grandpa dearly, but he was poor. And once again, I was puzzled. He lived in what I considered an old, run-down shack, with potbelly stoves for heat and no air-conditioning for the summer. From what I saw, he had little material wealth, yet he had a reputation for regularly helping others. Why didn't he help himself? It was a mystery. Because of this, his offer shocked me. Knowing he didn't have much money to spare, I asked, "What's the catch, Grandpa?"

"Well, there is one condition," he admitted. "I want you to go to Anderson College. You know it's a small Christian college in Anderson, Indiana. The people you hang around with aren't good for you. This college and location will be a better place and influence for you. I'll pay for your tuition and board." (Grandpa was familiar with the college because of its affiliation with our Church of God denomination. Today, it is Anderson University, although it still has fewer than three thousand students.)

Wow! Not only could I use the financial assistance, but it was thrilling to think that I could escape my current circumstances and be able to start a new life. My situation had become dire. I had come too close to seeing two murders. The aftermath left me sickened, struggling, and feeling as if I were being caught in a prison with the doors clanging shut. This college news was terrific!

"Grandpa!" I exclaimed. "Are you sure? Yes!"

Before I left, we chatted some more, and I gave Grandpa a big "thank-you" and a hug.

No sooner had I applied to Anderson College than they sent me an acceptance letter on the condition that I arrive sometime during the next couple of weeks and start the summer session. This was even better! I could leave right away. While preparing that week for college and for moving to central Indiana about five hours away, I notified my Mafia bosses about my college plans. Not only did they like that I was going to college (they were always seeking legitimate businesses and partners to cover their criminal enterprises), but they encouraged me to contact their associates in a nearby town, with even stronger Mafia connections, if I needed any help.

A SHOCKING START

Driving out of town, giddy with excitement to start my new life, I'm sure I put the accelerator down so hard that I left skid marks. I was free!

However, my feelings were short-lived. Each day, for my first three days of college, held its own stunner. On my first day, a school official informed me that students were not allowed to curse, smoke, or drink alcohol on campus. All students had a curfew. I didn't know what a curfew was, but I quickly found out. Students had to be in their rooms by 10:30 on weeknights and midnight on weekends! I couldn't believe what I was hearing. But that wasn't all. To top off my misery, freshmen couldn't drive their cars on campus. I had to turn in my keys and license plate to the dean.

It didn't take long to start breaking these rules. On my second day, I was being fined twenty-five cents for every curse word I uttered (a quarter was worth a whole lot more back then), and a dollar for saying "Jesus Christ."

I quickly made friends with Gary, a tough guy down the hall, who was struggling to conform to these stupid rules, too. Gary grew up on Chicago's South Side (infamous for being tough and mean). For the past four years, he had been an enlisted serviceman in the US Air Force. Once he earned his degree, he would return as an officer and become a fighter pilot. On our first evening as buddies, Gary and I began going to the cemetery next to the church for a smoke and drink. Technically it was off campus.

On the third day, after finishing my classes, I paid my obligatory fines and headed for the cafeteria. Standing in line, waiting for the hamburger I ordered, I was fuming and wondering what I had gotten myself into, mumbling to myself, "This lifestyle is going to be impossible." After taking a sip of my Coke, I was about to set it down on my tray when a student walked past and bumped my arm, causing me to dump my drink on a pretty young lady next to me.

Automatically I hollered, "What the f--- are you doing?" You could have heard a pin drop.

Everyone in the cafeteria turned and stared at me. Completely embarrassed, I wanted to run out of there, but I also wanted my hamburger, so I stood there, trying to be invisible. Suddenly, one of the school's preacher students came up to me, grabbed my left hand, knelt down, and started praying out loud, saying that I needed Jesus in my life.

"Hey, Preacher Boy," I snapped. "Let go of me."

He squeezed my hand tighter, prayed louder, and with even more passion. Not knowing what else to do, I walloped him with my right hand. As he collapsed to the floor, out cold, I lit out for my dorm room, hungry, embarrassed, and angry.

Gary, hearing me come into my room, came over. When I shared what happened, he said, "C'mon, man, we've got to go to the cemetery." That sounded good to me.

Just then, a knock sounded on the door. I opened it, and one of the dorm residents told me that he needed to escort me to the dean's office. When we arrived, I took a seat. Practically shaking, I thought, *Man, I really need a cigarette and a drink.*

After the dean called me in, he asked me if I thought I was pretty good at "fisticuffs." I told him I wasn't sure what that meant.

"Well, I see here in your file that you did some boxing."

When I replied I had, he told me that he enjoyed boxing in the navy, and we talked a bit about the sport. Then he asked what happened in the cafeteria. I told him everything. As I finished, I asked if his "Preacher Boy" was going to pay a fine for saying "Jesus Christ."

"No, son," the dean said with a smile, "although he was very wrong in what he did, and I expect him to apologize to you. However, you cannot go around campus hitting people. I understand how embarrassed you were, but I can't condone what you did. I must place you on probation."

It was dawning on me that college, unlike high school, wasn't going to be a breeze. In fact, one of my first mandatory classes was called "How to Study." It shocked me to discover how much I didn't know about studying.

AN UNCOMFORTABLE INVITATION

As a Christian school that produced a flock of preachers, Anderson required every student to attend chapel services twice a week. After a few, I started skipping them and was placed on disciplinary probation to go with the one for fighting. That didn't bother me until the dean called me in and threatened me with expulsion if I didn't attend chapel. Now I had to listen to the gospel being preached.

Although I was still resisting God, I was learning truth along the way. The word *gospel* literally means "good news." God is perfect and holy and gave us His perfect righteous law. All of us have broken His law and fall short of His glorious standard. God declared that the person who commits sin and breaks His law deserves punishment, is separated from Him, and will die this way, but God didn't stop there. The gospel is the good news that God loves us and sent Jesus to pay the debt each of us owes for our sin, dying the death we deserve and, if we accept and receive His gift, He gives us a new life, along with a new heart, a restored relationship with Himself, and spiritual blessings. It takes a lifetime to unpack and grow in these gifts.

But we have a choice. Our choice is either to accept God's truth and receive Christ's free gift of forgiveness, supernatural help, and new life or—to face the Lord, His righteous standards, and His penalty for our sins on our own. This will mean when we die, separation from Him for eternity, and from everything good. If we don't accept His truth, we're saying we don't believe God, we don't need Jesus, and we think we're good enough on our own.

If we accept His way of grace and mercy, the Bible instructs us that we start this new life by not only believing in Jesus and calling on God, but also verbally acknowledging our trust in Him to others. God then begins to work in us, helping us to learn about, and live, this new life.[7] A few Scriptures regarding salvation and verbally affirming our belief to others follow.

> Everyone who calls out to the Lord for help will be saved. (Romans 10:13 GNT)

> If you declare with your mouth, "Jesus is Lord," and believe in your heart that God raised him from the dead, you will be saved. (Romans 10:9)

> Whoever acknowledges me before others, I will also acknowledge before my Father in heaven. But whoever disowns me before others, I will disown before my Father in heaven. (Matthew 10:32–33)

---

[7] A few verses regarding the work and many gifts of God's Spirit for believers include Ezekiel 36:26–27; John 16:12–13; Acts 2:38; and 2 Corinthians 3:18.

At my college, just as in gospel-believing churches today, the speaker, at the end of every service, gave an appeal, inviting anyone who wanted these gifts to come forward and speak with a pastor. Sometimes, individuals responding would stay after the service to talk further with the pastor; other times, the pastor shared with the chapel audience that the individual had already prayed and received Jesus as their Lord and Savior. The pastor would then ask them a few questions, providing them the opportunity to declare that—yes—they believed in and were receiving Christ into their lives.

The invitation time always made me uncomfortable. I believed in God. I even believed that Jesus was His Son, but I wasn't ready to surrender my life to the Lord and His ways because I knew it would mean changing my habits. While I didn't understand it fully, God was calling me to surrender to Him. I responded to the tug of His Spirit, saying, "Not now, maybe later in my life."

Several times, I felt God respond to me, "Not only do I want you to follow me; I also want you to go into ministry."

This scared me even more. Surely, I wasn't hearing Him correctly!

Gary struggled with the invitation time as well. Once we knew they had taken attendance, and the invitation started, he was often the one to whisper in his deep voice that still seemed to carry, "It's time to cut out."[8]

A REAL CHRISTIAN WITNESS

Cole was another good friend who lived across the hall. He was short, stocky, quiet, and possessed a faith that was real and active. Cole never condemned me, even when I shared stories about what I had done through the years and wondered aloud how God could forgive me. Besides being extremely worried about going to jail for my deeds, I struggled mightily with guilt and shame.

"There's nothing you've done that God won't forgive," he would tell me after I had confessed something else. Although I would kick myself for

---

8 Gary and I stayed in touch. One day, many years later, he called and exclaimed, "Dale, I accepted Jesus!"

telling him my activities, I never felt judged by Cole, only cared about, as he patiently explained Christian topics to me.

One time he asked me the reason I left during the invitation. "Because they already took attendance and recorded my name," I answered flippantly. When he repeated the question, I said, "I don't want to go forward. I'm not going to be weak and cave and surrender." Cole calmly shared, "God is convicting you. He's drawing you, and you're fighting against Him."

During the first year, Cole received the shocking news that both his parents had been killed in a car accident. It was awful. It distressed me to watch him endure his great pain, loss, and grief. My strained relationship with my own parents and desire to be closer to them gave me a deep empathy for him. I reasoned that if I had lost my parents the way Cole had, I would leave skid marks as I left campus, get drunk, and never come back.

Not only did Cole lose his parents, their comfort and guidance, and his childhood home, but he also lost their financial assistance. Now he had to work his way through college. I watched him up close—as he grieved and wondered whether or not to stay in college. Cole's life, and his honest emotions of anguish and even anger at God, along with his persistence in faith, offered a strong witness to me. Cole would talk about feeling alone, but later say, "I know I'm not alone." Sometimes he would collapse into tears, and then come back and express the peace he sensed in the midst of devastation. As I watched this long, ongoing process, the peace and anchor that helped him survive spoke volumes to me. The only way to explain it was God. Whatever it was, however it worked, it was real.

God's grace was on display for me every time He put authentic Christians like Cole in my life. They haven't always had every answer, but they have had an honest walk with the Lord. Additionally, they have been so busy applying God's truth to themselves, they haven't judged me, but have shown me patience and kindness. It's difficult to describe the impact that these followers have had on my life.

MORE GIFTS OF GRACE

College is a monumental symbol of achievement for families who have never had a college graduate, and it was this way for our family. Everyone in our family, including me, was surprised that I was the one going to college. Larry was the one who had made straight As, yet he had no desire to go. I was also amazed that being a "college boy" improved my relationship with Dad. He told me I could work for him in the summer anytime I was home, as head lifeguard-manager.

This was huge. In my younger years, he always told me that I wasn't receiving special treatment at the park because I was his son and that I had two bosses: him and the head lifeguard-manager. Now, he put me in charge of all hiring, firing, scheduling, and resolving conflicts. If there was a problem, he told the complainer, "Go talk to my head lifeguard-manager." I realized that Dad was proud of me and depended on me (especially as he wasn't good at handling conflicts). It felt good.

With Grandpa's funds limited, during my second year, Dad told me to simply ask him if I needed any financial help. I did ask Dad and, true to his word, he helped, although I still had to work side jobs. That first year, when I knew Grandpa was paying my tuition, it irritated me that Dad wasn't assisting me with college. Later on, I realized that it was part of God's grace; otherwise, I never would have attended Anderson.

Even though the college's restrictiveness bugged me, I found myself enjoying everything—including the people I met, my studies, and my professors. Naturally, I had to take many classes on the Bible, Hebrew (the original language of the Old Testament), Greek (most of the New Testament's language), and church history. I frequently complained and bugged my adviser with such questions as, "Why do I have to take these Bible courses? I'll never use them." Little did I know that God's grace was preparing me for a different and unimaginable future!

Although I graduated from Anderson University, I stayed on probation for one rule violation after another. Many times I couldn't understand why I didn't get expelled, especially when I saw other students sent packing for fewer, and less serious, offenses. Something was going on. I marvel at God's grip of grace not just to get me there—but also to keep me there with all my infractions. He was definitely working overtime on this.

Years later I was surprised to find that the Preacher Boy, whom I slugged in the cafeteria on my third day, was the pastor at my sister Judy's wedding. John told me that the incident taught him a great deal. It amazed me that John was a victim of God's grace, as well!

HER EYES & SMILE

Another summer rolled around and, once again, I was the summer lifeguard-manager and actively hiring. It was a Wednesday and her big, sparkling brown eyes and warm smile captivated me. Karen was an eye-catcher! She was eighteen and applying for a summer lifeguard job at Pleasant Valley Lake prior to starting Ohio State University in the fall. I had just hired Lois, Karen's best friend, the day before. When Karen passed the swimming test, I hired her on the spot.

By Saturday, I couldn't get Karen out of my mind, so I asked her out that night. After this, I asked her friend, Lois, and my best friend, Jim, on the same date. I hadn't figured out all the details and how we would pair up, or even bothered to tell the girls. Consequently, it felt a bit awkward when they saw each other and realized I asked them on the same date. Fortunately, for me, they were good sports.

We all worked at the park and changed there—Lois and Jim changed into casual clothes, with tennis shoes. Karen came out wearing a red, white, and blue blouse, and blue shorts, with her hair in pigtails. When she looked at me with those big sparkling brown eyes and engaging smile, I thought my heart would beat out of my chest. I was in love!

However, my Mafia-inspired dress code brought a quick look of surprise to Karen's face. Not many guys stepped out in pleated black trousers; a white-on-white, short-sleeved shirt; and shiny black Florsheim shoes, topped off with a black fedora. I really did wear this outfit everywhere.

While I liked Lois, I was thrilled when Karen climbed in the front seat with me before we sailed off in my huge, gold, 1964 Oldsmobile Cutlass with a white hardtop. Back then, trampolines were the new rage; we knew a place where we could rent two side-by-side. The rectangular monstrosities were set down in holes, so people actually jumped at ground level. After a laugh-filled fun fest, we went for hamburgers and ice cream.

Karen was smart and a good person—the kind I would have called a "Goody Two-Shoes" in high school. She didn't smoke, cuss, drink, or use drugs. A good Catholic and a rule follower. I, on the other hand, have always had rebel tendencies. (How true is the saying—opposites attract.) I found Karen's inner confidence attractive, too; for years, I called it "audacity." While a good person, she was no pushover, and would do whatever she set her heart to do. I held a certification in scuba diving and, before I knew it, she had earned her certificate and began diving with me.

Quickly falling head over heels in love, I often made the three-hour drive (one-way) to Columbus on weekends to see Karen. But coming up with extra gas money posed a challenge. One day while walking from my dorm to the cemetery and passing the college president's beautiful home, inspiration struck. I could siphon some gas from his car! Dad had taught us how to do it when we needed to transfer fuel from one piece of heavy equipment to another. All it required was a siphon hose and a one-gallon gas can.

After siphoning gas from the president's car for several months, one time I decided to return for a second helping. However, I forgot about the leftover gasoline in the tube and sucked it in. Immediately, I began choking, throwing up, and gasping for air. Hearing the ruckus, the president came out to see what was going on. Worried about me, he helped me inside and got me a glass of water.

Just as I finally thought I might live, he asked, "How long have you been doing this?"

"Awhile," I coughed out.

He quickly called his wife downstairs, saying, "Honey, you have to hear this." (I can only imagine the heated discussions they had about where he had been going that took so much fuel.) After briefly relating the tale to his wife, with an "I told you so" raise of his eyebrows, he asked me, "How much gas do you think you've stolen?"

When I told him, he declared that I had to pay him back four times that amount. (At least it was more lenient than repaying seven times the stolen amount, which is the biblical mandate in Proverbs 6:31.) I started fussing about it until he reminded me that he could kick me out of school. This wasn't the first time he threatened to expel me. He was also the one who lectured me about cutting chapel and questioned me about why I left so quickly when the invitation time began. Yet, despite my reprobate ways, I felt he liked me. He had encouraged me a number of times and told me that I was growing into a fine young man.

Rats, I thought after I walked out. *Now I've got another bill to pay.*

For a time, I saw Karen less until I acquired an extra job. Still, it was often enough that, two years later, I asked her to marry me. She says, technically, I never asked her; I told her. (We joke, too, that I hired her for life.)

GRACE FOR A BAD DUDE

It's truly a miracle and an act of grace that God can change a heart, especially for such a bad dude like me, who was constantly getting into fights and all kinds of trouble. All I knew was acting tough, and trying to "prove myself" as I battled mightily against the shame that stalked me. Until God got ahold of me and changed me from the inside, just being around Christians, rather than the Mafia, didn't make the slightest dent in my character. My college days were filled with crazy stories.

On a double date once, our group stopped at a bar and wanted a table, but there wasn't a vacant one. Telling my friends, "I'll be back," I went to a table up front where a foursome was sitting and told them we wanted their table, knowing that I would have to take on both men. Outside in the parking lot, I put both men down, with one guy's head taking out a car's headlight.

On another occasion—drunk as usual—I was driving the wrong way on a one-way street. When the cops pulled me over, I ran down a gravel alley. Although I tripped the officer coming up behind me, I ultimately lost the race and the battle. Three cops beat me severely with their nightsticks, leaving my body aching and banged up for a long time. To this day I occasionally feel the effects of that beating.

Because of various episodes over a number of years, police escorted me out of several far-flung towns, telling me, "Don't come back." These locations included Fort Pierce, Florida; Sparta, Tennessee; and a small town in Indiana.

Despite my habits, Christians like Cole never gave up on me, even after I stumbled into the dorm hallway at six one morning—drunk, bloody, beaten, and nursing a black eye.

My injuries came from a fight at a jazz club, which was actually a barn in the middle of nowhere, called Club 21. I loved listening to jazz at this great after-hours joint, which opened after the other bars closed. Occasionally, musicians like legendary blues guitarist B. B. King and saxophonist Charlie Parker played there. The dance floor, tables, and band were downstairs. An upstairs loft contained more tables and the "crow's nest," where the main order-keeper sat, armed with a tommy gun.

The action inside was bad enough, but getting from the barn to the car could be worse. It didn't help that I was usually the only white guy there. This particular night, a guy named Black Jacks and I got into a fight, which always had to be taken outside. Most fights start over a minor slight or ridiculous comment that offends someone, something such as, "Whatcha lookin' at?" This fight started over a comment Black Jacks made about my motorcycle jacket, which Larry loaned me and told me not to lose. With its leather, well-worn appearance, look and feel, and the fact that it was Larry's, I loved it, but I lost it in the fight.

When I entered the dorm, all banged up, Cole happened to see me. He helped clean me up and kept an eye out so I wouldn't get caught, although he did pepper me with questions. I'm sure he wondered if I would ever change.

COLLEGE GRADUATION DRAWS NEAR

Nearing the end of my senior year, I still didn't have any clear postgraduation plans, but I knew it didn't involve God or preaching, even though Anderson produced ministry leaders. Being a preacher was the last thing I wanted to do for several reasons. The leading one was money—that is, the lack of it. My grandfather went down that path, and where did it get him? Poor—it seemed to me. He had to work a second job, like the apostle Paul, who made tents just to make ends meet. I didn't want to struggle, working two jobs, so I could preach. Plus, I was still resisting God.

With graduation fast approaching and wanting to marry Karen, I knew I needed a job. So when Anderson hosted a job fair, I was one of the first through the doors. When I was walking past an education booth, a recruiter with the Cleveland Board of Education stopped me and asked if I had thought about becoming a teacher. I told him I wasn't qualified; I hadn't taken education classes, nor did I have a teaching degree.

"What is your major?" he inquired.

I told him science and psychology. (My roommate had been in pre-med, and I took many of the same classes.) The recruiter explained that the city had a shortage of science and math teachers, and I was qualified to become a science teacher. They would also pay for my graduate work for a master's degree in education if I taught in the inner city. This was a no-brainer. I signed up on the spot.

I will always remember 1969. It was the year I graduated from Anderson University, lived with my parents for six months, and started teaching in June. In November, it was topped off with the best event of all—marrying Karen.

Chapter 7

THE TEACHER LEARNS

A month after graduating from Anderson College, I was teaching summer-school biology at Kennard Junior High. While not happy with my modest $13,000-a-year salary, at least I would be working toward my master's degree in education and not having to pay for it.

I needed that small morale boost in the midst of the desolate-looking teaching environment. The buildings at Kennard Junior High were antiquated and pockmarked, with broken windows looking down over a trash-strewn parking lot. I felt depressed and hadn't even walked through the doors.

During my first week, as Mr. Summerville, my supervisor, talked with me, I began piecing together a mental list of rules I would need to survive:

- Rule #1: There will be fights.
- Rule #2: As a teacher, I need to help break up the fights.
- Rule #3: Don't jump in too soon to break up a fight; let the students wear themselves out a bit.
- Rule #4: But don't wait too long, either.

Fights broke out nearly every day, and I was expected to help stop them. My background in the boxing-ring and roughhouse-bar environments helped prepare me for this, but one day I came on a situation I had never encountered before. Hearing the sounds of a crowd, indicating a fight, I ran into the hallway to find two girls tussling, battling with knives, and slicing wildly at each other.

I froze. I fought for years—in the boxing ring, in street fights, in bars, and as an enforcer for organized-crime bosses and loan sharks. My nose was busted more than once. Fights didn't bother me, even when they involved knives or guns. Normally, I would step in and put a guy out cold. But I didn't have a clue how to break up a fight between two girls. What was I supposed to do? I almost got sliced standing there, trying to figure it out.

Fortunately, Mr. Summerville appeared. When one of the girls tripped, or maybe was tripped, he went for the one still standing and executed a perfect 1-2 maneuver—grabbing her arm with the knife (directing it away from himself) and slamming her against the wall. As the other girl lay on the ground, I managed to step on the hand clutching the knife and squeak out the question, "Where have you been? How come it took you so long to get here and help?"

"Why didn't you do something?" Mr. Summerville asked.

"I didn't know what to do."

"What do you mean?"

"I've never hit a girl," I replied. "What was I supposed to do?"

Mr. Summerville told me later that I should consider teaching at the school where he taught during the regular school year, Thomas A. Edison. There were no girls, just guys, mostly African Americans, in seventh-through-twelfth grades. Everyone called it The Bad Boys School. It was more desolate than Kennard was, the kids were more troubled, and nearly everyone carried a gun or a knife. Several armed guards patrolled the grounds. Once the bell rang, signaling the start of classes, the doors were chained shut.

Given these bleak circumstances, the education department's director was stunned that—given the fact that I was white—I volunteered to teach at Edison the following year. The school board hired two other white teachers with me, but by Thanksgiving I was the only one left.

A CRAZY PLAN

At my new school, I took up residence next to Summerville's room. He meant it when he told me, "Son, the only thing I want to hear that first day of class when they come out of your room is, 'Man, that guy's crazy.' You won't make it here unless they think you're crazy."

It didn't take me long to come up with a plan—that I really liked—because it included using my switchblade. In my collection of knives were a World War II combat bowie knife and several switchblades, which are those severe-looking weapons that, with the push of a button, eject a long sharp blade. (The knives are now illegal in most states.) While still living at home as a young teenager, I regularly threw knives at a target that I set up behind a garage door. I threw at it with either my combat knife, about thirteen inches long, or my favorite Italian-made switchblade that was about ten inches long when open. My target was essentially a silhouette of my father because I drew in his crew cut. When Dad discovered it one day, he stopped and slowly took it in.

"What's that?" he questioned, pointing. "You want to kill me?"

"No. But I get pissed at you, and it's how I get rid of my anger."

After thinking it over for a minute, he let it stay.

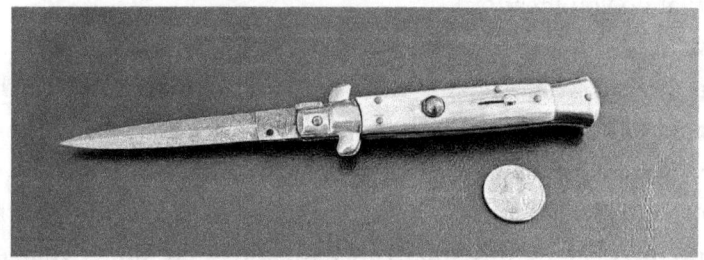

My Italian-made switchblade

Besides my knife throwing at home, my college dorm room had a nice solid-wood door, which made for great target practice. I taped matchsticks to it and threw knives at them, cutting off the match head. College buddies always wanted to try and wanted me to teach them my secrets.

Not everyone was impressed, though. In my senior year, the school hired a new dean, whom I had already met because of another infraction. He called me in and told me that if I wanted to graduate, I had to pay three hundred dollars for a new wood door. I whooped and hollered, "Three hundred dollars? I don't have three hundred dollars! I'll sand it and stain it myself, and it'll look like new."

The dean laughed, but insisted: "I want a new door. No new door, no diploma."

Several years later, when my sister Judy followed me to Anderson, she shared that she was mortified at her college-entrance meeting. A faculty member gasped, "You're Dale's sister? Maybe we should frisk you for a knife."

Now my knife throwing would come in handy.

The first day of classes at Edison, the boys traipsed into my homeroom with every disgruntled and belligerent attitude imaginable. After establishing some semblance of order, I pulled my Italian switchblade from my pocket, popped the blade open, flipped the knife in the air, caught it by the blade (which is how you throw it), and flung it straight into the wooden locker at the back of the room. Then I declared: "I've got a knife, too. I guess we're even."

Working my way over to the blackboard, I wrote my name on it. Then I leaped onto my desk and back down again. As the kids left at the end of class, Mr. Summerville was standing outside his classroom. He heard the words he wanted to hear.

On the third day of school, class had already started when a tough kid named David, who was at least six feet tall, swaggered in and promptly ignored my directions to sit down. I got up really close to him and, even more sternly, ordered, "Sit down!"

Ripping his shirt open, he said, "Come on, you white …," and threw a punch at me. I always knew in the Mafia, and here with these kids—you can't bluff. You must be willing and ready to go "all in." Still, I couldn't believe this was happening and thought, *Oh, brother!*

We went at it. I grabbed for his neck and his vulnerable parts and threw him up against the wall. Except the wall was actually the fire escape. We busted it open, set off the fire alarm, and now battled on the metal landing. Mr. Summerville told me that when his class heard the commotion and asked what was happening, he looked out the window and said, "Oh, it's just Mr. Fiegland out there, talking to a student."

Finally, I got David pinned down, but he was fighting mightily, so I said to him, "If you get up, I'm gonna climb up and down you like a tree."

David, bursting into laughter, declared, "You're okay, Mr. Fiegland!"

That was another example of God's grace. This kid was as tall as a tree and a pretty tough fighter, but from then on, he and I shared a strong connection. David watched out for me and sometimes even sat on the hood of my car to protect it. We stayed in touch through the years. I wish I could say his life turned out well, but eventually he was arrested for ninety counts of armed robbery. When I visited him in jail, I said, "Ninety counts?"

He explained that he would stand at the bottom of interstate cloverleafs and hold up drivers, commenting, "Yeah, it was getting pretty easy."

Despite his habits that sent him to prison, David became a talented wood-carver and made me a beautiful detailed box, crafted with tiny pieces of multicolored inlaid wood. He sent it to me from prison for my fiftieth birthday.

LESSONS ABOUT PEOPLE

Five years of teaching at Thomas A. Edison gave me a number of crazy experiences and lessons about people. Mr. Summerville, who was a tall, good-looking African American with slightly graying hair, taught me many of them. Besides being smart, with a background in chemistry, he possessed considerable common sense. He deeply cared about the kids and had a toughness that helped him deal with them. It was a great combination.

Once I told him my plans to bring in a cooler of dry ice and Fudgsicles for the kids.

"No way," he replied. "Don't do it."

"Why not?" I asked.

"They won't appreciate it," he answered. "Plus, you're white, and you'll be sending a message we don't want to perpetuate—that they're entitled."

That was a valuable lesson, as was his example of respect and believing in others, regardless of their background. He inspired me to sign up my students for the science fair. It was the first time that Cleveland's Bad Boys School had participated. And we won! I don't remember if we came in first or second, but just entering was a big deal in itself. Winning was huge.

Among other lessons I gleaned were those that came from my studies for my master's degree and my instructor, Dr. Gatewood. One profound lesson came when I helped him conduct research concerning students and discipline. He had me divide up my classes and try different styles with each class. In class A, I was to have no extra verbal interaction or touching contact with the kids—just teach. In class B, I was to meet and greet them at the door and say something positive to the students. In class C, besides being friendly and saying something positive, I was to add a simple touch, like placing my hand on their shoulder or back.

The class in which I stayed behind the desk and showed no warmth posed the most discipline problems. The more warmth, kindness, and connections I established with the students, the better their behavior and attitudes were. The class where I spoke positively and placed a hand on the kids' back or shoulder had almost no discipline issues.

I wish all my experiences were that pleasant, but there were sad, painful ones, as well. Raymond comes to mind. He was a major-league troublemaker with a smart mouth and a cleft lip. Daily in the teachers' lounge, one teacher or another would complain about his latest disruption. Yet every year, he had perfect attendance. Many of us wondered, "Why does he even bother coming to school?"

Then a story and photos appeared in local newspapers. Raymond had been machine-gunned down in a horrendous, gang killing. The police made remarks about blood covering everything and dripping from the ceiling. One picture showed Raymond—he made it halfway under his bed when he was shot.

My heart sank. I realized the main reason Raymond came to school every day—it was the safest place he knew. Regret flooded me for how I had mistakenly judged him and hadn't been kind to him. In fact, I had been mean to him, especially when I paddled him. Raymond's death and my actions affected me greatly. Even though I wasn't yet a Christian, this event was pivotal. I was convicted that I can't judge others (because I don't know their hearts or lives), and compassion for others and their struggles began to stir within me.

A GEM OF A HOUSE

While I may have been learning a great deal on the job, I considered my salary pitiful. Every time I looked at my paycheck, I thought, *You've got to be kidding me*. So I decided to start a remodeling business on the side, which I could run throughout the year. Sometimes I made more money remodeling during the summer months than I earned all year by teaching school!

As newlyweds, Karen and I had been renting a house for ten months when we decided we were ready to buy our own home. While doing a remodeling job, I found a gem of a house on the west side of Cleveland. The elderly owner was preparing to put it on the market. I suggested that if she sold it to us, and held the mortgage, she could receive ongoing monthly checks. She agreed. The house had character-plus, with beautiful leaded glass windows, tall ceilings, and gorgeous wood trim.

Wanting to surprise Karen, I bought it without her seeing it. I didn't know any other husband who bought and surprised his wife with a house their first year of marriage. She would be thrilled and think that I was the best husband ever!

When I took her to see this beautiful house, she was definitely surprised. She saw a lone pitiful lightbulb hanging from the ceiling, with a frayed string to yank it on; a sad-looking kitchen with broken-down plumbing and a rickety faucet that spewed brown water; a solitary, puny electrical outlet—in the entire house; and gas chandeliers. Everything needed work or replacing.

She burst into tears and sobbed. Then she cried for a whole week after that. I learned a big lesson that day—Karen would be happier with a say in our decisions. Thankfully, we survived that unpleasant encounter and I got right to work fixing the house.

Life took a major and wonderful change four years later when Karen gave birth to our first child, Brianna. We were still living in this house, although it wasn't yet fully remodeled, when we brought Brianna home from the hospital. The howling wind blew snow, so that it came in underneath the windows and piled up inside on the windowsills. Just then, the furnace went out. We had to stay with Brianna in the kitchen with the oven lit and its door open to keep her warm.

Despite that rocky welcome home, what joy it was having a child. I felt a flood of awe and amazement looking at our perfect little baby and her ten little perfect fingers and tiny toes. After coming home late from work, I would lie on the couch and place little Brianna on my chest and rest for a while as I held her. That first week, snuggling my face into Brianna's, my mustache poked her and she started crying. I got up and handed Brianna to Karen, who looked at me, puzzled. I headed upstairs and came back clean-shaven. For years, Karen had tried to persuade me to shave my mustache; all it took from Brianna was one small cry!

Even though it took four years, we turned our diamond in the rough into a comfy home, including redoing all the plumbing so our water didn't come out brown. It turned out beautifully, and Karen loved it. However, I think our neighbors on Clybourne Avenue thought the "Beverly Hillbillies" had moved to town. We had to turn our coonhound into a house dog and, instead of pretty grass, I planted half our backyard in corn.

REASONS TO STOP TEACHING

Having a family, with little Brianna, and working in a tough inner-city school just didn't seem to fit together. It became increasingly clear to both Karen and me that my days in the classroom were numbered. The reasons to leave kept mounting.

In addition to the physical risks every day at school, the more I discovered about the politics of the school system, the unhappier I became. During my second year of teaching, I entered a program to try and become an assistant principal. Each year I was passed over and protested to my principal. Finally, he told me, "I put your name in every year, but unless you become fluent in Spanish or change your skin color, it's not happening for you."

Then two shootings happened at school fairly close together. I witnessed the second one from above the court on the gym's catwalk and track. I can still see the student shooting his .22 revolver at a teacher, who was running for his life. Mr. Orr ran to one end of the gym and tried to get out the door, but it was locked. He ran back the other way, looking like one of those ducks in a carnival shooting gallery—whizzing by in one direction and then flipping around and going in the other direction. The armed guards arrived after the kid had emptied every round and succeeded in shooting the teacher in his hand. Mr. Orr took time off from work, but I have no idea how you recover from that.

The final straw took place when I went to break up a fight and violated unwritten Rule #3: I broke up the fight too early. The guys still had too much power and punch. One jab, landing on my mouth, sent a couple of my teeth to the floor. Holding my teeth and trying to stop the bleeding, I went to the principal and garbled out the words, "I'm going to the dentist."

I'm still shocked that he asked me, "Can't you wait until the end of the day?"

I won't repeat exactly what I told him, but it ended with, "I'm going to the dentist. Now."

Although I finished the school year, I didn't renew my teaching contract. I was done with teaching and left with symptoms of post-traumatic stress disorder (PTSD). Events from my past probably made the condition worse. I was constantly on edge wondering what life-threatening event might happen next.

Chapter 8

TRANSITIONS & FAMILY MEMORIES

No longer teaching, I transitioned to the fast-paced business world of hard work and sales. For the last several years, I had worked on side jobs for Karen's father, Mike, in his cut-stone business. In addition, he had watched my remodeling business grow and was impressed with my ambition. Learning that I wasn't returning to the classroom in the fall, he invited me to work with him. We made a good team: Mike, an older, more cautious leader; and me, a younger risk-taker.

Together, we expanded Medina Cut Stone into seven small businesses. Among them were a leasing company for large equipment; an equipment-rental firm for smaller tools; and a fireplace and stove company. The late 1970s proved to be a good time for business. When a recession hit, some of our businesses—like the fireplace and leasing companies—became more profitable. We acquired Ohio Marble and Slate Company and bought an old railroad-station building, renovating it for our business offices. Thanks to our respective business skills, cash flowed like the Ohio River.

For example, our fireplace and stove company sold wood-burning stoves and kerosene heaters. One year, we borrowed a hundred thousand dollars to buy two container loads of heaters from Japan. It seemed no time at all before we resold them to our local Kmart stores.

Another example: we would buy a forklift for fifteen thousand dollars, use it for several years, then sell it for twice that amount. I remember one time selling a forklift to an Amish farmer who also owned a business. When I delivered it, we sat down at his kitchen table to finish the paperwork and sale. At the end he said, "Hold on a minute." He left the room and returned with a Mason canning jar stuffed with the cash.

While still functioning, I was now a full-blown alcoholic and addict. Besides working hard, I was partying, drinking, and drugging hard. Unfortunately, drinking and drugging helped me secure more business contacts and make even more money. The more I had of that lifestyle, the more I wanted of it.

On top of this, Larry had died several years earlier, which increased my world of loneliness and pain. Larry and I had become very close during the last eighteen months of his life. About two years before he died, Larry's alcoholism had grown worse; his life began spiraling out of control. In addition to experiencing blackouts, he crashed his GTO into a light pole and was arrested. His wife, Donna, kicked him out of the house, and she began attending Al-Anon meetings. After a while, Larry started attending AA. He worked the program wholeheartedly and found sobriety and peace. Those final months of his life, when he was sober, were Larry's best years. His relationship with Donna was the best they ever enjoyed, and he and I had a great relationship, as well.

But then at the age of twenty-seven, in a freak chain of events, Larry had a boil and lanced it himself. It became infected and turned septic. He lived for ten days. During that time I did everything I could to try to keep him alive. Even though he was in ICU in the hospital, I hired a private around-the-clock nurse to help care for him. When Larry passed away, I blamed God and the doctors for his death and began drinking even more to numb my pain and anger.

So this fast-paced business lifestyle that I was good at, and a world of hurt from which I was running, made for a perfect storm, as well as pretty tough times with Karen. Married to my business, instead of to her and our family, I was a terrible husband and father. I worked from 7 a.m. to 7 p.m., then went out to bars until the wee hours of the morning, doing selfish things. My self-interests made me a physically and emotionally absent husband and father.

Plus, I enjoyed other hobbies, like hunting and trapping with my trapper-bachelor friend, Shorty. Fur-trapping wasn't necessary for our income and, in fact, I often felt rich with cash in my pocket from the business, but I always got a thrill from selling skins to the furrier. Red-fox skins fetched forty-five dollars; coons brought thirty bucks. Muskrats earned three. I managed to get only one mink, which brought me the hearty sum of thirty-five dollars. With muskrats, I typically threw the whole animal in a garbage bag in the freezer, until it was full, then took it to Joe. Although I received less money, it saved me time from skinning the difficult rascals.

Old Man Joe, the furrier, was sharp. He caught me every time I tried to slip in a summer pelt for a winter price. He regularly bargained Shorty and me down on our prices, but made us laugh while he did it. Once he came out to Shorty's to show us ways to skin the animals better, especially around the feet and tails, and how to keep the face intact. The better the job we did, the more he was willing to pay us. Karen and I used these "fur funds" as our Christmas-gift money.

Another hobby I loved was antiques. I often found great pieces in the houses that I remodeled or by the side of the road. I would refinish them and sell them at the flea market on Sundays with Shorty. After the flea market, Mike always had Shorty and me over for lunch. I'm sad to say that it was just us guys—not Karen and Brianna.

Maybe you see the pattern in all this. Whether it was my activities or starting one new business after another, I kept seeking something that would fill the emptiness inside of me and give me fulfillment and peace. With all the good things I had, I should have been happy—a great wife, a beautiful daughter, money, a beautiful house, and even prestige. Why did I feel so empty?

GRANDPA KEEN & MEMORIES

In addition to leaving the classroom, another change in our lives was having Grandpa, Gottlieb Keen, come live with us, which we greatly enjoyed. It happened because Grandpa—all five feet, one inch of him—was an active, agile man. He preached until the age of seventy-five and climbed plum trees to pluck their fruit until he was ninety-seven. That's when he fell out of a tree and broke his arm. Because he needed some help, Karen and I were blessed to be the ones with whom he lived for several years.

Since I was a child, Grandpa and I loved being together and taking walks. When I was young, we frequently walked to the Brookside Zoo, which in those days offered free admission. (Today it's the Cleveland Zoo.) We always loved talking and swapping stories. Now, we both reminisced.

I often thought about the times I spent the night with Grandma and Grandpa. When I got up early, I would find them praying in the parlor, each of them kneeling by a chair, with their big German-language Bible open on the floor between them. They started every day this way—seeking God, thanking Him for His blessings, and asking for His help. Grandpa's relationship with God was the cornerstone of who he was.

As a pastor, Grandpa frequently ministered to church members and dealt with congregational business. When those duties arose during my visits, he or Grandma would send me to another room; yet I could still hear him gently resolving issues and conflicts. He could mediate problems and reconcile differences with the skills of a Fortune 500 executive and a highly skilled counselor.

Through the years, Grandpa regularly told stories relating how God protected him and was active in his life. Gottlieb was born in Prussia (which eventually became Germany). He worked in a mill, grinding wheat and corn until he was sixteen, when the Russian army invaded their town and forcibly drafted him, along with other males. Russian troops simply showed up and, at gunpoint, ordered all the men and boys, "Get on the train." Once on board, these new soldiers rode to Moscow, where they became part of Czar Nicholas II's army in a war against Germany. Gottlieb drew an assignment to work as a pharmacologist until he broke out in a severe rash. Not knowing what contagious disease he had contracted, the army released him and sent him home. A month later, his rash cleared up. He realized that the rash was from the chemicals he had been compounding and it was God's grace!

Grandpa prayed constantly, even for small decisions. He often ended our conversations with, "Let's pray and ask Jesus what He wants us to do." An authentic follower of Christ, he was humble, honest about his struggles, and small in his own eyes. He followed the counsel of Jesus, willingly accepting last place and never being offended or shocked if others put him there (Luke 14:8). He displayed no pretense or spiritual superiority, and was always open to constructive criticism. In addition, he seemed to be liberated from the need to be associated with people of importance.

From Grandpa I received unconditional love and comfort, while Mom and Dad came down hard on me. A familiar story I often heard concerned my mother's longing for a daughter. After the birth of my older brother, Larry, Mom's yearning for a girl increased. When I was born, she was so disappointed, she cried for weeks. She exhibited such despair at the hospital that Grandpa finally went to her room and told her, "You have a healthy boy. That is good. Be happy. He may be the one who will take care of you someday."

During my childhood, Dad routinely said that I was an accident, while Mom claimed I was possessed. But Grandpa cared about me, stood up for me, and went out of his way to point out good things he saw in me. He never lectured me or told me how bad I was; even speaking truth, he spoke kindly. After my arrest for breaking and entering at the age of twelve, I never felt condemned when he said, "There's a fork coming on the road you're on, and you'll have to make a choice."

Grandpa also had a way of talking about Jesus and his relationship with Jesus that didn't offend me. When he talked about God's love, it made me curious because I saw little evidence of a loving God or loving people around me. Grandpa was different from everyone I knew—family, friends, and church members.

MOM'S FAMILY

One reason Grandpa stood out as such a good role model was the stark contrast he offered to Grandma, Emma Keen. She seemed the polar opposite—usually in a bad mood and constantly critical of others, even though she was the pastor's wife. She upset so many people that Grandpa's church disciplined her, requiring that she not attend Sunday morning or evening services. Later, they relented slightly and let her come on Wednesday nights.

Now, Grandma did have some good traits. Good with animals, she loved her dogs and cats. She was a great gardener, too; her flourishing, beautiful yard and flowers amazed people. Added to this, Grandma was a great cook. Like others of her generation, who lived through the Great Depression and knew hunger, she didn't want to think anyone was going hungry. She encouraged everyone, "Eat up! Clean your plate because people are starving in other countries." As a skinny little kid, I had no problem putting away her food. She always praised me for getting seconds. Even though she was tough, I felt she had a smile, a twinkle in her eye, and a hug for me, plus, oftentimes, an extra piece of pie that she put aside for me in the kitchen.

Grandpa and Grandma Keen had five children. Their two daughters were my mother, Arline, and Aunt Lydia; their three sons were Uncle Val, Uncle Al (Alex), and Uncle Zig. The following are a few stories about Mom's family, which had its share of crazy characters.

While Mom was a perfectionist, Aunt Lydia was even more of one. She was always cleaning. She also insisted I take a bath every night and double-checked that I really did bathe and didn't try to just make it look like I took one. Still, I enjoyed visiting her, Uncle Louie, and my cousin, Ellen, every summer for a week. Aunt Lydia was gifted musically and, when I stayed with them at their house in the city, every morning she would play the piano. Then she, Ellen, and I would sing hymns, praising and worshiping God. I enjoyed those visits and times together, singing.

Uncle Al was the one who abused me. Ultimately, I forgave him for a number of reasons. I came to realize that, thankfully, the abuse stopped after I told my mother. Plus, it seemed that there was a bit of time afterward, when he was not around for a while. But he and Mom were best friends and did a lot together. He was often at our house. Uncle Al was also funny and just darn likable. A cutup who joked constantly, he could always make me laugh.

Uncle Al never married and lived mostly with his parents, although he would stay with us a couple of times a year, for several months at a time, usually before Christmas and in the spring. At Christmastime, he and Mom would spend two weeks baking cookies, boxing them up attractively, and giving them as gifts. Uncle Al sometimes worked for Dad, at the park or around the house, fixing things. Storm windows needed to be installed in the winter and removed in the spring. Eaves and soffits required painting. Something always needed repairing.

I tagged along with Uncle Al because he made everything fun—even the flies that buzzed annoyingly around us when he was painting. He would say such things as, "See those two flies? That's Susie and Johnny," and off he went, concocting some crazy, silly tale about two flies.

His joyous exterior masked the truth: he was a binge drinker throughout his life. He ultimately died from a perforated, duodenal bleeding ulcer, which studies reveal can be caused by excessive alcohol consumption.

Uncle Val—short for Vandaline—also struggled with alcohol. He was a functional alcoholic who lived a fascinating life. He was officially married twice. His second marriage was a short, ill-fated match to a trapeze artist. While he held a good job and drove a flashy car, he lost the job and the car—along with his third, common-law wife. She ran off when his drinking left him unable to support her. Uncle Val, like his own grandma, was a kleptomaniac. His pilfering often got him into trouble with family members who had to search Val before he left their house. Most of the time, he picked up dumb stuff, like pens or paper, but occasionally the searches turned up items of value, making the person glad they checked his pockets. Uncle Val died in a nursing home from "wet brain," which is brain damage that is caused by alcohol.

Although all three sons of Grandma and Grandpa Keen were alcoholics, Uncle Zig—we called him Ziggy (his real name was Sigismund)—was the most functional and stable, with a wife and family. While his stability means I'm short on Uncle Ziggy stories, it was good for our family because his stability was needed, especially later on. With his gentle ways and great wit, he was a refreshing respite for our family.

Life was tough on Grandpa when he was in his early nineties. Grandma had to live in a nursing home, and Alex and Val were not doing well due to their alcoholism. Grandpa took them in and cared for each of them for several years until they passed away from alcohol's effects.

UNCLE JULIUS—THE BOOTLEGGER

Grandpa also told stories about his brother, my great-uncle Julius, the bootlegger. While I know Uncle Julius sold illegal booze, I'm uncertain whether or not he manufactured moonshine. In the roaring 1920s in Cleveland, it wasn't difficult to get into the bootlegging business.[9]

Uncle Julius always had plenty of cash, wore fancy clothes, and purchased our family's first-ever car—a yellow convertible. He gave generous gifts, often cash, to family members. Because of his business endeavors, he always carried a gun in his shoulder holster underneath his ever-present, double-breasted suit jacket. The family thought of him as the black sheep, and Grandma especially didn't like him, but Grandpa loved him—just as he loved everybody. I'm pretty sure Uncle Julius never felt condemned by Grandpa, either. (In my younger years, many relatives said I looked like Uncle Julius.)

One day, Uncle Julius tried to teach Grandpa to drive. He had Grandpa practice backing up and pulling forward in the driveway. As Grandpa pulled forward once, he stepped on the gas pedal too hard and sped all the way through the back wall of the garage. Given that his only experience driving was with horses, he kept shouting, "Whoa! Whoa!" Grandpa never again attempted driving after he took out the back wall of the garage.

As many good traits as Grandpa had, in his later years, he acknowledged that he had not been a very strong disciplinarian with his sons. He had been too easygoing with them, when he should have corrected them. Grandma possessed the strength and disciplinary muscles in their marriage. Being overly kind and trusting of people backfired on Grandpa another time. He and Uncle Julius loved sharing the story about their trip to Niagara Falls, when they encountered a hitchhiker in the rain. Grandpa insisted that they needed to give him a ride, especially because it was raining. Uncle Julius tried to talk him out of it, but Grandpa wouldn't

---

9 Incidentally, Prohibition, which banned alcohol sales in the United States from 1920 to 1933, was the catalyst for the growth of organized crime and the Mafia.

be deterred. After picking the man up, he robbed them at gunpoint. Uncle Julius always concluded, "Yeah, you think everybody is good."

Grandma and Grandpa both had a good sense of humor and enjoyed gently teasing and laughing about their differences. When they would hear a noise outside, Grandma would grab the butcher knife and exclaim, "Don't worry, Pa. I'll protect you."

However, besides the hitchhiker escapade, Grandpa stood strong and wouldn't budge another time. At the end of Uncle Julius's life, when he desperately needed help, Grandpa took him in. Grandma pitched a fit, yelling and saying, "No way! I'm not having that man in my house." Grandpa held firm and won the battle. Mom said, "It was amazing. He put his foot down and stood strong about Uncle Julius."

MORE CHANGES

As much as Karen and I enjoyed having Grandpa live with us, he had one habit that annoyed me. His bedroom was across the hall from ours. Whenever I stumbled in from the bars, usually around 2:30 a.m. or later, he would often be on his knees next to his bed, praying—out loud—for God to save me. As I went to my room, I would hear him praying for God to bless me, Karen, Brianna, and any other children we might have.

Ultimately, Grandpa's energy and agility got us all in trouble. Grandpa loved playing with Brianna and it included, at the age of ninety-nine, running in the snow, pulling her on the sled. When Aunt Lydia saw Grandpa doing this, she immediately called Mom. They both pitched fits, declaring that I was a bad influence on Grandpa, and that he needed to live with Uncle Zig. They caused enough of a ruckus that Grandpa finally agreed.

More changes occurred during this season. Dad was only fifty-five when he decided to retire and leave the frozen north. He didn't want to just escape from the snow; he didn't even want a chance of frost. After reading an article in *Kiplinger's* (a leading financial publication), stating that Fort Myers, Florida, was a growing town full of business opportunities, he decided that was the place for him and Mom. Because it was growing, he could buy apartments and rent them for income. They found a mobile-home park they liked for themselves and moved.

Although I was happy that they could enjoy retirement in Florida, and even with our past disagreements and disputes, it was sad having them move away. Plus, it meant that, besides selling his excavation business, they were selling Pleasant Valley Lake. Now, I wouldn't be able to one day build a home on the spot that I had chosen and dreamed about for years.

They sold their home and their Pleasant Valley Lake property to Jim Chapman, a pastor and businessman, and his wife, Liz. Jim became the pastor of the Pearl Road Church of God. This was the English-speaking congregation spun out of our German-speaking, Daisy Avenue Church of God, which my grandfather had pastored. Karen and I were married at Pearl Road Church, a modest-sized congregation of about one hundred people. Jim and Liz would live in the house with its five acres, while the church members would run the park. The income would help pay for a new church to be built overlooking the lake.

I liked Jim and Liz. The son of a full-blooded Cherokee mother, Jim hailed from the Appalachian Mountains in Virginia. He possessed striking looks, was down-to-earth, and easy to get along with. He was also a hard worker, usually in overalls, who wasn't afraid to get dirty. My kind of working man. Not only did I enjoy working with him, but it made me feel good when he requested my help to fix something or show him how something worked on the property.

While he and Liz were settling in, I was allowed to retrieve things I wanted from the property. I put these belongings in an old Fisher Foods trailer that Dad had on the property and would eventually haul it away. Jim laughed when I told him, "I'm going to leave only dust behind for you."

I said this in part because, before I finished, I planned to take a two-ton boulder, which was underneath a beautiful oak tree. The stone was gray granite, the kind with sparkles in it. Dad had given it to me for my sixth birthday. I wasn't happy about it back then, even when he told me I could chisel a seat out for myself. But I came to love it. When I outgrew the seat I carved, I would sit on top of my rock and think.

I didn't know it, but I was headed for my biggest transition yet, and this rock would be a part of that story.

Section Three

STARTING OVER

Chapter 9

I SURRENDER

Before any of us can fully receive God's help and regeneration, we need to call on Him and surrender. This means we are turning from self-reliance, and the ways we think are right, toward the Lord and His ways.

Surrendering is difficult.

I believed in God. Even knew He was real. My problem was that I didn't want to surrender to Him. I had been fighting my whole life. Fought to survive. Fought against put-downs, beatings, and abuse. Grew up angry, hot-headed, rebellious, and combatting everything and everyone before striking out on my own at fifteen. I fought my way through college and inner-city school teaching. Battled to succeed. I had never asked anybody for help. The mere idea of surrendering signaled weakness to me. I didn't need assistance, and I didn't need anybody telling me what to do.

Although my self-oriented wisdom and rebellion weren't leading me anywhere good, I still liked doing what I wanted. I kept trying to do everything on my own and manage life on my own terms—except nothing I did was making anything better. Indeed, it was making everything worse.

God had been working on me since I was young—it felt like overtime—to break through this thick head of mine. He placed numerous Jesus people in my life, like Grandpa Keen, my friend Cole at Anderson College, and many others. I always saw something different in them that I couldn't ignore or explain away. But the idea of a personal relationship with God scared me. I may have had a Midas touch in business, but I felt there was no way I could be successful as a Christian.

So, God pulled; I pushed. God sought me; I ran. God asked me to surrender; I fought. Not only was God asking me to respond to Him and yield myself to Him, on more than one occasion, I felt Him telling me that I was to be a pastor. I was running from this crazy and ridiculous idea, too.

None of my reactions were surprising. I fit the biblical definition of human waywardness. The Bible is full of crazy, difficult truths. One such truth is its description of human nature: every one of us has a fatal flaw in our heart. Twisted, baffling, cunning, and deceptive, it's the disease of sin or love of self. We want what we want, and we don't want to submit to anyone other than ourselves, including God.[10] In short, we want our way, rather than God's way. We want to be in charge of our lives and decide what is right and wrong. In this manner—we become our own god. This love of self is, in fact, rebellion toward God. Rebellion is a state of heart that opposes and defies authority, including God's. All these aspects were certainly true for me.

Even when we want to do the right thing, our hearts often have mixed motives. We lean on our own wisdom, rationalizing that we are acting with God's purposes. The disease of sin or self runs so strongly through our hearts and minds that we can't discern all the ways it is off track from God or all the ways we seek our own desires and greatness, instead of God's. Everything we do strives to keep this deception alive, just so we can keep living for ourselves.

ADDICTION'S GRIP

But wait. It gets worse with addiction. This desire for self becomes even more twisted, insidious, and powerful. *Webster's Dictionary* defines addiction as "a pathological [detrimental, deadly, poisonous, toxic, unhealthy, harmful] relationship with a substance, activity, practice, or habit." Because we're enslaved to our addiction, it's in charge, not us. It seems impossible, but our decision-making process becomes more faulty and demanding. Remember that our underlying devotion is to self, and we will go to any lengths to keep it that way. Addiction compounds these issues.

---

10 A few verses about these truths include Jeremiah 17:9; Romans 1:21; and Romans 10:2-4.

My addictions totally controlled and consumed me. While my drinking made me feel awful, it fueled my desire for more of it. Anyone who has struggled with an addiction of any kind (whether it is to a substance or even a habit, such as workaholism, shopping, or gambling) knows how the dependence and cravings transcend all reason, logic, and self-discipline. Said another way—throwing reason, logic, and self-effort at our addictions doesn't work because they are, at their root, spiritual problems. We require God's supernatural mercy, grace, and power to help us out of this miserable mess!

On top of all this, I still thought I was "fine." Flaws? What flaws? While others could name them, I couldn't even see them, much less acknowledge them. Blind—that was me. I gave no thought to my life, my actions, and how they might affect others. I considered myself well-adjusted. After all, I worked diligently to provide for my family. Inwardly, I resented others and shifted blame for my problems to everyone else. I accused others, but excused myself. Outwardly, I considered myself as a "law-abiding citizen" because I obeyed the law most of the time. There it is again—my foxy, deceiving human nature. "Most of the time" is a slippery slope, all in an effort to try to be in charge of what was right and wrong for me. The law, of course, interprets it another way.

So round and round I went—wanting to believe that I was in control of my life and drinking. I reasoned that if I wanted to, I could quit. I could manage my life. I could keep things under control by drinking just beer, or having only one or two (or three) next time. No matter how many times I failed, next time I would simply try harder and then succeed. We can be quite creative in coming up with excuses and possible solutions to our problems.

All this is denial—a defense mechanism to avoid accepting the truth that we have a problem bigger than us and we need help. From here, we move on to the minimizing trick and say, "Well, maybe I do have a little problem, but it's not that bad. I can handle it." Minimizing is still denial.

I lived in a state of denial. I denied that I had a problem, even when it was apparent to everyone else that my biggest problem was me. Denial reassured me I could stop whenever I wished, if I just tried harder and conjured up enough willpower. There were times I attempted to work my own program my way, thinking I was keeping my freedom, but I was trapped. Self-effort and willpower would never be enough for my full-blown addictions and brokenness.

For me to enter recovery, I would need to leave rebellion and denial behind and admit I needed help, from God and from others. But for this to happen, it would take a dark pit of desperation. Thankfully, because of God's conspiracy of grace, I experienced a crisis. Otherwise, I would have remained in my broken, blinded, and rebellious state and gone straight to my grave, forever in that condition, except for God's good intentions. It just didn't feel good at the time.

TROUBLE STARTS

In August 1976, Brianna was two and a half. Karen was still six weeks away from her due date with our second child, Larry, when her contractions started close to midnight. This wasn't good, particularly because we lived in the country an hour away from the hospital.

After getting ready, I helped Karen wobble out to our 1972 Chevy Chevelle. I had backed halfway down our long driveway when our radiator hose burst. Running back up the driveway, I frantically retrieved our '67 Ford pickup and helped Karen climb in. Taking off again, I sped down the highway at ninety miles an hour, in part, hoping to attract police attention. They always seemed to be around in my rowdy single days and quick to throw on their blue lights. But now, no such luck, even when I flew past a highway-patrol car and a "county-mountie." Neither one stopped me.

Halfway to the hospital, our truck started sputtering and lurching. Fortunately, we had reached a small town. Seeing a combination police and fire station, I whipped into the parking lot and pulled up so close to the door that I almost couldn't get in the door myself. I ran inside; Karen said later that she heard me from the parking lot hollering, "I've got to get my wife to the hospital! She's having a baby!"

A couple of EMTs came outside, loaded Karen into an ambulance, and let me ride up front. Needing a smoke badly, I lit a cigarette. Instantly, the driver started yelling, "Hey, buddy, put that out! We've got oxygen tanks in here!" I tried arguing with him, in my typical tough-guy manner, explaining that I needed a smoke really bad. He threatened to pull over and kick me out, so I grudgingly tossed my cigarette out the window.

Once at the hospital, the EMTs quickly pushed Karen on her gurney toward the elevators for the maternity ward, located on the fifth floor. While I was signing the papers to admit Karen, I heard them discussing which elevator was working. After I finished, I entered an elevator and pushed the button. The doors shut and the elevator whooshed to life, but then quit. My anxiety now ramped up another couple of notches; I yelled like a lunatic. Finally, a maintenance worker freed me from the elevator and I ran toward Karen's room.

As I neared her room, a nurse wheeled an incubator past me with a tiny, almost-blue baby in it. "Congratulations! That's your son! But he's having trouble breathing. We may call a medical helicopter and fly him to the children's hospital if he doesn't improve." With that, she hurried down the hall with our precious bundle.

By now, a total wreck, I nearly collapsed. Two nurses helped me into a wheelchair, gave me a shot of sedatives, and dumped me in a bed next to Karen's. Lying there, heart pounding, and mind racing, I pleaded, "Please, God. Please save this little boy. If you save his life, I will turn my life over to you."

Shortly after this, while the doctors and nurses continued working on Larry, he began breathing on his own, although the doctors, to be safe, kept him in an incubator and monitored him closely for twenty-four hours. Karen was doing better, too. We spent some time together but, back then, hospitals limited visiting hours, even for new fathers. Finally, giving Karen a hug and a kiss, I left the hospital.

WHAT A MESS

I needed a drink. I needed to calm my nerves following my newborn son's close call with death and subsequent recovery, and to celebrate his birth. Brianna was safe at home with a young Japanese exchange student staying with us. My Rotary Club, which I was active in, sponsored foreign-exchange students every year. The previous year, Karen and I had hosted our first student, from Mexico. Figuring Brianna and her caregiver would be all right a little while longer, I headed to my favorite bar for a cold one.

Sitting in the bar with my drink, I thought about little newborn Larry, which made me think about his namesake, my brother. Here I was, seven years later, still desperately missing him. The fear, relief, and happiness over my son's birth collided with unresolved pain over Larry's death, propelling me on my emotional roller coaster. As always, I was using alcohol to deal with every mood—glad, sad, and mad. One drink led to another until what started as a quick drink to celebrate my son's birth turned into a three-day binge that included blackouts and memory loss. Not only was I not with Karen and my family during this important time, but this bout again signaled my downward spiral.

When I finally came to, after clearing as much of the fog from my head as I could, I called a friend for a ride and for help with my broken-down, abandoned truck back at the fire station. It turned out it had a plugged fuel filter. While we worked on it, a few firefighters gave me grief over my erratic parking because they hadn't been able to use the door I had blocked.

Their jibes were minor compared with facing Karen once I got the truck running and drove home. Our marriage had been rocky for a long time. Saying that we had problems would be an understatement. She had contemplated divorce on numerous occasions. So had I. Only by God's grace were we never ready to call it quits at the same time.

I couldn't blame Karen for wanting a divorce; she deserved one. But I didn't want to lose her or our children. And yet there was the other side of me—the one enmeshed in self-pity and casting blame on others. Sometimes, in my clueless self-absorption, I thought my marriage was the problem.

It was worse than you know. I had been unfaithful to Karen. Before my binge, she found out and had confronted me. Though I never intended to have an affair (most people don't), my twisted thought processes led downhill. Confiding in a female friend, I felt heard and understood. This led to emotional closeness, and the destructive trap sprung and caught me.

What a walking mess I was.

Now this was the final straw. When I showed up at home several days after Larry's birth and my alcohol-fueled binge, Karen gave me an ultimatum: get help for my drinking, and go with her to marriage counseling, or she would file for divorce. If I said no, there was no hope for our marriage.

Although I knew she was right, how I hated those words: "Get help." Those words made me mad. I never needed help. I was a successful businessman and talented overachiever. Me—need help? I wrestled with my feelings; even though I felt stuck, I didn't want to lose Karen.

Though the truth felt like a sucker punch to my pride, I spent a long bout looking at my life. I saw my selfishness and how I was hurting everyone I loved. Everything had always been all about me and what I wanted. I had plenty—a good wife, children, a good job and wages, even a little success—but none of it made me happy. I was married to my business, yet felt empty. I always wanted more, but more gave me nothing but additional emptiness and hurt. Nothing brought me peace. Forced to acknowledge that my ways weren't working, I thought, *Maybe You're right, God. Everything I've done up to this point is making it worse, not better.*

During the previous year, I had been to church a number of times. I had even prayed to receive Christ three times. Though I felt remorse for the mess my life was in and even cried, what I really wanted was to be fixed and get people off my back. I wanted an easy way out, without really having to surrender and participate with God. My prayers weren't fully honest. Rather than just believing in God, I realized that I needed Him. For me, this was a huge difference. I couldn't get my life in order and then come to Him; I needed God to help me get my life in order. I needed a Person and a power greater than myself to help me stop drinking and drugging. In turn, God required the whole package—me and my life—if He was going to help me.

A ROCK & A HARD PLACE

As the day wore on with Karen's ultimatum looming over me, I was a wreck wrestling with my choices. By that evening, after she laid down the law, I set out for my old homeplace, with one destination in mind: my treasured rock under the old oak tree. It was dark, and I knew it would be quiet and peaceful there. I needed to talk to God. Sitting there with thoughts and painful emotions running through my mind and colliding like spattering paintballs, I finally surrendered.

"Okay, God, You can have my life," I said, choking back tears. "I'll do what I'm supposed to do, but I need help. Please help me. I'll go to any lengths that You want me to. Just please help me."

Tears flowed.

When they finally dried, I felt peace and God's presence.

After spending some time there, I drove back to my place.

The next day, I realized that for the first time since I could remember, I didn't want to take God's name in vain or say *Jesus Christ* as curse words. *Well, that was really different.* I felt a lack of pride, too. Talk about a 180-degree turn! Up until then, I wanted to control everything, but now I had a staggering sense of powerlessness. Yet, I felt all right about that.

How different that day was.

In the evening, I thought about the religious teaching I had heard and the church services I had attended; I learned enough to know that a Christian should read the Bible. Figuring there was no better time to start than the present, I dug my Bible off the shelf, opened it randomly, and read: "Whoever blasphemes against the Holy Spirit will never be forgiven; they are guilty of an eternal sin" (Mark 3:29).[11]

What? I read it again.

Fear and dread gripped me. Whatever blaspheming the Holy Spirit was, I felt certain I had done it. *I'm toast*, I thought. *What should I do now?*

I was desperate and needed help. My anxiety wouldn't let me rest. I needed an answer—now. But it was 11:30 at night! The only thing I could think of was to go see Pastor Jim. I drove again to his property and this night, I knocked on his door. When he opened it, I blurted out in a rush, "Jim, I gotta know, what's blaspheming the Holy Spirit? I surrendered 'cause I need Jesus, and I need help. I started reading the Bible, which says it's unforgivable, but I'm sure I've done it."

---

11 The passage and story are found in Mark 3:20–30 and Matthew 12:15–37.

Holding the door open, Jim replied, "Come on in, son. We'll open the Bible, and I'll explain it."

Before we sat down, a sleepy-eyed Liz came out to the living room, greeted me warmly, and disappeared into the kitchen. Before long she brought out fresh, hot coffee and, a little while later, returned with a plate of warm, freshly baked cookies.

With his Bible open, Jim explained more about Jesus and how people had various reactions to what He said and did, and the miracles He performed. Some people followed Him, but others—preferring their own ways and traditions—didn't want to surrender and acknowledge Jesus is who He claims to be. If Jesus is God's Son, they would have to admit their shortcomings, sins, and needs, and turn from their ways to God. They tried to deny Christ's truth, power, and miracles and explain them away.

Jim shared that when Jesus cast out evil spirits from captive, hurting souls, some observers not only dismissed the miracles, but they brazenly claimed they weren't from God and that Jesus had an evil spirit from Satan. He added, "These people, besides resisting and rejecting the kindness and goodness of God, slandered God and blasphemed His Spirit when they claimed His goodness was evil at work."

He pointed out that I was not rejecting God's grace. Because I was turning from my ways to Jesus, and I feared God, I had not blasphemed His goodness and Spirit. Great relief and hope washed over me while we talked. My salvation became more real as I sensed the punishment Jesus took on Himself for me, and saw glimpses of freedom and peace that I was to have.[12]

---

[12] When it comes to considering Jesus's life, actions, and words, we aren't to simply think He was a good person and great teacher. We are to have a reaction to Jesus and all that He did, said, and claimed. He was a religious and good man who hung around sinners, and went to their parties, eating and drinking with them; yet all the while, He performed miracles, raised people from the dead, claimed to be God, and then lovingly—and with authority—said how each of us must turn back to God and be forgiven. Jesus's actions and claims shocked and greatly upset religious and political leaders, as well as everyday folks. He so turned dearly held religious beliefs and traditions upside down that they crucified Him. Even today, the things Jesus said surprise us and make us react. Hopefully, we marvel at and turn to this incomparable God-man and Savior!

BATTLE INSTRUCTIONS

Jim said he was glad that I was serious about my relationship with Jesus, and my earnestness was important because I was engaged in a war. Drawing on his Cherokee-Indian heritage, he gave a vivid picture, asking me, "Dale, if we had two dogs that were going to fight, and one was not fed and was malnourished, and the other one was fed the best meat, food, and vitamins, and was exercised so its muscles were strong, which one do you think would win?"

"The strong, well-fed one," I responded.

"That's right. Up until now, your flesh side has been fed the most and is winning. Your spirit side is malnourished. You must feed your spirit by reading God's Word and coming to church. You need to hear God's Word and spend time with those who love God."

Before I left, Pastor Jim told me that he would be calling me again for assistance and advice about things around the park. They planned to reopen it soon, so they could begin receiving the income to help build the new church.

It felt good to be in this house where I grew up, sitting at the kitchen table with people who accepted me and cared about me. What a contrast to earlier encounters at this table! Jim encouraged me to return with any questions and to come to church. As I left, all sorts of thoughts and feelings swirled within me, including Pastor Jim's crazy description that I was in a war.

Besides being in a war, I was very much in the throes of addiction. The roller-coaster ride I was on? It was getting ready to take me for another wild ride.

Chapter 10

A FLOPHOUSE & A FEATHER

Not only would it be a while before I told Karen that I had accepted Jesus, but it would be longer before she would notice any changes in me. In fact, she had watched me walk the aisle at church a couple of times, so what she needed to see was change. However, considering the condition of my life, my personal issues weren't going to be fixed any time soon. A spiritual change can take place in an instant, as it did for me under that old oak tree, but transformation is another matter entirely.

As I reflect on all of it, the fact that we're still married is a miracle. Karen had divorce papers drawn up, although she hadn't signed them yet. My drinking and my moods were continuing to get worse. My life was a complete and total mess, and I felt miserable. In this state of mind, for some reason, I decided I needed to move out for a while, so I rented an apartment. While I was gathering some belongings to take with me and loading my truck, three-year-old Brianna watched me with sad eyes.

"Daddy has to move out and can't live here right now," I remarked. I will never forget the pain I saw on her little face. (It still pains me.) When I left, I did what I had always done to deal with my emotions—I went for a drink. It turned into a heck of a drink and my second binge with a blackout.

When I came to, I was in a smelly flophouse with a bunch of other drunks. I didn't know where in town I was or where my car was. I still had on my three-piece suit, and my socks, but only one shoe. All sorts of questions flashed through my mind about what could have happened during my binge and how I ended up at the flophouse. I needed help in a number of ways.

Ten years earlier I had attended six months of court-mandated Alcoholics Anonymous meetings. The problem was I never invested any part of myself into the program. I never worked the program or leaned on the help available. I sat, barely listened and, not seeing any reason to hang around or ask questions after the meeting, I left rather quickly. Well, the truths taught in AA (and those in Scripture) don't jump onto our head like a tick and simply burrow their way into our brain to enlighten and change us. We have to choose to employ them. We need to think on them, practice them, and work at them as if we're mining for buried treasure. I hadn't made the slightest effort to do anything, except warm the chair with my butt.

However, I had met Bob at AA. He was a bit of a conundrum; I couldn't decide if I liked him or not. He definitely irritated me, and I thought he dressed weird. Bob stood five-feet-nine and, as the old saying goes, "was as rough as a cob." Picture a rough, dried corncob, and add in toughness. His military-style buzz cut reflected his army days. He had been an army paratrooper and a prisoner during the Korean War.

Now Bob was a mailman. When he wasn't working, he always wore a suit, tie, and a tweed hat with a small feather on the side. Besides the fact that almost every word out of his mouth was about Jesus or the Bible, he also carried a leather-bound edition everywhere he went. While Jesus Christ was part of my vernacular, it wasn't as my Higher Power, which is AA's descriptive term for God.

Even with his quirks, I liked some things about him. At my first meetings ten years earlier—when I was young, scared, and uncomfortable—Bob chatted with me and helped me feel welcomed and accepted. He was a no-nonsense, straightforward kind of guy, who didn't beat around the bush or try to put on airs. I liked these traits. He was what he was.

Once he admonished me straight up: "You're headed down a bad path with your drinking, and one of three things will happen to you. You'll end up incarcerated, in a mental institution, or dead. Remember those three things are waiting for you. Here's my card. Call me before it's too late." His card, which I stuck in my wallet, had his name and phone number, along with a verse and cross. I thought about calling him several times, but never found the courage.

Trying to clear my foggy brain after my binge and blackout, I didn't know where I was or where my car was, but I had Bob's name and number. While thoroughly ashamed of my actions and current predicament in a flophouse, I was desperate and hoped like the dickens he would help me. As soon as Bob answered the phone, I blurted out, "This is Dale Fiegland. I want to go to a meeting." I explained that I wasn't sure where I was, and had lost my car and a shoe. After we figured out the location of the flophouse, he said, "If you can wait till noon, I'll help you find your car, and we'll go to a meeting. I'll bring a pair of shoes. What size?"

AA MEETINGS

Bob showed up just as he had promised and brought a pair of tennis shoes. Years later, he told me that when he walked in, I was in my three-piece suit, missing a shoe, and telling the other drunks how to run their lives. They were intently listening.

Because AA meetings are conducted everywhere, every day, at various times—morning, noon, and night—finding one wasn't difficult. After we went to our meeting, we located my car, but I never did find my shoe.

AA abounds with many slogans and refrains. They are spoken and shared repeatedly inside and outside of meetings. Although they had never sunk into my thick skull the first go-round, these valuable sayings are intended to help an alcoholic take in, and act on, needed truth. These are a few key refrains for newcomers:

- If you want to succeed, get ninety days of sobriety.
- Get a sponsor, and work the steps.
- You need a Higher Power; you can't do this on your own.
- Stick with these things if you want to succeed.

Like any other addict, I desperately needed detoxification, followed by an ongoing stretch of sobriety. These would help me obtain much-needed clarity of mind. My challenge would be learning to go to any lengths to avoid getting high from drinking or drugs. For this, I needed a sponsor.

AA suggests that to choose a sponsor, you look for someone who has what you want. I didn't have to look far. Bob was still involved in the same meetings and talking about his Higher Power—Jesus Christ. He was also still talking about the Bible a lot, including the valuable but strange principle that God blesses the poor in spirit.[13]

Bob still embarrassed me, both in the way he dressed and his boldness in talking about Jesus. But Bob had peace and wisdom, too. I craved those qualities. I could still relate to what he said and how he said it. The way he expressed truth made complete sense. Figuring I could get past his quirks, I asked Bob to be my sponsor.

THE CONDITIONS

Bob agreed to be my sponsor, but said there were two conditions, although they sounded more like three or four to me. He declared, "You need to take the cotton out of your ears and put it in your mouth. You have to listen to what I say and do what I tell you. And you must go to ninety meetings in ninety days."

After a slight pause, he continued, "Oh, and you're going to church with me."

I began resisting from the get-go, protesting, "Do I have to make ninety meetings in ninety days?"

"Look, Dale, you're dealing with a serious problem," he responded. "To succeed, you need ninety days of sobriety, all strung together, or you have to start over. As soon as you get sober, denial's going to kick in. Your mind will want a drink, and denial will tell you, 'You don't have to go to the meeting; you're fine; you can handle it now.' Denial is a battle you can't win alone, so the meeting you don't want to go to is the meeting you really need! You must make a commitment and attend enough meetings that

---

13 Though it would take me awhile to understand this principle, the poor in spirit know they need a Higher Power, trust He is good, and seek Him. God richly blesses these humble people with grace, mercy, and help. Matthew 5:3 GNT expresses it this way: "Happy are those who know they are spiritually poor; the Kingdom of heaven belongs to them!"

you understand what's going on. No one likes meetings in the beginning; you go till you wanna go, and you keep going."

After a moment, he added, "Of course, you don't have to do any of this unless you want to succeed."

Then he told me I had to call him daily, plus whenever I felt "stuck." Sometimes, I called him several times a day. Checking in with our sponsor gives us accountability. It also helps reinforce that we have to reach out to others and request assistance when we need it. Asking for help is the hardest thing to do and why AA calls it the "thousand-pound phone."

Besides attending meetings every day, Bob and I got together a couple of times a week after the meetings to talk. Known as the "meeting after the meeting," sponsors and their sponsorees discuss sobriety, the 12 Steps, and specific problems. Bob and I usually went to McDonald's, bought a cup of coffee, and sat in the car and talked.

At one of our first get-togethers, Bob gave me three books: a Bible, an *AA Big Book*, and a *Strong's Exhaustive Concordance of the Bible*. In the *Big Book*, he wrote, "Read this, dumb ass." He recorded the same inscription in my Bible. Inside the concordance, he wrote, "All the answers you will ever need are in the Bible."

Bob showed me how to use my concordance. I would consult it similar to using a dictionary. For each word given, there is a list of Bible verses that mention the word and topic. Then I was to look up those Scripture passages in my Bible.

Bob told me to write down the date. Inside my AA book, I wrote, "September 9, 1976."

At the end of our first post-meeting, before parting, he said, "Let's pray." As he started to pray, he took my hand to hold it! My eyes popped open, and I thought, *Oh my gosh, this guy's weird!* I had a flashback to the college cafeteria and that preacher boy who grabbed my hand when he prayed. Bob was lucky I didn't deck him. For some time, when Bob prayed in the car, I kept one eye open, watching him. I've since discovered that a lot of Christ's followers hold hands when praying.

When I was almost to my car, I heard Bob call out, "Tomorrow, make sure you're at a meeting, Dale."

Our times together looked like this:

- I would ask Bob questions and complain a lot.
- Bob asked me questions.
- During the week, he had me read portions or chapters of the Bible and the AA *Big Book* and we would talk about them.
- Bob would often choose a Scripture, have me read it, and then ask, "What is God telling you?"

Bob also encouraged me to write down my thoughts and journal. Again, I complained and whined, "I don't like journaling."

"Look, Dale, if the God of the universe speaks to you and tells you something, don't you think you should write it down?" He followed it with, "At the very least, when you read a book, write in the margin your thoughts and God's impressions to you."

Today, I'm thankful for every habit that he prodded me to practice and develop.

KEY LESSONS

A great deal of my efforts in the beginning focused on not drinking and staying sober. This took some white-knuckled efforts, making ninety meetings in ninety days, and Bob's assistance. There were a few bumps and restarts along the way. I was also going to church and Sunday school with Bob, which happened to be the church Jim pastored.

Bob and AA helped me learn to "live one day at a time," a key repeated slogan that comes from Scripture. Jesus told us in His Sermon on the Mount that we are not to worry about tomorrow, but focus on today (Matthew 6:34).[14] In my struggle to stay sober and not drink, I often called Bob. Some days he would ask me, "Can you stay sober for today?" When I would reply yes, he would respond, "That's all that counts." On

---

14 This great godly prescription—live one day at a time—has helped me through the years. It has helped me make it through tough times and find blessings in each day. Instead of dwelling on the past or overly focusing on the future, which isn't here yet, I'm to live today. The website https://alivetogod.com/notes/living-one-day-at-a-time offers a great short article with Scriptures about living one day at a time.

my worst days, he would tell me, "You can drink tomorrow; just make it through today."

Besides helping me not drink and live one day at a time, the next big lesson that Bob worked with me on—for a long time—was honesty. Addiction of any kind is an indication that we're not honest and that we don't know what to do with our hurts and feelings. Most addicts have experienced pain that they've never known what to do with, so they try to numb it, kill it, hide it, ignore it, and shove it down. They mask their emotions through work, play, distraction, substances, and habits. Addicts are attempting to make their pain and confusion tolerable. Pretending they don't feel the way they do means they are dishonest with themselves and others. All these aspects were true for me.

I couldn't not lie. For example, if I went fishing and had a good catch, maybe ten fish, I would embellish the truth and relate that I caught twenty. Besides the reasons just mentioned, I was dishonest because of my childhood; from not being believed when I said I had been molested; and from pretty much zero self-worth. To compensate, I wanted to say things so someone would believe me and listen. I lied more than I told the truth.

Pesky old Bob constantly caught me in lies about everything—from work projects to buying vehicles. After hearing the often-conflicting versions I told Karen and others, he kept insisting that I had to be honest in everything with everyone. When I complained, he inquired, "Well, how is your way working for you, Dale? You're trying to earn back Karen's trust and, to do this, you must tell the truth."

Besides Bob, the *Big Book* reinforced the message. I must tell the truth in everything. When we try to change a lifelong habit, our flesh and mind scream out, "This is really stupid and not a good idea." Ultimately, telling the truth, no matter what, meant I would have to trust God.

One night, Bob again advised me with words reflecting the *Big Book*, "Dale, you've got to learn to be brutally honest. You've got to learn to go to any lengths to be totally honest with yourself and with others, or your chances of succeeding are slim. You must develop the capacity and manner of living demanding rigorous honesty, no matter what your consequences might be, even if it means losing your position, losing your reputation, or facing jail. You can't shrink back from anything other than complete honesty."

Then he added, "I want you to write out a simple prayer, asking God to help you be honest. I want you to write it out now."

After doing as Bob requested, I was totally unnerved when he asked me to show him what I wrote. This was my prayer:

> God, You've got to be shitting me. All my life, I've lied about everything, and now You want me to tell the truth, knowing it will get me into more trouble. Jesus, please show me the way.

Bob read my prayer, smiled a bit, handed it back to me, and said, "Good job, son."

Chapter 11

MARRIAGE MESS

As I said earlier, as much as I didn't want to lose Karen and my children, I was filled with pity for myself and blame for others. Some days I wanted to stay married, and some days it seemed too hard. Sometimes I thought my marriage was the problem and if I just married someone else, I could live happily ever after. Of course, I was clueless that I would be dragging my miserable self and all my problems with me wherever I went.

Bob was now showing me how to look to God's Word for direction, protection, and consequently, avoid the hidden land mines that could blow up my life. When I continued to complain about my marriage, Bob told me he wanted me to look up and read every verse about marriage and divorce listed in my concordance. He finished with, "Consider what God has to say, then come back to talk with me."

I followed his instructions and was totally dismayed. God gives reasons that He allows for divorce, along with guidelines for remarriage. I discovered that although I could maybe get divorced, I did not have any grounds that would allow me to marry somebody else and find blessings in it from God.

Well, I knew I didn't want to be single for the rest of my life; so, I decided I would stay married, work on our marriage, and continue working on myself. Once I settled this issue and my inner wrestling match ended, I was surprised at the new focus I had for our marriage and Karen. It affected me in a startling way.

TELLING KAREN ABOUT JESUS

Before my conversion, I knew I was headed for hell. Now that I was saved, it felt good knowing that I was forgiven and headed for heaven. It was exciting to have assurance and comfort, mixed with a bit of thrilling eternal anticipation.

Suddenly, it scared me to think that I would go to heaven—but Karen wouldn't if she trusted in her goodness and not on Jesus's righteousness and sacrifice. I had to tell her she needed Jesus and felt a great urgency to do so.

When I shared all this with Bob, he held up his hand like a stop sign and said, "Dale, you need to wait. Don't tell her now. It's not a good idea." I kept insisting; he kept telling me to wait. When I kept pushing, he finally said, "Well, let's at least pray about it."

My reaction? Something like, "Pfffft . . . what's there to pray about? This is really important, Bob. I've got to tell her."

At this stage in my walk with God, I still had a lot to learn about praying and asking God for His help and wisdom in everything, much less waiting for His answer. Nor did I have a clue that maybe I should let God change my life and let it catch up to my faith. Nope, in my wisdom, I drove over to tell Karen about Jesus.

At this point in our relationship, she wouldn't let me inside the house, so we stood outside on the front steps. Excitedly, I jumped right in and declared, "I'm saved, and now I know that just because you're a good person, it doesn't mean you'll go to heaven. You can't be good enough to get to heaven on your own. You must be born again; you need Jesus."

"So let me get this straight," she responded, her voice tense. "You're an SOB, and you're going to heaven because you accepted Jesus? And I'm a good person, and I'm not going to heaven because I don't have Jesus?"

Well, this was not going as I hoped. After thinking it over for a minute, I replied, "Yeah, basically. That's about right."

Mad is what she was. She went inside and shut the door on me.

DIVINE HELP TO RECONCILE

Once again, leaning on my own wisdom didn't bring success. Bob kept telling me frequently and in various ways, "Dale, your best thinking got you here. You need God's thoughts." He showed me and instructed me to ponder on God's thoughts in Proverbs:

> Trust in the LORD with all your heart and lean not on your own understanding; in all your ways submit to him, and he will make your paths straight. Do not be wise in your own eyes; fear the LORD and shun evil. This will bring health to your body and nourishment to your bones. (Proverbs 3:5–8)

As I thought about this passage, I noticed that God tells me twice not to seek my ways. It was a truth sandwich! Around the slices of "Don't think I know the answers" and "Don't be wise in my own answers" came the filling: "Seek God and His ways."

Because my meager efforts at reconciling our marriage weren't going so hot, thankfully, Karen was still willing to seek counseling with me. It took a few counselors before we found one we liked and who offered sound advice. We both grew as we sought wisdom and help other than our own.

Why is it that many times we require someone to point out truth to us that then becomes obvious? Karen and I needed to have someone point out the places we were stuck and help us through them. Thanks to a counselor's assistance, we discovered that the way we handled our anger was unhealthy. I know—that's crazy! This was followed with more helpful guidance.

- Our explosions frequently originated from, and were fueled by, our insane craving to be right. We both needed to be right and, in the midst of this bubbling pot of nasty stew, Karen stuffed her anger, while I exploded. None of this offered a recipe for marriage success. It also meant the same issues surfaced and sparked more rip-roaring fights.

- Our anger, fear, and poor communication skills added to our problems. We needed to learn new and better ways to handle our anger and better ways to communicate. We had to learn about our emotions, be able to identify them, and recognize what was going on within ourselves and each other. Being aware of what is going on within ourselves is not the same as seeking our own wisdom; it is simply learning to be honest about our emotions, fears, and needs.
- We learned that anger can be driven by hurt, fear, or frustration, or all three simultaneously. As a result, we had to consider where our anger was coming from. What need were we experiencing? Possibilities include the need to be heard, acknowledged, understood, reassured, or comforted. (The need to be right doesn't count.)
- We learned that we needed to resolve our conflicts, instead of recycling them. At times, this meant asking for a counselor's help if we couldn't make progress on our own.

As we worked on our present issues, sometimes we discovered that we had to deal with difficulties from our past. Unresolved, past hurts can cause any of us to react disproportionately to current problems. This painful exploration of the truth regarding our own respective emotions, backgrounds, and family dysfunction helped open my eyes to the tremendous hurt I carried from my mom and her passive-aggressive manner.

Counseling helped Karen and me slowly heal our broken marriage. It took considerable time for Karen's hurt to heal and for me to earn back her trust. Marriage takes time and effort, and when we're trying to heal the pain of an affair and trust issues, it takes extra effort and time. Both people have to try, which is why Karen and I spent much time together. We did fun things together, including activities we each enjoyed. We kept learning to take care of what we have (each other) and treat each other kindly. Pastor Jim's words of encouragement were of great help to Karen, especially the needed reminder: "Remember and think on Dale's redeeming qualities."

GOD PROTECTS & BLESSES

It is truly amazing that as we seek, know, and follow God's Word, He protects and blesses us. I'm still surprised at the number of ways that God's truth comes to light in these events.

The Bible tells us that we are not to be double-minded or waver (James 1:5–8). As long as I was thinking one way one time and one way another, I would never have found peace and success. My life would have stayed a mess. Just think—if a captain of a boat steered the rudder according to every whim he had, he wouldn't make any progress and his potential for capsizing and drowning would be high.

When I became single-minded in following God's ways and promises, it put another spiritual truth into effect. I was resisting and shutting the door on Satan, so that he fled (James 4:7). The evil one is real and seeks to draw us away from God and destroy us—every way he can—which is another reason we need the safety of Jesus and God's Word. As I sought, learned, and followed God's heart about forgoing divorce and committing to our marriage, He protected us. Later on I learned that the woman who I thought might be the answer to my problems—well, her life went down the tubes. If I had continued on my adulterous path, my life would have imploded with hers. Besides protecting us, He blessed us. He continued to transform me, and was now transforming our marriage, as well.

The Lord still had more lessons for me to learn, including teaching me to depend on Him—in everything—no matter how crazy the circumstance.

Section Four

NEEDING GRACE

Chapter 12

A MESSY BABY CHRISTIAN

I thought that by becoming a Christian and going to church, my life would magically get fixed and I would automatically have peace and joy. It's true that God was empowering me to live more in accordance with His will. However, this new Christian life didn't simply make all my brokenness, habits, hurts, and shame disappear as if they never happened. There was much I needed to learn about walking every day with Jesus in grace.

At this point in my life, I had a few months of sobriety and that's about all I had. I was still struggling with all my effort to go to any lengths to stay away from alcohol and drugs and wondering if Karen and I would reconcile. To be honest, I was trying like hell not to hit anybody. I felt miserable, had a bad attitude about everything and everybody, and was filled with self-pity.

I was also a new, baby Christian, and just as babies are messy, so was I. Not only did I want myself "fixed and fine," but those around me at church did as well. If we're "fixed and fine," we don't have to be humble, get honest with ourselves or others, forgive, or grow spiritually. Although most folks at my church were good-hearted and well-intentioned, sadly they offered only religious solutions for my bad habits and brokenness. These solutions fit primarily under a label I call Perfect Christian Behavior, or PCB, for short. The message I felt was try harder, fix your external problems, and be perfect.

While I struggled with a number of issues like staying sober, smoking, swearing, and anger, church members would ask me, "Are you still dealing with that?" The question didn't make me feel good for several reasons. I felt that it came with a dose of smug superiority and judgment. Though I knew they cared about me, I sensed that they wanted me "fine" and fixed. If I demonstrated perfect Christian behavior, I wouldn't be so messy.

It seemed that these people didn't want honest acknowledgment of my struggles and had no idea how to give me grace and encouragement. This was strange to me because honesty and grace were aspects I experienced in my 12 Step meetings. Many of these church people seemed to lack the understanding that all of us (especially addicts) are growing as fast as we can, which is usually slowly.

This performance-based mentality pushed me into a cycle of straining mightily to achieve self-improvement and feeling hopeless when I failed. Dealing with my flawed behavior felt like an uphill battle. The struggle and feeling of failure would lead to another cascade of unhealthy choices and behaviors. Trying hard just wasn't working, and the inability to fix myself had me discouraged.

All this made the intense shame that I felt inside even worse. My shame was already screaming at me that I wasn't good enough. The discouragement piled on, making me think, *Something must really be wrong with me because I'm still struggling and have so many issues.*

A time or two, I slipped and drank. Each time, I had to start all over with my sobriety. Bob warned me that I was headed down a slippery slope. He also told me I had "head-in-butt disease," which—if you think about it—is a pretty accurate phrase. Those who are so wrapped up in themselves and their perspective have little concern for others. Because all they can see are themselves and their problems, they tend to show their backside a lot.[15]

---

[15] A few other truths regarding "head-in-butt disease" aren't pleasant, yet they are a reality concerning those mired in addictions and denial. When individuals are deeply stuck in problems and themselves, they can't pull themselves out. They need help to get unstuck, but it is hazardous for helpers, who frequently get "messed on" in the process.

A HECK OF A HANGOVER

One Friday night, tired of listening to my endless series of complaints, Bob handed me a bottle of scotch and said, "Here—I'll gladly refund your misery anytime you want it." This is an AA old-timers' wake-up reminder. Sure, recovery can be hard, but it's nothing compared to the misery we had in our addictions. I happily took the bottle.

You need to understand that my relationship with Bob wasn't always easy. Sometimes we got on each other's nerves. Bob was tough, and I was hotheaded (as he frequently reminded me). A couple of times we had to take a break from our sponsoring relationship. He would tell me, "Dale, you need to spend some time improving your conscious contact with God. Let me know when you're ready to start again." After a respite, we would resume.

This particular Saturday night—feeling sorry for myself and definitely angry at Bob and wanting to spite him, as well as numb my pain—I accepted the solution. I drank the scotch. The whole bottle.

An entire bottle of scotch gives a person a heck of a hangover. On Sunday morning everything hurt, especially when I breathed, even my eyelashes. Still, Bob would be expecting me at church. Plus, another of AA's frequent reminders was rolling around in my pounding head: Stick with the Steps, the meetings, and your sponsor. Even if you fall and go around the desert again, you can learn something valuable. Well, I certainly made a desert loop.[16]

Despite my stumble, God's grace was still with me and I still wanted God, sobriety, and a new life. So I got up and went to church. I also went because I didn't want to have to answer to Bob, or confess to him that I

---

16 Going "around the desert" is a reference to the story in the Bible about God's chosen Israelite people. They had been slaves in Egypt for generations and had been crying out to God for help and deliverance. He stepped in and miraculously rescued them, pledging to take them to the Promised Land—a beautiful, fruitful region—if they would trust and follow Him. On the way to the Promised Land, God led them through the desert. He wanted His chosen people to see His care and provisions for them and test them in following His directions. They circled the desert for forty years because they complained, stumbled, and resisted learning what God wanted them to know and do. The scriptural story is located in Exodus and Numbers.

drank the whole bottle. Hangover and all, I showed up for church. Of course he took one look at me and knew. Our conversation went something like this:

> Bob: "You drank it, didn't you?"
> Dale: "Yep! Every drop!"
> Bob: "You look like hell!"
> Dale: "Thanks."
> Bob: "I'm glad you came! Come on, let's go to church."

SMOKING EVIDENCE OF GOD'S GRACE

At this point, I was still smoking like a chimney—about three packs a day. It was all I could do to abstain from smoking for an hour in church. By the time the service ended, I badly needed a drag of nicotine before proceeding to an hour of Sunday school. This particular Sunday I was practically running for the front doors. I already had a cigarette to my mouth but, out of respect for God and the church, I was waiting until I got outside to light up. As soon as I hit that fresh air, I had my lighter to the cigarette.

Just then, a little old lady grabbed my arm, yanked the cigarette out of my mouth, and lambasted me, saying, "Sonny, you ought to know better than smoking in church!" I started to tell her that's the reason I waited until I was outside on the steps, but she wouldn't take a breath or let me answer. She kept lecturing me, concluding with, "You really need to trust Christ. You know, maybe you're not a Christian after all."

Normally, from embarrassment and shame, I would have cussed out this lady, but a supernatural peace from God came over me. I smiled, took out another cigarette, lit it, and took a drag. Blowing smoke, I said, "Lady, you don't have a clue how hard this last week has been for me, and smoking is the least of my problems right now." Finally, at a loss for words, she shook her head, turned around, and left me alone to finish my cigarette in peace. Afterward I headed to Sunday school.

I would like to think that I would never hit a little old lady, but I also know the awful sin nature in me that was dying a slow and painful death. Though it wasn't perfect Christian behavior, I felt Jesus's presence and grace with me. In fact, it surprised me how relaxed and calm I felt and I knew this definitely wasn't from me.

While that bottle of scotch was the last time I used alcohol to escape my pain, there is a scotch ring on the cover of my AA book from that night. When I see it I think of God's grace for desert loops because, with His grace, I still wanted Him and sobriety. Bob, AA, and God's Word all encouraged me to keep going in the right direction. Bob and AA kept reminding me, "Stick with the Steps, the meetings, and your sponsor if you want to succeed." Scripture encouraged me with stories of how God holds up His people (Psalm 37:23–24). Even heroes of the faith stumbled, but God helped them as they kept walking with Him. The stories include spiritual giants like Abraham, Moses, David, Peter, and Paul. These examples gave me hope and inspiration to not give up.

RELYING ON TRUTH & GRACE

I was learning that Jesus's solution is not about trying to be good enough, or even trying unnecessarily hard to fix my imperfections and brokenness. Certainly, we aren't to slack from making changes when they are within our power, but Christ's solution for my seemingly impossible issues and shame is for me to be honest, focus on Him, and depend on Him daily. I'm not to run ahead of Him or lag behind. We want ourselves and our problems fixed—God wants us to learn to rely on Him and His grace and power.

I used to feel that acknowledging my imperfections meant that I was not a good-enough Christian. In reality, confessing my shortcomings simply means I agree with God: I need His grace and help. The blessings and victory, which we're promised and given in Christ, come to us as we accept how much we need Jesus, His mercy, and assistance. In fact, the best part of our spiritual lives is what God does in and through us—not the changes that we are able to make on our own.

I used to roll my eyes and think it was hogwash when I heard someone say that he (or she) was a "grateful recovering addict," but now I know what they mean. Today, I gladly call myself a grateful recovering addict because, if God hadn't helped me realize my great need to be rescued, I would have missed His salvation and grace. He showed me how desperately I need Him and, after forty-plus years as a Christian, I still need God—just as much as I did when I started.

I'm always amazed how—as I walk with Jesus—I don't feel condemned by Him; instead, I feel accepted, valued, and loved. He cleanses me, heals me, and lifts me up. (I don't feel judged by Jesus, even when He has me tell stories about myself that include my failures, which He then uses for good purposes!) With AA, I don't feel judged either. There is no condemnation when we slip. We simply get honest, face our issues, and seek to grow with the assistance of God and others. We learn from others what we need to do to take a different path. And as we face and are real with our issues, we help others get honest with theirs.

Religion acquires a bad name when people miss God's grace and focus only on outward behavior, rule-keeping, and self-righteousness. This kind of religion is a soul-killer and joy-stealer. On the other hand, grace without truth enticingly lies to our fleshly human inclinations, telling us we can do whatever we want because God loves us and doesn't require anything from us. Do-anything permissiveness is nonsense. It does not lead individuals to understand their accountability to God, the ultimate outcome for their sin and, therefore, their need for Jesus.

Experiencing truth and grace together is what helps us surrender and call on God, change directions, and grow. But speaking both truth and grace, or speaking truth gracefully, is difficult to do. It is why over the years as people have tried to help me and set me straight, I've had to find some kind and honest responses. The following are a few of them.

Before I kicked my cigarette habit, people would keep asking, "Are you still smoking? You shouldn't be because you're a Christian." I began to say, "God hasn't convicted me of smoking yet. He is convicting me about other things, and I'm working on those with His help."

When I have introduced myself and shared the famous phrase, "Hi, I'm Dale, and I'm a grateful recovering alcoholic," I've received a range of responses, including, "You're insulting God. Don't you know He's healed you and who you are in Christ?" I frequently respond with, "I'm as powerless today as I was when I began. I need Jesus and His help and grace just as much today as I did when I started." Sometimes I add, "What is it that you need Jesus for in your life?"

I've come to realize that many don't understand the insidious struggles that those with addictions face. Yes, at times we are miraculously healed from an addiction, never to think about it again. However, sometimes God allows weaknesses of our flesh to remain, so that we depend on Him until He finally calls us home to be with Him. Second Corinthians 12:8–9 tells us that the Lord's grace is sufficient for us and His power is made perfect in our weakness.

LOOKING FOR A WAY AROUND GOD'S INSTRUCTIONS

As I continued to grow, Pastor Jim talked to me about being baptized and shared God's Word on the subject. Jesus, Himself, was baptized. He was fully immersed in the Jordan River by John "to fulfill all righteousness" (Matthew 3:15). Jesus's followers are to do as He did. In addition to this, baptism is to symbolize and make real to us several aspects of God's truth. It represents our sins being washed away and our hearts and consciences being made clean and right with God. Baptism symbolizes dying to our old life and being resurrected and raised up to a new life in Jesus, as we are "buried" in the water and raised up out of it (Galatians 3:27 and Romans 6:3–11).

A few Scriptures on baptism tell us:

> Peter said, "Turn back to God! Be baptized in the name of Jesus Christ, so that your sins will be forgiven. Then you will be given the Holy Spirit." (Acts 2:38 CEV)

> Anyone who believes me and is baptized will be saved. But anyone who refuses to believe me will be condemned. (Mark 16:16 CEV)

> And now what are you waiting for? Get up, be baptized and wash your sins away, calling on his name. (Acts 22:16)

Sometimes Christians struggle with being baptized, but God calls us to obey Him, be different from the world, and even stand out for Him. We are to profess God's truth, commands, and promises with our words and our lives. Christian teacher Watchman Nee declared, "Baptism is faith in action."

I struggled with getting baptized. Not only would I be getting baptized in front of people, but Pastor Jim baptized members in Pleasant Valley Lake and the park was open every day. I was to change into a long white robe in the bathhouse, then walk through the crowds of people down to the lake in this white flowing robe. Not only was Pleasant Valley open on Sundays, but it was busy! Just thinking about it made me uncomfortable.

I tried questioning, reasoning, and arguing my way around being baptized. Technically, one can suggest that baptism is not needed for salvation because the thief who was crucified on the cross next to Jesus wasn't baptized. He called on Jesus and Jesus promised him that he would be with the Lord that very day in heaven.

When I mentioned this to Jim and Bob, they both pointed out that I wasn't the thief on the cross. They said that my pride and my fear of what people thought were again causing me problems. My pride and fear were getting in the way of what God wanted me to do and, consequently, affecting my relationship with Him. They said I had to choose whether or not I was going to obey God.

My pride and fear made me wrestle with baptism longer than I should have. Finally, I surrendered and agreed to be baptized in the white robe, in the lake, and into Jesus and His life.

God was surely working to break my pride. The day I was baptized, the park was so crowded I could hardly get out of the bathhouse. Then it was difficult walking down to the lake. There were so many people milling around that I had to weave my way in and out of what seemed like masses of visitors. I even had trouble getting into the lake because so many people were crowded onto the beach. Later, Karen told me she had never seen that many people at the lake. She also said people were staring at me with their mouths open.

It was a 100 percent humbling experience, but it came with numerous blessings, not the least of which was that I was learning to follow and walk with God—to fear God, not man. As I was baptized, I felt connected to Jesus, new and clean, and I felt peace and joy.

Not bad for a Sunday "dip" as I followed my Savior in obedience!

Chapter 13

GRACE GIFTS EVERYWHERE

Grace. Sometimes people struggle to grasp the meaning and significance of this word. Simply put, grace encompasses all of God's gifts, kindness, and love for us, especially in light of our fallen, lowly, rebellious spiritual state.

By comparison, imagine that the owner of a nice restaurant franchise has an employee in an entry-level position. Despite giving him breaks several times for showing up late, slacking on the job, and other miscues, the employee steals from him. When the employee cries out for mercy from the owner, not only does the owner grant his request, but he gives this broken employee a generous gift—along with a promotion. That's grace.

Grace in its purest form, whether it is from God or people, is undeserved and unearned; it is given to those in great need (picture a destitute beggar). God is more than merciful—He pours out His loving-kindness toward us. We don't deserve it; we can't earn it; and we can never repay Him. Amazingly, God has provided a way to uphold His holiness, save us from His justice, and give us free will, all the while offering us salvation—including a new life, heart, and relationship with Christ.

Sometimes, God's spiritual blessings, gifts, and grace are not always easy to recognize. We stumble over them. They don't always come in the shape and form we want and are looking for, so it can be difficult to realize when we have been given a heaping helping.

It has taken me time to recognize and appreciate many of God's grace gifts to me. Slowly, I have stopped complaining and learned God's ways of working. As I have grown, journaled, and reviewed God's activities in my life, I have come to value His abundant gifts that are everywhere and have grown to appreciate His good, rich, giving nature. I'll share a few of these gifts and stories.

Pastor Jim was someone who showed me a lot of patience in many ways, as he embraced me for what I was—a baby Christian. Take, for instance, when I retrieved my boulder-rock from Pleasant Valley. My rock now held even greater meaning because it was where I talked with God and surrendered to Him. I decided to get my rock on a Sunday morning. Hopping in my pickup truck, I headed to Medina Cut Stone and loaded up a trailer with a bulldozer and forklift, which I needed for my task. I happened to pull into Pastor Jim's driveway just as he was leaving for church.

He seemed a little surprised, but asked fairly nonchalantly, "What's the bulldozer for?"

"I'm getting my favorite rock," I replied.

I saw a bit of a smile cross his face as he inquired, "Any chance you're coming to church after that?"

"Next Sunday," I said. "I'll be there!"

I had told Jim that one day I would get my rock, but he probably thought it was all talk. Looking back, he could have harangued me, told me I needed to establish better priorities, or scolded me in any number of ways, but he didn't. He gave me grace that day and in other ways, too.

When we would meet for breakfast or lunch, he always prayed before we ate. In the beginning, it made me uncomfortable for people to see us praying.

"Do we have to pray over every meal?" I grumbled one time.

"Dale, drop your napkin, and by the time you're done getting it, I'll be finished praying." He gave me grace—and stayed faithful to God.

Jim's friendship meant a great deal to me. In addition, it was great to feel needed when he asked for my help in fixing something or showing him how something worked on the property. I also treasured the times he shared how blessed he felt in purchasing our beautiful Pleasant Valley Lake property and the wonderful house my dad built.

Karen and I experienced grace gifts together, which included attending church as a family with Brianna and Larry. This was important to me because, as a child, I didn't like it that Dad never came to church with Mom and us kids. Now, Karen and I were enjoying our family, Sundays, lunch together, and new friends.

Besides church, we participated in fun get-togethers with our new friends, which were often held at our house. Sometimes we held sing-alongs, with Jim furnishing musical accompaniment on his guitar. Both Karen and I felt loved and that we belonged in this new family. These were wonderful feelings to experience!

Jim and his wife included us in their family and took us under their wing. Karen and I, along with Brianna and little Larry, went to lunch with them almost every Sunday after church. When the Chapmans sent their daughter to summer church camp, we sent Brianna. Karen also went to camp to help, and to keep an eye on Brianna. Karen excitedly called me from camp one day, exclaiming, "I understand what you were trying to explain to me. I accepted Jesus!"

God's grace was at work, blessing our family. When Karen got home, she was baptized in Pleasant Valley Lake.

LEARNING TRUTH & GRACE IN SCRIPTURE

I was learning truth everywhere—at church, in Sunday school, and from the Bible, as well as from AA, the *Big Book,* and Bob. It surprised me how often the lessons from church and the Bible were the same lessons in AA. Because members who aren't familiar with AA often complained to me or tried to dismiss AA and the Steps, it was thrilling every time I saw the principles of the Steps in Scripture for myself! They're everywhere! The Steps then enable us to put God's wisdom into action in doable portions.

It's not by accident that the Steps and Bible fit together so well. The founders of AA, including the original group known as the Oxford Group, were Christians who desired to live out God's power and truth. As these founding men daily sought help from God in prayer and through His Word—and followed Him and His word—they received miracles of sobriety and healing. These men studied and practiced Scripture, particularly Jesus's Sermon on the Mount found in Matthew chapters 5–7 which begins with the blessings of being poor in spirit; 1 Corinthians 13 (the love chapter); and the book of James.

Bob helped explain spiritual, biblical truths to me and showed me two key aspects of God's will for each of us. First, God's intent and desire for us in this life and the next are that we know and experience Him. Scripture tells us:

> Now this is eternal life: that they know you, the only true God, and Jesus Christ, whom you have sent. (John 17:3)

Besides knowing God, His will is that we are to be transformed into the image of Christ. Bob would often share passionately and almost breathlessly about a well-known passage. "This is amazing. We're told in Romans 8:28 that God works all things together for good for those who love Him and are called according to His purpose. Now look at what is shared in the verse that follows, Romans 8:29. God's purpose is that we're to be conformed to the image of Jesus. If we desire for all things to work together for good, then we are to seek to become more like Christ. Many church folks know variations of Romans 8:28, but they have no idea that God shares His design and intentions with us in that next verse."[17] Together, the two verses tell us:

> We are confident that God is able to orchestrate everything to work toward something good *and beautiful* when we love Him and accept His invitation to live according to His plan. *From the distant past, His eternal love reached into the future.* You see, He knew those who would be His one day, and He chose them beforehand to be conformed to the image of His Son. (Romans 8:28–29 VOICE)

The *J. B. Phillips New Testament* gives this beautiful rendition for the last bit of this passage: "He made them righteous in his sight, and then lifted them to the splendour of life as his own sons."

---

[17] Appendix G shares a few more Scriptures about "Being Conformed to & Transformed by Jesus."

In everything that happens to us, God's good purposes include revealing Himself to us, utilizing every circumstance for our good, and shaping us into the image of Jesus. As these events unfold, God, His goodness, and glory are continually enjoyed and shared.

GRACE PRESCRIPTION: MORNING & EVENING

Bob, AA, and the *Big Book* helped me learn to seek God's grace daily, starting with practicing spiritual principles in the morning and the evening. (Much of this section about daily practices also reflects the *Big Book*, chapter 6, "Into Action." The chapter includes these morning and evening practices, and shares about Step 11—seeking God with prayer and meditation.)

Turning our lives and wills over to the care of God in all our activities doesn't come naturally, nor does it happen once and become an automatic habit. We begin by practicing it—daily. Bob and AA taught me to turn my will and life over to God's care every morning and ask Him to direct my thinking. I was to ask God to give me inspiration, wisdom, and direction in my decisions and to help my thoughts be divorced from self-seeking, self-pity, and dishonest motives. As I sought His will, I was to relax, take it easy, and not stress and struggle when facing decisions. During the day, I would pray, "Your will, God," as I turned my life over to His care through Jesus.

Like so many before me and as the *Big Book* says, I was surprised to find how often right answers came to me after I tried this for a while. I found myself with much less fear, worry, anger, and self-pity; plus I was making fewer unwise decisions. Life became easier. I didn't tire so easily because I wasn't foolishly burning up energy, worrying, and trying to figure out everything using my own strength and wisdom.

In the evening, I was to review my day and my actions. Instead of brooding about what everyone else did or didn't do, I was supposed to look at myself—my thoughts, actions, and motives—with these questions:

- When had I been afraid, scared, fearful, or worried?
- Did I get mad at anyone? Was I still angry, resentful, or holding grudges against anyone? Do I owe anyone an apology?

- Had I been dishonest in any way?
- Did I keep something to myself when I should have spoken up? Is there something I need to discuss with another person?
- When had I been selfish and thinking about only myself?
- Was I kind and loving to everyone with whom I interacted? Could I have done something for someone? Could I have done anything better?

We could condense it like this: When was I afraid? When was I mad, angry, or resentful? When was I dishonest, selfish, or inconsiderate? Had I been kind, loving, and peace-seeking?

This may sound like a lot of trouble at the end of a long, tiring day, but AA focuses on self-examination and honesty. These are important if we are to grow and live well, yet they are difficult to do. As we willingly consider our actions and attitudes, eliminate weeds and trash, and seek God's help and sustenance, we find that our lives begin to produce good fruit.

As I sought God in all things and carefully considered my ways, I began to see amazing progress and results. Once so out-of-control I wound up in a flophouse with only one shoe and no idea what had happened to my car, I became a sober, thoughtful, and more caring person. In everything, I aimed for rigorous honesty as I leaned on the help and accountability of my sponsor and the caring group of men I learned to trust. As I learned to confess my sins, I experienced healing just as the promise and instruction tell us in James 5:16. Previously, I had been wholly undisciplined; now I was letting God teach and discipline me in gentle, simple ways through daily habits. I was doing what I could, while God was doing for me the things that I couldn't.

Amazing things were happening, including finding freedom, happiness, and thankfulness. Considering the criminal activities, conflicts, fights, and drunken behavior that used to characterize me, these were blessings worth more than all the gold in Fort Knox. No longer was my past something from which I was running or trying to hide. Rather, from it, I was experiencing God's care, power, and love for me. My past helped me connect with others and find peace with God. Life, with God and His help, was becoming pleasurable!

These changes didn't happen in monumental leaps or overnight; they were gradual—but they were happening.

BOB'S GRACE

Bob's encouragement and prodding helped me come to know God's Word, grow in it, and love it. To appreciate why Bob hungered to know God and Scripture so deeply, it helps to know a bit about his story.

As I've said, Bob was sharp, rough, and tough. Not only had he been a paratrooper and prisoner during the Korean War—he had survived the infamous Tiger Death March. This was when a North Korean general forced 845 prisoners to march ninety miles in nine days in the Siberian-like winter of 1950. The general earned the name "The Tiger" because of his brutality. While mostly military men, the prisoners included about eight civilians, some of whom were women and children.

The prisoners were starved, dehydrated, beaten, and tortured; some were simply shot and killed. Many had summer clothes and no shoes. During the night, from two to ten would freeze to death. Bob woke up one morning to find both men on each side of him frozen. Those unable to keep up with the marching pace were shot. Prisoners had to grab handfuls of snow, when they could, for water. One news report called these nine days an "icy hell." When the death march reached its destination, those still alive were held prisoner for three years. Two-thirds of the prisoners died by the end. Bob was one of 260 survivors.

Bob knew that God had spared his life numerous times, but he struggled with the memories and questioned why God kept him alive. (This feeling is called "survivor's guilt.") One time, guards forced the prisoners to wave their T-shirts. When they did so, those waving white T-shirts were shot. Since Bob had a khaki-colored T-shirt, his life was spared.[18] After the war, when Bob came home, he became an alcoholic

---

18 As Bob and I became good friends, his wife often expressed surprise about the stories he shared with me.

and progressively grew worse as the years passed. One counselor told him that he had a death wish both before he became a POW and more so afterward.

However, Bob's life changed dramatically the night he attended a Rex Humbard gospel revival. At the end of the service, Humbard extended an invitation for anyone to come forward who wanted to receive a new life in Christ, and Bob was there. He prayed and received Christ. Volunteer counselors then spent time with each person privately and helped disciple them.

From that night on, Bob was a different man. He became active in AA, obtained sobriety, and grew in his walk with Jesus. He became not just an avid Bible reader, but a serious and insatiable student of the Bible—so much so that he was virtually a walking Bible encyclopedia!

Bob loved taking classes from Rex Humbard's church, the Cathedral of Tomorrow,[19] and enjoyed listening to its Southern gospel quartet. Added to this, he took every class he could at Moody Bible College's satellite campus in Akron, Ohio. Amazing Bible teachers were brought in for the classes. Some sessions were single events, while others met once or twice a week and could last from one month to several months. If a class was offered, Bob was there.

GRACE, CLASSES & QUIZZES

Because Bob loved God's Word so much, he helped me grow in it. This was a real gift of God's because I rarely felt eager when Bob would first mention, "Let's do a word study." Complaining did no good; he loved to remind me, "Dale, you agreed to take the cotton out of your ears, put it in your mouth, and follow my instructions. Remember?"

---

[19] The Humbards—including Rex and his brother, Clement—were an influential Christian family who held gospel tent revivals. Many family members were pastors, evangelists, and musicians. Rex eventually started his own church, the Cathedral of Tomorrow, which became one of America's first megachurches. He was the first televangelist to nationally broadcast weekly services and was known for his familiar admonition, "What America needs is an old-fashioned, Holy Ghost, God-sent, soul-savin', devil-hatin' revival." He was the pastor who delivered Elvis Presley's funeral eulogy in 1977, in Memphis. In its December 27, 1999, issue, *U.S. News & World Report* named Rex Humbard (who died in 2007) as one of the twenty-five shapers of the modern era. Although Rex was involved in some financial troubles, he and his family made a difference for God.

Bob had me study a number of topics in Scripture, including anger, fear, and forgiveness. He would talk to me about what I read, test me, and ask me, "What did God tell you?"

Once he had me conduct a word study about sin; I had to look up every New Testament verse referencing sin. When we sat down to discuss it, he had me use my concordance. I had to tell him about each sin listed and what God said about it. At the end, he let me know that I missed one—the verse that says, "If you don't do what you know is right, you have sinned" (James 4:17 CEV). Once again, this is more proof of how much I need Jesus's forgiveness and help!

In fact, the Bible describes the law, righteousness, and truth as one entire unit. If we break just one part (which we all do), we stand guilty before God. It doesn't matter how good we think we are; before God, we are broken, ungrateful, resistant people, in need of forgiveness, grace, a new heart, and a new life. God pours out His grace to us because He loves us, and He wants people who love Him, and who reflect His glory and image.

Bob and I talked a great deal about our sin and our sin nature. He often enthusiastically shared about a passage in Romans, declaring, "It's the best description ever of our bent toward sin, the tendencies we can't break on our own, and addiction!" The passage tells us:

> I know that nothing good lives in me, that is, in my sinful nature. I want to do what is right, but I can't. I want to do what is good, but I don't. I don't want to do what is wrong, but I do it anyway.... When I want to do what is right, I inevitably do what is wrong. (Romans 7:18–19, 21 NLT)[20]

He would finish by reminding me, "That's the bad news, but the good news is that Jesus rescues us (Romans 7:25). With Him we have ample grace and help, for every struggle!"

Now, every time Bob took a class at Moody Bible College's satellite campus in Akron, he signed me up too and we were both there. One day, he signed us up for a class on Romans that continued for several months.

---

[20] The full passage in Romans 7:14-25 and the entirety of Romans chapter 7 contain much about sin and our sin nature.

"Why do I need to take a class about Romans?" I moaned.

"Because you need to be a student of the Bible, and Romans is a key book," Bob answered. "It includes the plan of salvation and everything you need to know about Jesus and following Him."

He enjoyed adding, "You agreed, remember?"

Our teacher was just as passionate about Romans as Bob was and, once again, I learned a great deal!

James was another favorite book of not only Bob's, but of the founders of AA, in part because all the principles of the Steps are in it. It can be a tough read. Bob had me camp out in it for some time. James was Christ's half-brother, and he doesn't let us off easy. The book happens to be the last book of the Bible that was declared (canonized) as Holy Scripture. I tend to think it's because other people struggle with James's hard-hitting grace, but it is hard-hitting grace that we all need.

Repeatedly, God's Spirit kept drawing me into His Word, helping me know Him more intimately. He had been at work on this for years, going back to when He first led me to take the Catholic-catechism class and then, through my mother, challenged me to read through the Bible—twice. God gave me the gift of a Christian college education, which required me to study His Word. Thanks to Bob, He was giving me another heavy-duty, robust course on His Word—complete with tests!

Bob always wondered why he survived being a POW of the Korean War and God didn't simply take him back then. I know the reason. God, in His grace, saved Bob for good purposes. God used Bob in my life—to disciple me with love—knowing that I needed Bob's tough grace to push and prod me, particularly with all my complaining and grumbling.

God's grace that He bestowed on Bob, combined with Bob's love for God and His gifts, made a drastic difference in my life. The grace that God gave Bob, and then Bob gave me, has flowed to many others. Now this grace has spilled onto you, too!

May we keep seeking to know God's amazing grace that is everywhere. It's all around us, showered on us, and woven into our lives even when it's difficult to recognize.

Chapter 14

STEPS ON THE ROAD OF GRACE

I had been sober for almost a year when Karen and I got into a heated argument. Mad as the dickens, I stormed out of the house, jumped in my car, and peeled rubber all the way down the street. I was becoming madder by the minute, in part because I wanted a drink, but I wasn't drinking. Not knowing what else to do, I headed for Bob's house.

We sat at his kitchen table, while he patiently let me unload. But then Bob asked me—as he always did—to read what God had to say. He had me read out loud Ephesians 4:26–27: "In your anger do not sin. Do not let the sun go down while you are still angry, and do not give the devil a foothold." After this, he had me read the third chapter of James, which instructs us about anger, our words, and wisdom. When I finished, he asked me, "What is God telling you?" With anger still overpowering me and without thinking, I picked up his Bible and threw it. It sailed right through his pretty bay kitchen window, shattering glass everywhere.

Bob surveyed the busted debris, looked back at me, and declared, "Son, it's time you learn what a dry drunk is and do a 4th Step."

"What's a dry drunk?" I inquired.

"It's what you are," he answered exasperatedly. "The only thing you've done over the past year is stop drinking. You still have all your character defects and the same thinking that you had when you were drinking. You've yet to work on your issues that led to your drinking in the first place. Your defects are still there, and now you're not numbing them. Your disappointments and hurts are leading to anger and resentments. These are all hazardous to your life and soul. They will eat away at you, destroying you and your relationships. You have to learn to deal with anger and resentments in a healthy way. You're ready to do a 4th Step."

Right then, Bob's wife charged in, exclaiming, "What's going on in here?" Although she normally tolerated me, this night when she saw the window, she exploded on Bob, "Why are you always helping drunks? I don't know why you let men like Dale in our house; all they ever do is make a mess!"

After she stormed out, Bob turned to me and said, "And I want my window fixed before dark."

I left to round up supplies to fix the window and thought about what Bob shared. It was true. It wasn't just my drinking and drugging; my self-centeredness was a consuming tornado, tearing through my life and the lives of those I loved. Even though I made a decision to follow Christ and He had enabled me to stop drinking, I still had a number of selfish habits keeping my life in chaos. I required more than merely theory and talk; more than ever, I needed to seek God's help, power, and His spiritual principles.

DESIRE FOR SOMETHING BETTER

For addicts to find sobriety and recovery, they must give up fighting and admit they need help. Then, they need rehabilitation. But simply being rehabilitated wouldn't be enough for me—it only restores people, mentally and emotionally, to the state or condition they were in prior to using alcohol or drugs. Individuals are simply refurbished to the level of maturity they had achieved before their addiction began. This wasn't good. I would be returned to the maturity of a twelve-year-old boy. My thinking, behavior, and emotions would all be like an adolescent boy's, except for my anger, which would be more like that of a five-year-old on good days. This was not a state I wanted to restore or return to.

I needed the regeneration that God promises—a condition beyond my own capabilities—and beyond what I could imagine. I needed to be made new in Christ. This, of course, requires ongoing commitment and cooperation with Him. The good news of salvation is that God saves us, fully and wholly, when we turn to Him, but this is just the beginning of our conversion and walk with Jesus. We must participate with God and the work that He wants to do in us.

For me, the regeneration process would include two key components—working to renew my mind and working the 12 Steps. Scripture instructs us to renew our minds with God's Word and truth because, apart from Him, our thinking is faulty and broken.[21] Bob frequently reminded me that I needed to stop pursuing my random thoughts and stop following my own wisdom, which most days is fairly worthless.

Sometimes, he would tell me that my mind had become a derelict plot of ground; it certainly wasn't a garden growing anything worthwhile. Left alone, it had become infested with weeds—unhealthy attitudes and selfish, jealous, depressing, and filthy thoughts had taken over—nothing good could grow.

Other times, he would tell me that, without the Lord, my mind was a dangerous place with dark alleys. Blaming others, resentment, stinking thinking, "what-ifs," fear, and pride were lurking and assaulting me when I gave them opportunity. My own reasonings were attacking my peace and sanity, destroying my relationships when I flared up in defensiveness and attacked back, and robbing me of joy.

Renewing my mind takes willingness and effort as I turn myself and my life over to God, seek His help, and digest the nutritional food from His Word. Slowly, I learn what is important to Him, and my focus and values begin to change.

CLEARING THE MESS

The 12 Steps have helped bring me much healing because they're biblical and they help me put God's instructions into action. They help me clean up my life and be amenable to God's regenerating work that He desires to accomplish in me. In this chapter, I'll share a bit about the Steps, along

---

21 A few of God's directives on renewing our minds and thoughts include Romans 12:1–2; Ephesians 4:21–24; Philippians 2:5 and 4:8; and Colossians 3:10.

with a few stories. (The 12 Steps of AA can be found in Appendix B. More information regarding enjoyable sobriety and AA is in Appendix D.)

In a condensed form, the 12 Steps help us to:

- See and admit that we can't fix ourselves or our circumstances;
- know that there is a God, He is good, and He wants to help us;
- call on God and turn our lives over to Him;
- review our shortcomings and admit them;
- make amends with those we have hurt;
- seek God through His Word, meditating on it, and praying;
- follow Him as He directs us;
- recognize God's love, new life, and hope that we're given; and
- share these gifts with others.

RELATIONSHIPS MATTER

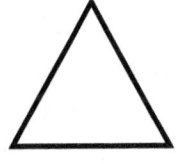

AA's program and goals are often illustrated with a triangle; each corner stands for a goal of recovery, unity, and service. I have come to picture a triangle for life and recovery in which the top corner represents God, one corner depicts others, and the other one symbolizes ourselves. The condition of our lives is reflected in these relationships. Being upset with the Lord, others, or ourselves will come out with fighting or hiding against the others. The 12 Steps not only help us heal and grow ourselves and our relationships, but we discover that the closer we draw to God and move up the triangle, the closer we draw to others. [22]

WORKING THE 12 STEPS TAKES WORK

To work the Steps, we must actually *work* them. We work them, think on them, and practice them on our own, and with the aid of a sponsor who gives us encouragement, grace, and truth. Bob, and the men at my meetings, all gave me these gifts that helped me do what I needed to do.

---

22 Through the years, as I counsel people regarding various types of issues, I frequently draw this triangle on my whiteboard, and we discuss how the health of our relationships affects our lives.

STEPS 1–3

In Steps 1 and 2, we admit we need help and come to believe in a God who desires to help us. In Step 3, we ask God for His aid and turn our lives and will over to His care. These Steps can be condensed to: I can't; God can; I need to ask Him for help.

These first three Steps may be a process for us and take time. We may still be in "self-effort mode," trying old and new things in various combinations to fix our problems, while desperately hoping for new results. We may be attempting to help God in how we think our recovery should go. We may be struggling to believe in God or that God cares and will help.

Ultimately we come to realize that living solely with our own wisdom, strength, and power is not enough to navigate this daunting challenge called life. We require help, power, and wisdom greater than our own—we need God. In fact, living life without the Creator-Owner of this life is part of why we struggle. God never intended for us to do life on our own—He wants a relationship with us.

In Steps 1 through 3 we come to believe that God exists and He desires to help us, but because God doesn't force Himself and His ways on us, we must call on Him and request help. We consciously and specifically invite God into our lives. We find a place and a way to talk to Him. We can believe in God all we want, but we need to call on Him for His help, and follow as He directs us. Calling on God sometimes happens only when we reach the pit of complete despair. Otherwise, we think about God; we want God; we are even looking, waiting, and wishing for God to intervene, but we haven't asked Him. Sometimes, it takes utter hopelessness, desperation, and fear for us to finally cry out to Him, "Oh, God, please save me! Please help me and show me what to do!"

Scripture promises us:

> Everyone who calls on the name of the Lord will be saved. (Romans 10:13 ESV)

> Therefore, if anyone is in Christ, the new creation has come: The old has gone, the new is here! (2 Corinthians 5:17)

STEPS 4-5

In these two Steps, we make a searching and fearless moral inventory of ourselves. Then, we admit to God and another person the exact nature of our wrongs.

The 4th Step helps us do some plowing of our hearts and lives. Instead of looking at the faults of others, we consider our offenses and issues that we try to blame on others. ("Well, I wouldn't be this way if they weren't that way!" Or, "I wouldn't be this way if life wasn't this way!") Well, this is our life, and this is the way we are; so we look at ourselves and where we fall short.

I love AA's *Big Book*, especially its disarming way of describing character defects that makes me admit, "Yeah, I do that too!" It inspires me to want to "clean up my side of the street" and gives me a motivating picture for conducting a moral inventory. The fifth chapter, "How It Works," reminds us that any business enterprise, if it wants to be healthy and successful, must list its assets and liabilities; then it must work to add to its assets and reduce its liabilities.

The 4th Step is tough and challenging, and can overwhelm us if we were to stop there and not complete it with another person. This is a place where our sponsor plays a vital role—by being a close friend who helps us talk about our defects, confess them, and pray for forgiveness and help. Along the way, we're surprised to discover that instead of feeling that we will die if our failings are exposed, with the help of God and our sponsor, we start to know God's freedom, grace, and peace! There are many Scripture passages about confessing our shortcomings and finding healing. Following are two key promises from God's Word (and Appendix F shares a few more).

> Repent, then, and turn to God, so that your sins may be wiped out, that times of refreshing may come from the Lord. (Acts 3:19)

> Therefore confess your sins to each other and pray for each other so that you may be healed. (James 5:16)

MY NOTEBOOK OVERFLOWS

The Saturday when I sat down to work the 4th and 5th Steps for the first time, Bob was with me. In addition, I had a blank notebook, which he told me to bring. Bob prayed with me before I started and asked God to bring things to my mind and help me write them down. He instructed me to write down my good traits. Next, I was to list everything I could think of that I had done wrong with regard to people, places, and things, and anyone I had hurt as far back as I could remember. I was to list everyone I was mad at or resented, as well as my fears and sexual sins.

When I finished, I was exhausted and drained. My notebook was full. Bob and I again prayed, requesting God's forgiveness, cleansing, and help. Before we were through, Bob listened as I shared some of my 4th Step. He encouraged me not to feel overwhelmed and reminded me that I would work on only one thing at a time, with God's help.

FREEDOM & BLESSINGS BEGIN TO FLOW

As I have mentioned, much healing and growth take place while we are working the Steps. This is especially true in Steps 4 and 5. For instance, much healing happens in the process of admitting our character faults. We learn to name, acknowledge, confess, and talk about them—rather than shoving them down and pretending we don't have any. Admitting is key. We're not just aware of our issue, or wanting our issue to go away, or hoping our issue gets better, or even knowing what our issue is—we admit our issue to ourselves, to someone else, and to God: "I have a problem with _____." We fill in the blank and confess it.

When we identify and name our issues and character defects it is like we give them "handles" so we can pick them up, consider them, talk about them, and deal with them. Instead of trying to fight against them, cover them with habits that don't work, or drown everything in a bottle, we consider the nature and patterns of our wrongs. For example, what exactly do we have problems with? Anger? Resentment? Bitterness? Lying? Fears? Doubt? Envy? Greed? Lust? Pride? We can't grow and deal with our defects when they come up if we avoid thinking about them and don't know what they are. We need to know where we are stuck so we can ask God for assistance.

Three of my big broken areas are pride, fear of not being worthy, and anger. I can swing quickly from pride to fear, or experience both simultaneously. I also have problems with anger—which snaps and crackles when my pride is stepped on and fear is triggered. All these ingredients are a recipe for fireworks and trouble. With the Lord's assistance, I would work on these broken areas of mine.

Bob continued, over time, to help me talk about my shortcomings. He sent me to the Bible to look up and read what God says about my defects, and consider the Lord's specific promises and instructions concerning them.

I discovered more freedom as I learned to talk about my failings with the men in my group (and as I heard them name their defects and share ways they were finding freedom and healing). Removing my masks with others, getting real about myself, and admitting my failings are, amazingly, good things. As I admitted my failings to Bob and to the men who cared about me and had walked this same road, I experienced fellowship, forgiveness, and love in tangible ways. This is life-giving; words cannot describe this experience and the feelings it brings. As I stop spending time and effort pretending to be what I'm not, I realize how much God and others love me. I find acceptance and peace—which inspire me and help me grow. If God accepts me, I can accept myself, and in return, I can accept and love others.

The 4th and 5th Steps have been so valuable to my life and walk with God that I have worked them many, many times. In the early years of my sobriety, I worked through them a couple of times a year. I still work them. They help me grow and be filled with more of Jesus. In this way, when I'm squeezed by life, instead of my own ick and junk coming out, Jesus and His good character traits can develop and emerge.

STEPS 6-7

These two Steps—being *ready* for God to remove our character defects and humbly *asking* Him to remove our shortcomings—may seem like one Step, but they are two different aspects. They may also seem easy at first but, like the other Steps, there is more to them than meets the eye. We discover this every time we stumble on a shortcoming that we are reluctant to relinquish (because it offers us a payoff or benefit), or we don't know how to overcome it. (Anger was the issue I struggled to relinquish.) Our defects can seem too difficult to remedy—impossible, in fact. If we don't possess the strength or the wisdom to do it on our own, we must seek God's aid. We may even have to return to the first three steps: I can't. God can. I will ask Him for help.

STEPS 8–10

In Steps 8–10, we make a list of people whom we have harmed, and make amends to them whenever possible (except when it would injure them or others); we continue to take a personal inventory and promptly admit our wrongs.

These Steps can be fairly tough for those who would rather undergo physical pain than apologize. In fact, making amends is more than apologizing—it is doing what we can to set things right with others. For example, if we have stolen something, we offer to pay for it.

Once again, *the process of the Steps* is important. We don't simply make a quick list and rush out making amends, willy-nilly. We use our completed 4th-Step inventory to make a list of names. We add any more names that come to mind. Then, we divide our list into three groups:

- People with whom we need to make amends as soon as possible.
- People who could be hurt if we made amends to them.
- People with whom we're willing to make amends if God provides us an opportunity to do so.

I MAKE AMENDS

After compiling my list, I met with Bob. We talked and prayed about my list, the people, and the situations. We asked God for wisdom, direction, and opportunities. I was continuing to make amends with Karen, doing my best to grow and work on issues with her as they surfaced. Now I began to make amends to other people.

One of the first amends I made was to the owner of the old candy store that I loved as a kid. It was an old-timey store with a long shotgun-style room, wooden floors, and wood counters, which held big glass containers filled with all sorts of colorful candy. There were several of these long, colorful, tempting aisles. As a kid, I had stolen candy from there.

The store had closed years ago, but I knew the owner and where he lived. When I arrived at his house and told him the reason I came, he started laughing, but he agreed I could pay him back. We agreed on fifty dollars. The experience gave me pleasant, peaceful feelings, and I felt God encouraging me to keep going.

Later, I went to make amends to one of the men whose arm I had broken as a Mafia enforcer. I sought him out and asked him if he could forgive me. He said that he could because he knew he had hurt people, too. This was another healing experience for me, which helped relieve some of the great regret and pain that I carried with me from those years long ago.

Some amends didn't turn out as well as these did. Bob reminded me that seeking to make amends isn't about the outcome. We're doing what we can to set things right with others and to clean our side of the street. If people continue to embrace their anger, refuse to forgive, and nurse a grudge against us, we can't change them—only ourselves. We take action, but we can't control the results.

I put some amends on God's list. He would need to provide me with the time, place, opportunity, courage, and strength if He wanted me to take that step. And God did. I marvel at the ways that God brought about some amends in His timing and His way.

In Step 10, I continued to take daily inventory and make amends as needed. When I was wrong (and when I am wrong), I try to promptly admit it. In the beginning, this was rather frequent; even today, I find myself messing up more than I would like. That's why I love God's forgiveness so much—I need it.

STEPS 11-12

In the last two Steps, we seek through prayer and meditation to know God and His will more, and we seek the strength to carry out His will. As we live out God's principles, we experience a spiritual awakening and realize that we have been given a new life! Consequently, we strive to share this message, grace, and hope with others in need, and continue to practice these principles in all our affairs.

Again, all the Steps seem easy to read and mentally agree with, but working them is as different as watching a video about climbing mountains versus actually scaling massive peaks. As I worked the Steps, I experienced, like others before me, what is descriptively called a "spiritual awakening." It is like waking up and seeing ourselves, God, and life in a whole new way and a new light. It is also receiving (and realizing) that we have been given a new life filled with unearned, undeserved blessings, privileges, freedom, and new opportunities that we're to explore and grow in.

In a number of ways, AA helped generate change and break down my walls and selfishness. Like most addicts, I struggled mightily with selfishness. Life had been all about me, at the expense of others. AA taught me how to participate with others in life and connect with them. At first, just showing up for meetings was a huge success. Then, I began participating in the meetings—sharing and revealing aspects about myself, peeling away the onion, and becoming vulnerable. I continued to ask for, and receive, assistance. Next, I was encouraged to begin helping in simple ways. I took my turn at setting up the room for meetings, serving coffee, or helping clean up afterward. Later, I helped take my turn at leading meetings.

Then, I began to help those who were behind me on this same road of addiction, and a surprising thing happened. Like others before me, I found that aiding other alcoholics provided the best incentive for staying sober. It brought me more connection with others and gave me joy! The more I received these thrilling gifts from God and others, the more I wanted to do all I could to share and pass on these blessings to as many people as possible.

I was experiencing a spiritual awakening! I really was being converted, transformed, and made new! Everything was different—my heart, desires, actions, and purpose. I was living for God and others. All the while, I continued to apply these principles—every day—in all my affairs. As I did, God's cleansing and healing continued to flow, removing the debris and dead places that had been destroying my soul and life.

And God was just beginning.

Gottlieb & Emma Keen
(Grandpa & Grandma)

Pastor Gottlieb (Grandpa),
third from left, with church elders

Uncle Julius,
our bootlegger

Pastor Gottlieb preaching

Arline & Reiny (Mom & Dad) shortly after they were married in 1941

Dad, Dale & Larry

Four years old and unable to stand after drinking a beer (which is on the running board)

Dale & Larry

Pleasant Valley Lake crowd (like when I was baptized)

PLEASANT VALLEY LAKE
INVITES YOU ! !

9511 W. Pleasant Valley Road

Parma 30, Ohio   R.A. FIEGLAND, prop.

Res. Phone - VI. 3-5945 .... Park - VI. 2-0848

" SHADED   PICNIC   AREAS "

Come out to Pleasant Valley Lake for your Summer Picnics and for a swim in a clean spring fed lake.

This is the spot to bring the whole family for enjoyable recreation away from the public parks and swimming pools.

Picnic tables available. Refreshment stand in the picnic area. Guards on duty at the lake at all times. Modern Bath House Facilities.

REGULAR MEMBERSHIP:
$2.00 per family, plus general admission each time when entering.
60¢ per person age 12 and over.
40¢ per child age 1 to 12.

SEASON MEMBERSHIP:
$15.00 per person age 12 and over. $5.00 per child age 1 to 12.

PARK HOURS: Sundays and Holidays 9:00 A.M. to
9:00 P.M. - Weekdays 12 noon to 9 P.M

LODGE, CHURCH and BUSINESS GROUPS WELCOMED.

Our Pleasant Valley Lake brochure

High school graduation in 1965

Hunting

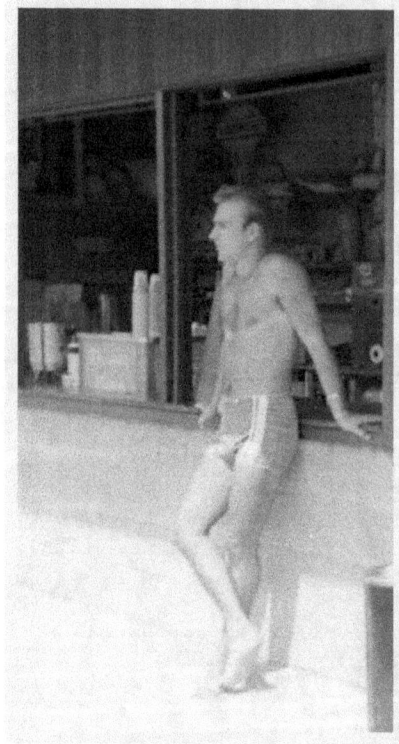

Lifeguard in August 1968

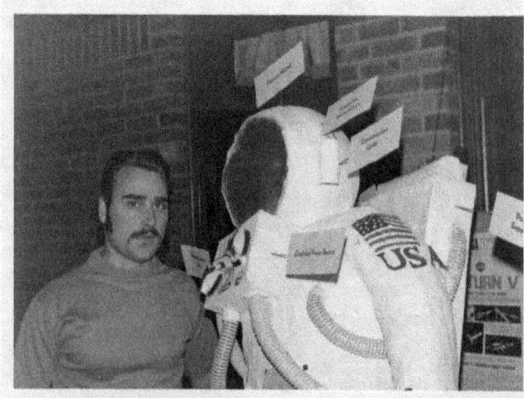

Teaching and our science-fair project

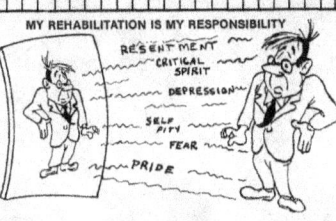

An AA Moral Inventory list

A church function

Dale's sideburns

Jail-counselor ID card

Riverside Baptist Church on Tarpon Street
(not the current location)

Dale Fiegland To Be Ordained July 6

Wednesday evening will be a special time in the life of our church as we ordain Dale Fiegland to the gospel ministry. One of the marks of God's blessing on a church is that He places a special call to ministry on men and women in that congregation. God has done that in calling Dale Fiegland into the ministry.

Dale has demonstrated a life surrendered to the Lordship of Christ and has been an example of a heart for service and what ministry is all about.

By ordaining Dale, we as a church are simply stating that we see evidence of God's call on his life.

Pray for Dale, Karen and the children this week as we celebrate together what God is doing in their lives.

Ordination bulletin

Pastor of education and principal of Riverside Christian School

Family photo (L to R): Trouble, Brianna, Double Trouble, Karen, Dale, Nathan, & Larry

Vali (6); Henry (9); Victor (4); & Adi (17)—the week they all joined our family

2011 Discovery Schedule

Monday:
1:00 Alcoholics Anonymous 1-2-3 Go Co-Ed Rm: 125-1
7:00 Alcoholics Anonymous Big Book Co-Ed Rm: 130-2
7:30 Alcoholics Anonymous Garden Group Co-Ed Rm: Church Patio
7:30 Men's Sexual Addiction Recovery Rm: 125
7:30 Women's Codependency Rm: 126-1

Tuesday:
6:30 AA 12-Step Beginners Open Rm: 116
7:00 Sexual Addiction Recovery Modular A
7:00 Men's Hurts Habits & Hang-ups Rm: 143
7:00 Women's Codependency Rm: 126
7:00 Women's Narcotics Anonymous Rm: 145-2
7:00 Food Addicts Anonymous Rm: 127-2
7:00 Transforming Prayer Ministry Rm: Modular B
7:30 AA Big Book Workshop Rm: 125
8:00 AA Tough Love Rm: 116
8:00 Al-Anon Rm: 129

Wednesday:
7:00 Just for Today Narcotics Anonymous Rm: Modular B

Thursday:
8:00 a.m. Men's Sexual Addiction Recovery Rm: Discovery Life Center
7:00 Food Addicts Anonymous Rm: 127-2
8:00 Wives of Sexual Addiction Support* (Held Off-Campus at Summit Church)
7:30 Gambler's Anonymous Rm: Modular B
7:30 GAM-ANON Rm: Modular B

Friday:
7:00 p.m. Overeaters Anonymous Rm: 130
8:00 p.m. Alcoholics Anonymous Modular A

Saturday:
9:00 a.m. Overeaters Anonymous Rm: 130

Sunday:
7:00 p.m. Narcotics Anonymous Modular B

Updated 10/25/11

Riverside Church
8660 Daniels Parkway
Fort Myers, FL 33912
Phone: 239-689-6884
Dale Fiegland
Discovery Pastor
E-mail : Discovery2@riversidechurch.org
www.riversidechurch.org

Discovery brochure

Dale's office (the Lazarus print mentioned in chapter 20 is on the wall at lower right)

Section Five

GOD'S PLAN FOR GOOD GIFTS

Chapter 15

SMOKING SURPRISES & EVERYTHING'S NEW!

Jesus and His grace kept healing me, growing me, and pruning my stray, scraggly branches. My job was (and still is) to keep paying attention to Jesus; stay at a walking pace with Him; and cooperate with Him and His nudging. No aspect was too big or small for His attention and direction, including smoking.

I had smoked for years, but never at the house. Besides the fact that I was not home much, Karen and I both grew up with parents who smoked. We hated walking into a room filled with foul nicotine haze and had long ago agreed: no smoking at home. Karen was smart and never started. However, when I was away from the house, I smoked like a choo-choo train—all day at work in our railroad-station office and when I went out at night.

I was feeling pressure to quit. Church and family members were pestering me constantly about my habit. On top of this, most of the people I knew had quit, including Dad and Mike. As the lone smoker in our office and family, I tried to quit several times, but wasn't successful.

However, I started noticing a few things about my habit. Every time I answered the phone, "Medina Equipment and Stone Company," I lit a cigarette. A bit later, I would look down and see several nicotine sticks already lit from the previous times I answered the phone. Every time I went outside to talk with a customer, I lit up. It dawned on me that my smoking was more from a nervous habit and feeling insecure than it was from my need for nicotine. When I shared all this with Bob, he said that God was showing me these things and we needed to pray about my smoking habit, which we did.

One day, soon after this, I left my office briefly to get something from outside. Immediately upon returning, I stepped into the office, and it was as if the Lord removed blinders from my eyes. With a jolt of awareness, I saw my foul, smoky haze hanging in the room like an unwelcome, toxic cloud. Then I noticed all four secretaries' eyes watering. Sadness washed over me. I cared about these cheerful workers, who always helped me. Here they were suffering for my actions, yet never complaining.

Later, Bob and I discussed these aspects more and prayed again, asking God for His help and wisdom to replace the oral-fixation part of my habit. Even as a kid, I liked to have something to gnaw on, such as a piece of hay or sassafras root, which grew on our property in northern Ohio and is the ingredient for root beer. I loved pulling up a stalk and enjoying the distinctive taste. As I pondered about what I could chew on, Olin Beech came to mind. He was the likable owner of a nearby feed-and-grain store who always had an unlit cigarette hanging from his mouth. While I considered trying that, I also remembered people regularly trying to light it for him and how it flapped when he talked. I nixed that idea; it was too awkward.

Then I had a brainstorm. I could chew on a toothpick! Karen was in favor of this and bought me a fancy metal flip-top toothpick holder to keep in my shirt pocket. It worked! My toothpick habit broke my cigarette habit.

My new habit worked great for several years until the morning Karen climbed out of bed and ran a stray toothpick deep into her foot, and the part sticking out broke off. Unable to remove the half-toothpick from her foot, I had to take her to the doctor to have it removed. That was the bad news.

The good news is the accident cured my toothpick habit in one fell swoop! Ridding my life of cigarettes and then my toothpick habit was huge. God, once again, was giving me more freedom!

It continues to amaze me how real Jesus is, how full of truth the Bible is, and how much light and grace God wants to give me as I walk with Him! God's grace heals me when I stay close to Him and pay attention.

He desires to set me free from everything that encumbers my life. Surely, this is what Jesus calls the abundant life with Him.

HEATED CONVERSATIONS

Although my relationship with Jesus was changing me in good ways, it created difficulties in my friendships with Mike and with Shorty, my trapper buddy. Now that Karen, the kids, and I were attending church together as a family and enjoying Sunday lunch together afterward, I had stopped going to the flea market with Shorty and eating lunch with him and Mike. While Shorty had been a good drinking buddy, he had absolutely no interest in hearing anything about God. Our friendship fizzled.

Mike came from a Catholic background and initially expressed curiosity about the changes in me. I eagerly shared about my relationship with Jesus and salvation, explaining that none of us are good enough to enter heaven on our own; we all need Jesus.

This bugged Mike. Just as I had been in the past, Mike didn't need anything or anybody. In fact, his life seemed to prove it. After all, he was a tough navy veteran who endured both the bombing attack on Pearl Harbor and of his ship, the USS *California*. Then he survived having two more naval ships sunk under him (the *Astoria* and *Santa Fe*) during World War II! You couldn't keep Mike down. Financially, Mike seemed to be a self-made man too. He started out with nothing and built a successful business through hard work and perseverance.

Mike had no use for religion; he didn't need help from God. He believed he would end up in heaven because he was a good person. When I told him that none of us are good enough to go to heaven on our own, Mike replied, "Look, I believe in God and that God sent His Son, Jesus, to die and pay the price for our sins. But I'm not one of those bad people or SOBs who needs saving. I'm a good man. Religion is for other people. Why would God send me to hell? I never murdered anyone."

Back then, I had very little tact, so our discussions often grew heated. Mike was fine with us going to church Sunday mornings, but it bugged him when we started attending Wednesday-night prayer meetings. "You just went on Sunday," he complained. "Why the hell do you need to go on Wednesdays?"

Mike told me that I was getting brainwashed, which is kind of true. My brain was getting washed and rejuvenated! When Karen and I began going to church on Sunday nights as well, he exclaimed some more.

Next came the aspect of money. Karen and I were continuing to learn that God's Word provides instructions for every area of life. Scripture has a great deal to say about money, possessions, and business dealings. It instructs us that giving a "tithe" to the Lord is important to Him. Tithing is giving back to God a well-considered, specific, and consistent amount from our income. He wants us to return a portion of the blessings that He has given us. Proverbs, chapter 3, shares instructions on ways we are to live for God and be blessed. The directives include honoring the Lord by tithing and giving from our firstfruits. Written in an era when many people farmed for a living, the Old Testament describes it as giving to Him from our crops (v. 9). I like the descriptive phrasing in *The Message*: "Give him the first and the best" (Proverbs 3:9–10 MSG). This applies to everyone, whether we are a fast-food clerk, a small business owner, or an entrepreneurial millionaire.

Whatever amount we choose to give, we are to do so thankfully. In giving back, we are showing our gratitude and our trust in God that He will care for us. Giving also helps fund the work of love that God wants to accomplish in the world. In Malachi 3:9–10, God states that when we don't give back to Him, we are robbing Him. However, when we do give back to Him consistently, trusting Him with our finances, He promises to bless us.

The following are a few verses on tithing.

> Honor God with everything you own; give him the first and the best. Your barns will burst, your wine vats will brim over. (Proverbs 3:9–10 MSG)

> Will man rob God? Yet you are robbing me. But you say, "How have we robbed you?" In your tithes and contributions. You are cursed with a curse, for you are robbing me, the whole nation of

you. Bring the full tithe into . . . my house. And thereby put me to the test, says the LORD of hosts, if I will not open the windows of heaven for you and pour down for you a blessing until there is no more need. (Malachi 3:8–10 ESV)

Then Jacob made a vow, saying, ". . . of all that you give me I will give a full tenth to you." (Genesis 28:20, 22 ESV)

Convinced by the teaching we heard, along with our own study of the Word, Karen and I started tithing. It was exciting to think that Mike's and my business could help our church, which was building a new sanctuary. I was happy loaning the church equipment and selling some construction products at cost. When Mike learned about it, he was hot. To Mike, money and how much you had of it symbolized your success and worth. When I suggested giving money from the business to the church, Mike went nuts, hollering, "I worked too damn hard for my money to give it away to the church!"[23]

The more I grew in my relationship with Jesus and tried to live as He would have me live in all my affairs, the bigger the wedge grew between Mike and me. Mike had never been upset with me for being a terrible husband to his daughter, but he thought I was a fool for the changes I was making in my life. Still, as a baby Christian whose life was rough around the edges and messy, I wasn't the best witness at times, and he saw these as well. Finally, he told me that he couldn't trust me anymore, and I had to go.

Once again, I would need to find another job. However, during this several-year-long conflict with Mike, plenty of other changes had occurred in my life.

SAD GOODBYES

One major change was Grandpa Keen's death in 1979. He lived a wonderful life to the great age of 102! Mom and I grieved over losing him, while at the

---

[23] Years later, Mike did donate a large, beautiful cross to his Catholic church in honor of his parents.

same time we were angry at Dad because he refused to fly with Mom and me to Grandpa's funeral in Ohio. Dad stayed home in Florida because he never much cared for Mom's father. Dad wasn't fond of Grandpa's enthusiastic, outspoken love for Jesus; plus, because Dad was the kind of man who could fix anything, it bugged him that Grandpa couldn't even hammer a nail. They were just too different.

Three days after Grandpa's death, Mom and I were at the funeral home making final arrangements when my youngest sister, Linda, called us from Fort Myers. Sobbing and weeping, she could barely choke out the shocking words: "Dad died!" Linda explained that she hadn't heard from Dad for several days and, unable to reach him, enlisted a neighbor's help to check on him. They found him in bed with lots of empty beer cans on the table next to him. Our family theorized that he had a heart attack, but was too inebriated to call for help. My father was fifty-nine.

We held two services for Dad—one in Ohio and one in Fort Myers; both had large turnouts. Mom was in shock for months, having lost her father and husband within days of each other. Before I could begin to grieve, it would take me time to work through my anger at Dad.

BLESSINGS & DECISIONS

When 1980 rolled around, I celebrated four years of sobriety and walking with Christ. God was still regenerating me and blessing Karen and me. We felt He was blessing our socks off. God had taken Karen and me from the edge of divorce to saving us, healing our marriage, and now—He was giving us another child! We were both thankful for all God was doing for us. We knew this child was special, so we named him Nathan, which means "gift from God." Karen and I, along with Brianna and little Larry, were thrilled when cute little Nathan was born.

Before Dad passed away, Karen, the kids, and I had taken a number of trips to Florida to visit my parents. We loved visiting them, especially in the winter and having brief respites from the cold and snow. We stayed with Mom and Dad in their three-bedroom home in the mobile-home neighborhood, Forest Park. It was located in North Fort Myers, a suburb of Fort Myers, on the north side of the Caloosahatchee River.

Dad had become good friends with the Bishops, the father-and-son team who owned and developed Forest Park. I liked them, too. After Dad's death, the Bishops began sharing with me that they were putting together an eighty-five-acre residential and commercial development project, with a couple of other investors. The project would entail clearing the land; building roads and eight hundred homes; and finally a shopping center. They invited me to join them in the venture both as an investor and the project manager. I would make a handsome salary and, with my buy-in, was expected to net several million dollars by the time we were finished.

This was terrific timing! Mike was making me leave and Karen and I had been saving for some time, so I would have cash for the deal. With Dad gone, living in Fort Myers would mean that I could help Mom. Plus, the idea of getting rich sounded great to me. I felt like a kid at Christmas!

However, Karen, Pastor Jim, and Bob didn't see it the same way I did.

Jim tried to caution me in my zeal, telling me it wasn't a good idea to put all my financial eggs in one basket. Bob pretty much just shook his head when I told him my idea. Financially conservative, Bob never cared for my affinity for financial risk-taking. He frequently shared with me Scripture's warning to avoid debt and owing money to others as much as possible. The ethic ran through his veins, motivating him to work diligently, double up on his mortgage payments, and pay off his house early.

Added to this, Karen wasn't keen about moving to Florida. I told her this opportunity seemed to be from God and would surely work out. "What could go wrong?" I asked during many late-night discussions. I promised Karen that I would get her a nice house. Finally, Karen agreed; she would stay in Ohio, and I would look for a home. I moved in with Mom, began working as the project manager, and initiated my hunt for our Florida digs.

LIFE IN FLORIDA

First, the eighty-five acres of land needed to be cleared. The heavy-equipment operators began removing the trees and brush, pushing them into enormous, fifteen-foot-high piles. One of my jobs was lighting the piles on fire, keeping an eye on them and keeping them stoked, so that they burned down by the end of the day. I had to walk around each stack and light the debris every several feet. It took a while to make my way around the house-sized piles. One day, I had the bright idea that it would go faster if I simply climbed to the top, started one fire, then jumped down. I tried it once. When the third rattlesnake—as big as my arm—crawled out, I figured maybe there are good reasons people in Florida take the long way around to burn brush piles. However, my coworker was thrilled with the rattlers he killed that day, which he took home to fry and eat.

Though I had been diligently searching for a house, at least seven months had gone by. Still living with Mom, it seemed like forever. In my cash-poor condition, it was impossible to buy a house. I had invested most of our funds in the development project; then, for good measure, I bought a few lots, figuring land in sunny Florida would make us even richer. Mom, though, hadn't gotten any easier to live with—a reality putting me on the edge of desperation.

I was beginning to think maybe I had been a little greedy. I realized I needed to pray for God's help. The circumstances of the move, the job, and the house had all seemed so logical. I thought I had the answers. What was there to pray about? Well, God keeps showing me how much I need His wisdom and guidance on everything.

I prayed and asked God for His help in finding and buying a house. Shortly after I prayed, I met a man with a nice house for sale, which I liked and thought Karen would, too. The details miraculously worked out. Not only would he accept our lots in a partial trade, but he was willing to wait for final payment when our house sold in Ohio! I thought Karen would like the house, but figured I had better make sure. She flew down and loved it. We bought the house, and got rid of our lots! (Unfortunately for this gentleman, it took us four years to sell our home in Ohio. Thankfully for us, we were able to rent it out while it was on the market.)

It was now the beginning of December. I was anxious for Karen and the kids to move down and join me. Brianna was seven; Larry was four; and Nathan was five months old. Karen said that it would be impossible to move by Christmas, which, to me, sounded like an adventure and challenge! Yes, we moved by Christmas, and yes, Karen deserves some heavenly rewards for dealing with me when I'm difficult.

This house, which God helped us find and buy, has been perfect for us in many ways, including its location. This is amazing, considering that our church has been at three different locations in Lee County, yet each time we were only a half hour away from the church.

In addition, this house has had the ability to accommodate numerous people who have stayed with us—family, friends, and many people we have helped in their time of need. To top it off, the lot was large enough, and the zoning was flexible enough that we were able to add an adjoining apartment when Mom needed assistance. Since her death, we've been able to rent the apartment for extra income. Even better is that currently, one of our sons, his wife, and their children are living next door. Not only are they a great help to us, it's wonderful having little grandkids scramble over for visits!

I'm continually reminded of God's amazing help, wisdom, and provisions for us in specific ways and details, like this house. Thankfully, God in His grace keeps helping me learn to lean on Him and seek Him in all things.

EVERYTHING IS NEW

Besides living in a new house, in a new state, we became members of a new church—Riverside. Mom loved Riverside, and we did, too. We enjoyed the people and felt the pastors did a great job of teaching from the Bible.

Shortly after we joined the church, Riverside hired Jay Strack as the new pastor. Jay, who grew up in Fort Myers, came from a broken home. This led to life as a troubled youth and drug addiction. When he accepted Jesus as his Savior, God turned his life around and called him to the ministry. Besides being down-to-earth, with a great love for Jesus, he is a powerful communicator and evangelist for God. During an early ten-month period at Riverside, he helped 321 people come to know the Lord and baptized them![24]

---

[24] It didn't surprise me that after leading our church for four years and then moving on, Jay increased in ministry work, writing more than fifteen books and achieving acclaim as a dynamic speaker in Christian, educational, and business arenas. He has addressed more than fifteen million people during his ministerial and speaking career. Since leaving Riverside, he has appeared on CNN, the *MacNeil/Lehrer Report*, and *The 700 Club*, and was the featured speaker at the 1998 NBA All-Star Game's chapel, to name just a few of his numerous compelling outreaches.

Jay often preached in an expository, verse-by-verse style. Karen and I hadn't experienced this kind of exploration through a chapter or book of the Bible, but we loved it. Jay spent a long time going through the book of Nehemiah and reviewing how the prophet spearheaded the rebuilding of Jerusalem's damaged walls. We could easily recognize the parallels with our own lives. Thanks to such messages and other teaching at Riverside, Karen and I kept learning more about God and continued to apply His Word to our lives.

During my earlier trips to Mom and Dad's house in Fort Myers, I had visited several AA groups. The first night I attended the group that I ultimately chose, I met a guy named Ron. Noticing that we were the only two men to bring our Bibles to the meeting that night, we hit it off immediately. Ron became a longtime sponsor and friend and, through this group, I ended up with many close Christian friendships.

Besides conducting vibrant, solid meetings, the group members took their 12th Step seriously—aiding other alcoholics and passing on to everyone they could the assistance and gifts they had received. In a variety of ways, the group ministered to men, women, and families affected by alcohol, and even hosted what is known as a "24-hour group." Our AA group kept one meeting room open around the clock, seven days a week, usually manned with one or more volunteers. Members took turns being ready with a hot, fresh pot of coffee for whomever might walk in, day or night, seeking help. I, too, took my turn with the coffee pot and found myself actively assisting other addicts in becoming sober and turning their lives around.

For the first time in my life, I felt I had a purpose. This was indescribable. As a child I was called a mistake, but now I had a purpose and value. I was helping men and women get free from their addictions, find a new life, and trust Christ. As my ministry grew, Jay Strack and other pastors began sending me alcoholics in need of assistance or family members of drinkers who wanted help regarding their loved ones.

I didn't know it, but God's plan was starting to take shape.

Chapter 16

GOD'S CRAZY PASTOR PLAN

My first six months as project manager went well until trouble appeared on the horizon—the economy was tanking. The question that I had asked Karen during our late-night discussions prior to moving to Florida: "What could go wrong?" Well, I was finding out a number of things. Economic conditions were nose-diving and interest rates were soaring. Our combined residential-shopping-center project was floundering and I had gone six months without a paycheck.

The three other investor partners kept hoping to turn things around and secure additional financing, but I didn't see that happening. I couldn't wait any longer. I had to find a job that came with pay. It's a good thing I didn't wait. One year later, the property went on the sheriff's auction block, while interest rates hovered near 19 percent.

Besides losing my job and income, I had lost a LOT of money in the investment. I had to start all over. Anger and fear fought for first place in my emotions. I felt that I had lost everything and protested vigorously to God, "Why are you doing this? I'm trying to be good and follow You, Jesus, and this is how You treat me?"

Yet, in God's strange way of working, in those fourteen months of dire straits I found myself having to rely on Jesus and His help more than ever. While it was a difficult and gut-wrenching season, especially financially, it propelled my faith and my walk with God to new heights. I prayed constantly, asking God to lead me and help me follow His will for my life, even when I wasn't sure exactly what that meant or where that would take me.

As I continued in daily prayer, I sensed the Holy Spirit directing me not to take on any more business partners. If I was going to be in business, it would be on my own, with God as my only partner. Soon after, a good friend told me about a dry-cleaning business for sale in the neighboring city of Cape Coral. Although larger than Fort Myers, the city had enacted a moratorium on additional dry-cleaning businesses. There were just three of them, and one was for sale. That sounded close to a monopoly to me! If Karen and I secured a second mortgage on our home, we could buy it and generate immediate income. I felt God's leading in this, so we purchased it.

Things began looking up, and the season of wondering if we would wind up living on the street slowly passed. As the dry-cleaning business grew and demanded more of my time, and also Karen's, we found ourselves in need of day care. The more we searched for a good facility, the more we recognized the need for a well-managed and well-staffed facility. We decided to start one with the profits from the dry-cleaning business. Soon, we owned two businesses, with both of them performing well. (When we sold the dry-cleaning business a couple of years later, we were blessed to make a healthy profit.)

CHURCH & LEADERSHIP

Life continued looking up. Besides our thriving businesses, my ministry of assisting people with addictions continued growing. I wasn't seeking people out; God kept bringing them to me. Our church involvement was expanding, too. Leaders and elders, observing my ministry and involvement at church, asked me to become a church deacon. Looking back, I was growing spiritually, but I wasn't all that mature in my walk with God. Still, God was in the situation. I agreed to serve and was voted in as a deacon.

Karen and I loved our Sunday-school class of young marrieds and singles and enjoyed frequent, fun get-togethers outside of class. My cheeks usually hurt afterward from laughing so much. Because our class kept multiplying, church leaders considered ways to split it into smaller groups, so people wouldn't get lost in the crowd and close friendships could keep forming. One Sunday, a leader shared with Karen and me that we needed to "move up to the next age group." In the car going home, I pitched a fit with Karen, fuming, "I'm not going to the new class. Who do they think they are, telling me I should be in the next age group?"

"Let's at least check it out," chirped Karen, who is usually content to follow rules. "Come on. We might like it."

That made me madder. I grumbled, "Have fun, and tell me all about it!"

I lost that battle. Karen and I checked out the class. Wouldn't you know it? We ended up loving the class and the teacher. In fact, Dr. Bob Sheffield (we called him Dr. Bob) was another Christian who greatly influenced my life. When he taught the Old Testament, he made it interesting, understandable, and brought it to life. Additionally, he encouraged and discipled me, helping me grow in my walk with God.

Now, because my ministry of helping alcoholics and their families kept growing, pastors and deacons were asking me to be ordained as a pastor. I wasn't interested! The requests came like an annoying swarm of flies. I swatted them away with a variety of replies, including "No, thank you" and "Not happening!" I was happy serving in my outreach to AA folks and other addicts and, the rest of the time, I liked doing what I wanted and warming the pew. But the more my addiction ministry increased, the more leaders urged, "Dale, you need to be ordained and become a pastor."

One reason I wasn't interested was that I saw preachers regularly come and go. The average length of time (in the early 1980s) that Southern Baptist pastors served in one church, before moving on, was two and a half years. To me, a pastor's job seemed high-risk, with little security, and not many long-term benefits or returns. I didn't want to put myself and my family through the ordeal of moving frequently. Besides, I liked Florida and didn't want to move every couple of years to who-knows-where. "It would be just my luck to end up in Alaska, freezing my rear end off," I would quip to Karen or others when discussing the request that kept coming.

Despite my repeated refusals, the deacons kept asking. As I kept resisting, Dr. Bob pointed out that it was God who was calling me to be a pastor, and I should consider it seriously. One time he asked, "How long are you going to run, Dale?"

During this time, Riverside Church discussed and voted to open a Christian school. The elders asked me to serve on the planning committee; oversee construction and setup; and then, help run it. They knew I had the skills for these tasks. Plus, since I ran my own businesses and had really good people working for me, I could devote the time needed. Because of my background in education, they continued to ask me to be ordained and then be pastor of education and the principal. Repeatedly.

Wrestling with God about this issue would be an understatement. Finally, I grudgingly conceded. The staff set a date for my ordination ceremony. But my heart wasn't in it; so, God took me on a loop around the desert.

NOTHING GOES RIGHT

The school's opening date was drawing closer. I had worked hard, helped from the first brick to the last, and kept it under budget. The inside was almost finished, so I began interviewing teachers, even though I wasn't yet ordained or officially principal.

About this time, Pastor Jay Strack had accepted a position in Orlando, Florida, to minister to youth, mentoring and training them to become Christian leaders. Now we had a new lead pastor. As the new pastor settled in, someone told him that I was slated to be the school's principal. The pastor did ask, "Fiegland who?" However, within short order, he hired a minister of education, along with the man's wife, who would help run the school. Having my own business, I understood. This pastor and leader wanted to choose his own people, whom he knew and trusted. I wasn't angry with him.

I was plenty mad at God. "What are You doing, God?" I wailed. "I finally agree to become a pastor, and now You take it away from me. Didn't I hear You correctly?" I wrestled with this turnabout of events, but figured it meant that I wasn't going into ministry and needed a new plan. I decided to start a second day-care business. After finding a great location and building, I signed the lease and began remodeling the rooms.

My hasty, snap judgments with my own "wisdom" cost me. I moved too quickly on all of it, especially swinging a hammer. The city's zoning commission denied my rezoning request. This meant I had to break my lease and lose all the money I had invested—the first and last month's rent and the great remodel. There went another quick five thousand dollars, which I wasn't happy about, to put it mildly.

The doors to everything—the pastorate and now this business—were slamming shut. Nothing was going right. Feeling as if I was in a small boat tossed by stormy seas, I kept asking God, "What are You doing?"

GOOD & BAD

Added to this, our church was in a tough place. The new pastor had initially seemed genuine and qualified. He even showed me how to read the Psalms, learn about God from them, and turn them into prayers. But he had another side. He was misusing church funds and seemed to be in ministry more for personal reward and financial gain than to serve God.

It can be difficult at times to reconcile people's good and bad traits, particularly with Christians. Several things have helped me in times like these. One was Bob's continual refrain, "Never put your eyes on a man; you'll be disappointed. Men mess it up. Put your eyes on Jesus, and you'll never be disappointed."

Scripture repeatedly warns us that we are not to seek ambition and power for ourselves. If we want to be great, we are to follow the example of Jesus, who did not come to be served, but to serve others (Matthew 20:25–28). When we bump up against difficult people and those who abuse power, we're to remember God's promise that He will one day judge everyone rightly.

In addition to all this, AA built its organization on the biblical goals of service, unity, and harmony, and members are continually reminded (through the readings shared at the meetings) to strive for these objectives. When these are our aim, power struggles and difficulties are diminished, and fellowship grows.

The deacons and I continued finding a pattern and evidence of wrongdoing with this pastor and voted—unanimously—that he had to leave. Though we were united in our decision, it was difficult to remove him. Not only did he stand over six feet, six inches tall, but he was an expert at intimidation, using all sorts of crafty tactics with church leaders, members, and people in the community. He worked members against one another, threatened lawsuits, and manipulated the media for his purposes. At one business meeting held after our church service, he brought a stenographer, his lawyer, and a newspaper reporter with him. He told those in the congregation who supported him to stand beside him, providing the reporter with a great photo opportunity. The picture of the pastor with his supporters made the newspaper. I had experienced lots of Mafia operators, con artists, and politicians in my life; this guy was a pro.

When it was finally time to tell him that he was fired, the elders asked another deacon and me to handle the job. The other deacon had more seniority, so I knew that I was there simply as a witness and support. When the pastor ushered us into his office and we sat down, Mr. Senior Deacon quickly said, "Dale has something to tell you."

While I was a bit surprised, thankfully, my boxing background helps me in unexpected and surprising ways. Because I was trained to size up and evaluate individuals and opponents, this pastor had always struck me as a bit physically awkward. I didn't feel intimated or threatened so, without much fanfare, I told him he was fired. He didn't say much, and we left. But this pastor wasn't through. He went back to the deacons and wrangled himself a generous severance package. I wasn't happy and thought we should have stood up to him, but it wasn't my decision.

This entire experience for our church was difficult. Sitting in the pew, watching the pastor during that Sunday business meeting in the church (which we later called "Black Sunday") was painful. However, the Lord's grace was still working in our congregation. Many sought God all the more and drew closer to one another. Plus, God had put a plan in place when the outgoing pastor made his best decision, one I especially liked. He had hired a new youth pastor, Tony Chester, fresh out of seminary.

I was teaching Sunday school in the youth program and enjoyed this "kid," with his easygoing, down-to-earth, transparent manner. In addition, he seemed to tolerate me fairly well. I kept discovering that many people in the church didn't know what to make of me. I ruffled feathers for several reasons—because of my ministry to alcoholics and addicts; I never fit the typical Christian mold; and I can tend to be blunt and outspoken. I was thrilled (and still am) to find people who don't easily get out of sorts with me or my ministry.

While our church searched for a new senior lead pastor, Tony served as interim preaching pastor. Man, was he gifted! He could take almost any verse in the Bible and explain it so well that everyone understood it. A year later, the whole church had fallen in love with him; we voted him in as senior pastor—a position he held for twenty-three years.

GOD'S PLAN

As the turmoil calmed down and Pastor Tony settled in as lead pastor, I began hearing the familiar refrain: "Dale, you need to be ordained as a pastor." This time, I willingly and wholeheartedly surrendered to God and said yes! God, in His sovereign grace, knew exactly what He was doing.

When the education pastorate had been promised to me and then taken away, suddenly I found myself wanting it. God didn't want me just serving Him outwardly; He wanted my heart—willingly and closely—following and serving Him.

On July 6, 1988, I was ordained as pastor. A Southern Baptist pastor, at that! To this day, I'm continuously shocked and surprised by all of it. I am quite aware that my becoming a pastor is all of God's grace, work, and timing. I can't take credit for any of it. God helped this street kid from Ohio, who knew nothing but carousing and fighting, be able to surrender and call on Him for help. God began to clean me up, made me new on the inside, blessed my life, and topped it off by calling me to serve Him in ministry. Truly, God's goodness for broken, undeserving people is amazing.

Through all of this, the problem pastor had created so much division and turmoil that, when he was fired, the principal of our school quit as well. In short order, I was ordained, became a pastoral staff member and principal of Riverside Christian School. But there was still more to come. I walked in the first day of school to discover that the principal and his wife, on their way out, had convinced a handful of teachers to quit their jobs with no notice. School would be starting very soon, and we were short a number of teachers! This wasn't good. Eventually, the school would enroll about two hundred children, but at this point, we had less than sixty students, many of whom were preschoolers. Thankfully, with my day-care business and my network of friends, I rounded up trusted adults to help care for the children until I could straighten out the situation.

When the next paychecks were ready, instead of mailing them, I held them and made all the teachers come to me to receive their pay. This enabled me to hire back a few of them. Slowly, peace was restored.

Pastor Tony and I grew in our roles and in seeking God's help to serve Him. In the beginning, as we struggled with surprises, challenges, and sometimes members who tried our patience, one of us would ask the other, "Do you know what you're doing?" The frequent reply was, "I haven't a clue." So we would pray and ask God for His help. We learned numerous lessons the hard way. In fact, we could probably write a book about how *not* to do church. We also discovered that for many who look up to you and hold you in high regard as a pastor, there will be plenty of critics. It's enough to keep one humble and leaning on God.

GOD'S GRACE SURPRISES

God's changes in my life and the fact that He called me to be a pastor amazed not only me—they surprised lots of people. We learned that several church members in Ohio had taken bets years ago about whether or not I really was a Christian and would Jesus really be able to change the life of this alcoholic, troublemaker, and Mafia runner?

Then, several years into my pastorate, someone from the Anderson College alumni newspaper, *Raven Pride*, called our house. When Karen answered the phone, the caller's questions went like this: "Is this the home of Dale Fiegland? Dale Fiegland from Cleveland, Ohio? The Dale Fiegland who attended and graduated from Anderson College? Did he really become a pastor?" Karen enjoyed answering yes to all the questions.

God's grace and power to help broken, fallen people are surprising—no matter what angle you look at it from. And God's grace would keep astounding me. For a long time, I kept expecting someone to say, "Dale, your time is up—you're done being a pastor." Finally, I realized that I needed to trust God and His grace. He placed me here; He would keep me here as long as He wanted.

I would also learn that God's grace for me would come with a seemingly steady supply of surprises.

Chapter 17

GOD WANTS ME TO LOVE HIM

It's true that God loves each of us, but it's not a bland love that is uninvolved. God's love is so real and passionate—He wants us to do more than simply know that He loves us. God wants us to know and experience Him through Jesus and to love Him back with our hearts and lives.

At this point in my life, I had been saved by God, followed Him, grown spiritually, studied His Word, and experienced the Lord and miracles. However, there came a day when God confronted me about how much I loved Him. He did this in a powerful way through a large man named Clyde Cranford.

Clyde would have been an opera singer, if he hadn't been doing the Lord's work. Besides having a great voice, he had the height and girth. Every inch of him seemed full of the Lord. Clyde and Pastor Tony had met in seminary; and now, shortly after my ordination, he came to Riverside to minister especially to our pastors and leaders. Clyde was a "pastor's pastor." He traveled to churches and remained in one place for several months at a time, encouraging pastors and leaders, ministering to them one-on-one, and leading retreats. The church from which he served—Bellevue Baptist in Memphis, Tennessee—was led by the highly influential Pastor Adrian Rogers. The church's ministry name said it all: "Love Worth Finding."

Clyde had been discipled himself by none other than Henry Blackaby, the coauthor (with Claude King) of *Experiencing God*.[25] Clyde lived and shared the message that runs through the book: Each of us is to enjoy God's love and fall in love with Him. More than just reading the Bible and knowing about God, we are to love Him wholeheartedly. We are to know Him through Scripture, seek Him in our circumstances, talk with Him, and listen for His guidance. We are to enjoy His purposes and plans, enjoy how He is at work in us and around us, and the tasks He has for us. We are to follow and cooperate with Him and His desires, over and above simply making requests of Him.

Loving God and learning to listen to Him are threads that He keeps weaving into my life and building upon. God taught me this through Grandpa's easy way of saying, "Let's pray and see what Jesus wants us to do." He taught me through my AA buddy, Bob, who encouraged me to read the Bible and inquire, "What are You telling me, God?" Then, AA encouraged me in various ways to improve my conscious contact with God. Along the way, I was given a wonderful little pamphlet titled, "How to Listen to God," written by John E. Batterson in the 1930s.[26] This short booklet offers practical steps to help us hear God. While we are still praying, we are to quiet our spirits and minds, listen, and write down everything that pops into our minds. After this, we are to consider our list with Scripture and godly friends. God may be trying to tell us something about the topic or issue, even if it seems random or unrelated to Him. We're not done until we act on what God is impressing upon us to do.

Now, here was Clyde sharing how the Lord is pursuing each of us in a love relationship and we are to love Him back with our heart, mind, soul, and strength. This imperative—to love God—is first declared in the Old Testament. Jesus reiterated this truth, stating that it is the greatest commandment.[27] We are to passionately seek God and love Him.

---

25 Released in 1990, *Experiencing God* is offered as a book and workbook. They are frequently favorites of church Bible studies and have become international bestsellers. The book has sold more than seven million copies, and the workbook has been translated into forty-seven languages.
26 John E. Batterson was a friend of Dr. Bob's and one of AA's cofounders. The booklet is easily located online.
27 The commandment to love God is found in Deuteronomy 6:4–7; Matthew 22:37–40; Mark 12:30–31; and Luke 10:27.

I was generally satisfied with my walk with God until Clyde asked me questions about my quiet time. While he was happy that I was a student of the Bible, he advised me, "Dale, you need to fall in love with Jesus. You can't just be an expert on God and Jesus."

It was true. I was becoming knowledgeable about God, but I was in danger of stalling out in interacting with Him and loving Him. In fact, there are several aspects regarding our relationship with God. Mentally learning God's truth, instructions, and promises is only the beginning. We need to personally take them in for ourselves. This means that we need to ponder on, wrestle with, and practice applying these aspects to ourselves and our lives. Hearing truth versus applying it is like watching a teacher work a math problem on a blackboard and thinking, "Oh, I get it; that's easy." But when we have to work out a problem on our own, we haven't a clue what we're doing. This is also the reason, when I attended Anderson College, I learned plenty of Bible facts, but I needed to have Bob and others help me comprehend and apply them through the years.

We are to keep growing with God, enjoying Him, and loving Him, but it's easy for Christians, and even pastors, to fall into the rut of head knowledge, past experiences, and being busy. I had facts and theory, but I wasn't having many conversations or experiences with Him. My heart wasn't engaged. Clyde reminded me that Scripture tells us that God wants to continually reveal Himself through:

- Creation, which reveals His beauty, glory, power, goodness, and provisions
- The Bible, which reveals His plans and purposes, proof of His truth, His provisions and promises, and His instructions and commands
- Jesus—His love for us, His life, work, powerful miracles, sacrifice, forgiveness, and new life and blessings we're to receive with Him
- God's Holy Spirit, which is given to believers to know His presence, comfort, and guidance
- Our daily circumstances, both good and bad

It dawned on me that I was spending very little time with God. When I woke up in the morning, my feet hit the floor, and off I was doing what I felt was important, but neglecting to stop and have time with Him. When I did read the Bible, it was more from duty and obligation than to know God. Pondering all this, I asked myself, "Why am I not spending time with God?" The first thought that popped in my mind was, "I'm too busy," followed immediately by, "I don't need to." Wow, there was concealed pride! I was saying to God, "I don't need you. I can handle things." But I knew when I had a problem, I needed God and spent time with Him. The truth is, the Bible tells me, I need God for life and breath. I like to keep breathing, so I need God every day.[28]

HEARING GOD

Clyde was right. To get to know God better and love Him more, I committed myself to consistently spending time with God and His Word, reading, praying, and listening for Him. I began in prayer, by acknowledging His presence, and thanking Him that He was there with me. (I frequently still do this.)

In Scripture, I watched for Jesus in every book of the Bible. The Old Testament provides glimpses of Jesus. The New Testament shares Jesus, His life, miracles, teaching, death, and resurrection, and reveals how he offers Himself (all that He is and has) to us if we want to receive Him! Finally, the future points to Jesus and His promised, and possibly soon, return as Savior and Lord for those who have taken Him into their lives.[29]

I began to purposefully pursue knowing the Lord. As I read His Word, I began stopping and meditating on passages as I read them. No more reading quickly and superficially just to be able to cross "read the Bible"

---

28 Numerous verses explain that God gives us our breath, including Genesis 2:7; Job 12:10; Job 34:14–15; Isaiah 42:5; and Acts 17:25.

29 For those who want to read more about Jesus, a few powerful, descriptive Scripture passages include John 1:14; Philippians 2:6–11; Colossians 1:15–23 and 2:9–15; and Titus 2:11–14. In the Old Testament, Isaiah reveals many prophecies regarding Jesus, especially Isaiah 9:6. An easy and interesting online search can be made regarding "Jesus revealed in every book of the Bible." For a powerful article on the diverse excellencies of Christ, see: https://www.monergism.com/blog/jonathan-edwards-excellency-christ.

off my to-do list. If I didn't consider and pay attention to what God was saying, I wasn't gaining anything. With this desire to know and experience the Lord, when I would read a passage, many times I would ask, "What do you want me to know about this, God?" I would be quiet and listen.

I had been doing this for a while and God had been helping me understand His Word. One day during a time of struggling with anxiety, I read the following passage:

Therefore I tell you, do not worry about your life, what you will eat or drink; or about your body, what you will wear. Is not life more than food, and the body more than clothes? Look at the birds of the air; they do not sow or reap or store away in barns, and yet your heavenly Father feeds them. Are you not much more valuable than they? (Matthew 6:25–26)

It wasn't an audible voice, but I heard God say, "Dale, when you worry, you are calling me a puny, little, good-for-nothing God."

Because of my past, I am keenly aware of how awful it is to feel this way; in fact, God knew it would capture my attention. Dissolving into tears, I said, "God, I would never call you a puny, little, good-for-nothing God."

"That's what you're saying when you worry, Dale. I am either a big enough God to handle your problems, or I am a liar."

That shook me more. "Oh, God, I don't want to call you a liar," I replied, brushing away a few more tears.

Loving God and experiencing Him this way changed me in several ways. Through this event, God became more personal to me, deepening my relationship with Him. Additionally, I experienced God's Word in a powerful, life-changing way. Before this, if someone would have asked, "Pastor Dale, is worry a sin?" I would have said yes and probably quoted Scripture. Although, in many people's eyes, I may have seemed like an "expert," I'm not sure I agreed with God. I didn't understand how big a deal worry is to Him or consider it a sin. I hadn't confessed it as a shortcoming and asked for His forgiveness and help in overcoming this common human failing.

Now, it hurts me when I find myself worrying because I don't want to offend or grieve God (Ephesians 4:30). When I catch myself worrying, I frequently look up and say, "I know, God. You're not puny, little, or a liar. You are big enough to handle my difficulties. You love me, and You want to help me." By the time I acknowledge that God loves me, cares about me, and is able to help me with every problem, my worry is often gone.

I desperately need a quiet time alone with the Lord, so I can hear Him, get to know Him, experience Him, and love Him more.

A GOD WHO LOVES

It's humbling and moving to know how passionately God wants a deep, personal love relationship with us and that He wants to talk with us as a friend. As I ponder this truth, and spend time with Him, it helps me fall in love with God and enjoy Him.

I gained several truths from my time with Clyde and from the *Experiencing God* workbook. Below is my list. Except for the first point on my list (which is Blackaby's second point), these are not the same key points that the book shares in several places.

- God wants us to know Him in a love relationship. He has forever demonstrated His absolute love for us on the cross.
- Being loved by God and loving Him back is the greatest relationship and achievement in life; it should be of the utmost importance to me.
- To know God, love Him, and live for Him, I need His Word and Jesus.
- I need to spend quiet time with God, grow in my relationship with Him, pray, and seek His will in all my circumstances. These aspects help me know, experience, and love Him.
- God gives me more of Himself, and blesses me and my life, as I follow and obey Him.

Because I don't want to fall back into a rut of "going through the motions," sometimes I need to change up my quiet time. There are times I study topics or reread my journal, reviewing what God has done in my life. Other times, I ponder, wrestle with, and meditate on God's Word, striving to understand His truth and the concept of a text. At times, I ask God to show me hidden treasures.

Besides thinking on Scripture, memorization is also important and valuable. Bob, in particular, pushed me to memorize passages. Even when I would choose the shortest verses that I could find, he would encourage me and say, "Good job."

Memorizing God's Word has brought me several benefits. First, it's helped me lean on God's wisdom, rather than my own wisdom and understanding (the truth sandwich of Proverbs 3:5–6). As I seek to be sensitive to God and fill my mind with His Word, He can more readily guide and instruct me. Besides this, it has surprised me to discover that memorizing God's Word has helped shape me into a vessel that God can more readily use. I have no wisdom of my own to offer, only God's truth, and amazingly people seek me out for this. (Of course, loving people is vital as well, so that I'm not just a Scripture-quoting noisemaker.)

LOVE GROWS

Before Clyde returned to his home church, he shared with Pastor Tony that I had a heart for God. This meant a lot to me. Clyde saw my desire to love God—even with my rough edges. Plus, it was Clyde's big love for Jesus that inspired me to grow.[30]

As I sought to know more of God's great love for me and follow Him, my love for the Lord continued growing, as did my love for the hurting people He kept sending my way. There seemed to be no shortage of those who called me or knocked on my door.

---

30 While Clyde Cranford was known for discipling many men through the years, he was one of the first men from within the church (and outside of AA) to disciple me. Clyde went on to write a book with Henry Blackaby titled, *Because We Love Him*. It shares Clyde's passionate message. We are to strive to know God, love God, and live to please Him. The book offers practical suggestions for empowering believers to "live their love for God out loud."

Chapter 18

POTATOES & GRACE

The Lord kept sending me people needing assistance. Sometimes it was alcoholics and, sometimes, family members of drinkers who needed counsel.

In fact, when families are dealing with an addicted member, there is much to learn, because addiction affects them as well—mentally, emotionally, and physically. Unhealthy relationship patterns morph out of control. Loved ones, when dealing with addicts, often develop a coping mechanism called codependency. The loved one living with a resistant addict is caught in a bad cycle; they keep trying harder to hold life together, help the addict, and fix the problem, but cannot do so. Life with an addict (who doesn't play by any rules, except their own personal whims) becomes an unending, crazy-making loop.

I shared with these family members of addicts their options for intervention, plus changes they needed to make, so that they weren't enabling the alcoholic to live self-destructively. People's desire to be nice and help others usually backfires with addicts. For instance, giving troubled people money or a nice place to live isn't helpful. Neither is calling their bosses or teachers with excuses that they are "not feeling well," when in reality they have a hangover. Addicts often have to "hit bottom." They have to be miserable enough that they want to change and want help. Instead of trying harder to rescue an addict while the relationship continues to deteriorate, we can learn better ways of interacting. Following are a few recommendations (from various resources):

GUIDELINES FOR FAMILY MEMBERS OF ADDICTS

- Accept the truth about what is going on; don't deny the reality.
- Don't enable them to keep doing what they are doing.
- Don't try to keep secret the truth of what is happening.
- Don't try to protect them from natural consequences of their behavior.
- Don't try to bail them out of their problems.
- Don't give them money.
- Don't take care of things for them that they should be doing themselves.
- Don't try to control situations (like talking to teachers, so they don't fail, or bosses, so they don't lose their jobs).
- Don't make excuses for them and their problems (don't blame the problems on shyness, adolescence, a broken home, life's problems, etc.).
- Don't believe what addicts say; watch what they do. (Remember, most addicts are habitual liars, meaning that if they're talking, chances are they may be lying.)
- Decide and choose boundaries of what you will and won't accept and what you will do if these lines are crossed. State your boundaries simply and clearly. (Arguing, reasoning, yelling, making idle threats, and giving addicts the silent treatment don't work. You need to find words that you mean and that you can say, which will include some form of, "This is not acceptable to me.")
- Let them decide what they are going to do regarding your boundaries. (Be prepared for all sorts of tactics to try and get you to change back the way you were.) Stand strong; speak up plainly and directly. Don't cave.
- Give them time to get healthy and prove themselves.
- Get healthy yourself. (Deal with your own issues, habits, hurts, and fears.)

THE DRUNKS

Besides the addiction counseling I was conducting, four friends from AA and I worked as a type of rescue team to assist alcoholics and their families. We called ourselves The Drunks. When people would ask us to help with drunken loved ones, sometimes we would go out and pick up these intoxicated individuals, give them a chance to dry out and get sober, then talk to them, share our stories, and offer to help them find sobriety for life—if they wanted it. Karen's and my house was frequently the place we took them to dry out because we had a spare bedroom with a door directly to the outside, which worked great for this situation.

One day, my friends and I came up with the idea (long before cell phones) to buy ourselves pagers and print business cards with the name, New Direction, and our pager numbers on them. When our cards were passed around and word got out about our pagers, people really began calling us for assistance. We stayed busy and learned along the way.

One woman had asked us to help her and her alcoholic husband when he went on a drinking spree. Sure enough, we found him in his favorite bar and loaded him in my car. Just then, we received another call on our pager for help; so we swung by my house, dumped the first drunk on the bed, and took off. The circumstances happened so fast that I didn't have time to call Karen and alert her. Karen came home that day and found an inebriated stranger in our house! Thankfully, it turned out okay, and Karen didn't stay mad at me for long. I'm blessed that most days Karen rolls with the flow and helps with grace and strength. Occasionally, she draws a clear boundary line for me in her audacious way.

ANOTHER POTATO IN THE POT

Karen and I know what both sides of the fence feel like. We know what desperation feels like, and we know the life-giving hope, help, and grace that Jesus-followers have given us. Consequently, we try to share these same life-saving gifts with as many hurting people as we can.

I can't count how many times I've come home and asked Karen, "Can we put another potato in the pot and take in so-and-so for a while? They need our help." Instead of bringing home stray dogs, I bring home wayward people. Sometimes it's for a short stay, and sometimes it lasts for years if they are getting their life on track.

Some rides have been bumpy, and I have had to learn along the way. At one point, I came to the conclusion that I needed to let Karen and our kids vote on whether or not someone could stay with us, but even in this, there was a learning curve.

One young teen boy, whom I'll call The Kid, needed assistance with his life and troubles. He shared that he was a Christian and said all the right things. Our family voted. Everybody agreed that he could stay with us, except Brianna, who voted no. I jumped in, happy to assert my fatherly authority, and said, "The majority rules."

The Kid lived with us for some time, when I discovered that he had been skipping school for just as long. Working with him didn't produce any change, so I told him he would need to leave. A night or two later, I heard someone stirring around in the house about 2:30 in the morning and got up to check. It was The Kid, who told me that a friend had given him money for a plane ticket, and he was leaving. After he left, something didn't seem right. I started checking and discovered that he had robbed us of a sizable sum of valuable and meaningful heirlooms. Not happy was an understatement. Because I knew he was very good at martial arts, I grabbed a baseball bat, and headed out in my car to find him. Whichever way you look at it, it's a good thing I didn't locate him.

Shortly after this, The Kid was arrested on other charges. A deputy friend let me know that The Kid couldn't be held any longer on those charges and was getting ready to be released. I asked the deputy, "If I buy a plane ticket to his home state, can you put him on the plane?" Together, the deputy and I made it happen. After that event, I figured maybe I should listen to Brianna and all my kids more often.

We have taken in quite a number of people, beginning with foreign-exchange students from Mexico, Japan, and France—in part, so we could provide our children with a variety of learning experiences. In addition, we have taken in many in need, including a single mom from Brazil with two small boys, seven people from Romania at different times, and one person from Bulgaria. Riverside's pastors and staff nicknamed our house IHOP—International House of People. (Even today, through the writing of this book, we have had houseguests.)

The following are a few of our adventures.

TROUBLE & DOUBLE TROUBLE

When our kids were young, we needed a good babysitter. Our church had an active and fun puppet ministry for children and a bus ministry (which picked up children and adults for church services). A church friend and I took turns driving the bus. My friend recommended identical twin sisters, age sixteen, who were active in the puppet ministry and used the bus ministry. We liked the girls, who turned out to be great babysitters. I affectionately nicknamed them "Trouble" and "Double Trouble."

Slowly, we learned that they had a pretty rough life, and we began offering our assistance. One day, Double Trouble called me from the bus stop. She said it was raining and she didn't know what to do. She had been sent home from school because she was sick and had a fever.

"Well, you need to go home," I said.

"Mom won't let me in the house."

I told her I'd be right there. I picked her up, took her to her house, and knocked a couple of times on the door, more loudly each time, and waited. Finally, a big, rough-looking dude answered the door. Imagine the Hulk—only really mad. Just then, her mother yelled from the back bedroom, "I told her to get the hell out of here! No, she can't come in and can't get anything!"

The more we pieced together about the girls and their living conditions, the bleaker the story became. We agreed—the girls could live with us. It wasn't long before we felt they were our daughters and part of the family. (They have a number of siblings who have struggled, too. Karen and I are thrilled to have connected with a sister of theirs.)

I tease the twins that we were able to experiment on parenting teenagers with them before our own children became teenagers. As they grew older, naturally there came a time when Trouble and Double Trouble developed a dislike for our rules. Deciding to rent their own apartment, they moved out. But the facts of real life collided with their young dreams of freedom. They soon realized they could afford an apartment, but not much else. After a bit, they asked if they could move back in.

Trouble and Double Trouble are great girls, have done well, and both enjoy working at a Christian school. We're proud of them!

OUR FAMILY GROWS AGAIN

A number of years later, in 2000, Brianna, Larry, and Nathan were all in college. I, too, had been continuing to pursue a college degree in counseling. Since becoming a pastor, I frequently felt inadequate in ministry, which prompted Pastor Tony to encourage me to continue my education.[31] Now, Karen joined the four of us in college. She wanted to become an occupational therapist.

It was during this time, when our three kids were away in college, that the Lord decided to fill up our house again. Not only did God bring two families of different nationalities to live with us, but He brought them the same week! It wasn't how we would have planned it, but God gave everyone involved an adventure with blessings. Only God could have orchestrated this kind of crazy plan.

Following is the story of how it happened, along with needed backstory, which will also help in chapters to come.

Riverside Church was growing. I was the lead pastor for our counseling and recovery program, which we called Discovery. Besides having several counselors available in various specialties, during the week our church opened our campus to a number of AA and 12 Step meetings. One night a week, we held a main Discovery meeting, which began with joyful worship from our Discovery praise band. After the large group meeting, we offered a variety of small, church-based 12 Step meetings and classes on various topics, such as marriage and codependency.

Addicts—actually, all of us—are broken people, emotionally and spiritually. Yes, we all need prayers, and sometimes God heals specific problems

---

31 It took many years and spanned the three different locations of our church, but I kept at it and graduated with my counseling degree from Liberty University in September 2003.

quickly in response to prayer. But God requires us to grow in knowledge and application of His truth. This takes time. It takes time to recognize our unhealthy patterns and learn better ways of relating. Our Discovery classes and fellowship were designed to aid people in these areas.

Besides Discovery, Riverside supported missionaries in various countries, including three in Romania, who happened to be friends of mine. We had a husband-and-wife team, Chris and Pam Mueller, living in the small town of Lipova. Then we had Rich, a young missionary, who lived five hundred miles from them, in the southeastern metropolis of Bucharest, the capital of Romania.[32] Rich became friends with Pastor Nicholas and his wife, Maria, who had been called by God to start a church in their apartment, which the Lord blessed. Alpha Omega Church grew so much that they rented a larger space for the church services.

Maria has many siblings, several of whom Rich befriended, especially Ana and Christine, whom he dated. When Rich and Christine talked about getting married, he helped her and Ana obtain visas and come to the United States. However, after the girls arrived here, Rich and Christine broke up. The sisters didn't have anywhere to go, so Karen and I took them in for a season. Once they had settled into our home, Christine and Ana told us about their family, especially their brothers—Vali, age six, and Adi, seventeen. Vali needed eye surgery for a torn retina sustained when he fell and hit his head on concrete.

Slowly, we found ourselves swept up in this story of a boy who needed an operation. We had been praying for Nicholas, Maria, and their church; now our prayers grew to include their family. Before we knew it, Karen and I began to research eye doctors in Fort Myers. We found one who was willing to see Vali, if we could get him to the States. Then, we began trying to get Vali and Adi visas, and were disappointed when their visas were denied twice.

---

[32] Rich and Chris, both engineers, began as church members who were wonderful helpers when I was the children's minister and principal of Riverside Christian School. The three of us were like three grown boys, coming up with fun activities to teach exciting Bible stories. For instance, when we taught about Jesus and the disciples in the boat when the storm arose, we placed the chairs in the shape of a boat and gave the kids squirt guns. What a blast. After a season of ministering to children, God called both Rich and Chris into full-time ministry and mission work!

THE UNITED NATIONS IN OUR HOUSE!

During this time, Karen and I met Claudia and her two boys, nine-year-old Henry and four-year-old Victor. Claudia had come to the United States from Brazil twelve years earlier. Now, she was a new Christian, as well as a member of our church and our Discovery program. She was learning how to stand strong and be wise in dealing with Alfonso, her husband at the time, who was an addict.[33] Although attempting to overcome his addictions, he struggled mightily.

The more Claudia grew with spiritual wisdom and confidence, the more controlling and abusive Alphonso became, even attacking her with a pair of scissors. He became jealous and confrontational with me as I worked with each of them. I tried convincing him a number of times and in different ways—being both nice and firm—that I wasn't hitting on his wife. One time, as his agitation was getting out of control and nothing I did was working, I decked him. His suspicions and attitude improved, although he was shocked that a pastor laid him out. On another occasion, I had to locate where Alfonso was staying and then kick in the door of the shabby house to retrieve Claudia's boys.

Claudia and her boys were in a dangerous situation, with nowhere else to go. Christine and Ana had moved out and, for the second time, the Romanian boys' visas had been denied, so Karen and I offered to the family of three that they could live with us.

No sooner had we helped Claudia, Henry, and Victor move in, than we received a phone call from Paris, France. Vali and Adi's visas had been approved, so they and Rich flew out immediately and were getting ready to board a plane for Miami. Adi asked, "Can you please pick us up when we get there?"

Well, we couldn't abandon them now! I drove to Miami and was there when their plane landed.

All of a sudden, we had five new friends—two different families, two different nationalities, and two different languages—moving in within days of each other. They would all become part of our family.

---

[33] Permission has been granted to use the names of Claudia, Henry, and Victor. Alphonso's name has been changed.

While Claudia spoke English, we could hear her chatting away in Portuguese at night with her boys in the bedroom; Adi and Vali were in another bedroom, conversing in Romanian! It was pretty amazing. Vali and Adi knew only a few words of English, but they were young and learned quickly. Thankfully, the Portuguese and Romanian languages are both Latin-based, which enabled the families and boys to have some understanding of one another.

MORE CRAZY TIMING

There is one more part to this story. They moved in the weekend before Karen started back to college on Monday. I had encouraged Karen that if she wanted to return to school, I would help pick up slack around the house. I just didn't know God would slip five extra people into our house in the meantime!

While Karen went to school, she was working part-time and still trying to help take care of our family and household chores. One day, halfway through her degree studies, I woke up to find yellow sticky notes all over the house with the word *slack* scrawled on them. Karen stuck them on dirty dishes, laundry, and stray items that needed to be put away. Yellow flags were flying, testifying to the fact that (except for cooking) I wasn't keeping up my end of the bargain.

While I needed those bright reminders to step up the pace assisting with responsibilities, I couldn't help but grow in appreciation for Karen and her abilities to run a household and keep track of people and tasks! I don't know how Karen was able to work, go to school full-time, and be a wife and mom. I couldn't even keep up with helping everyone have clean underwear. Karen's my hero, picking up my slack through the years and loving me. I couldn't do what I do without Karen.

FOUR ENERGETIC BOYS

The four boys were good, bright, and energetic. Karen and I added school drop-off and pickup, as well as doctor's appointments to our schedules. Besides keeping us busy, they kept us on our toes.

Once, walking into Adi and Vali's room, I was surprised to hear a

Romanian channel on their television. Just as I was asking them how they received that channel, I saw a cable coming from behind the TV. Following the cable out the window, I found it went up the roof to a satellite dish that hadn't been there previously. Because Romania is a country without a lot of conveniences, ingenuity there is a needed commodity. The boys had a good, active supply of it. We let them keep the channel as it provided them with news and a connection to home. I'll also say that Adi and Vali were typical brothers, with the requisite roughhousing and brotherly fights.

In the meantime, Claudia's boys, Henry and Victor, discovered that our plastic dinner plates, if placed in the microwave, came out looking like a washboard. We kept telling the boys more strongly each time, "Don't put those dishes in the microwave!" After yet another plate appeared looking like a washboard, I called Victor over, looked him in the eye, and inquired, "Victor, do you want to live to be six?" His eyes got as big as those dessert plates. I added, "Then stop warping the dishes in the microwave."

The summer heat that year turned brutal, even on our back porch. We regularly talked about it. One day, I found one more warped dish on our kitchen counter. It had a note on it, written in Victor's five-year-old scrawl:

dear pistor dale the heat from the roof did this

UPDATES

We all survived, and I think I can say that I didn't mess up our new family members too much. Here are some updates:

Claudia, Henry, and Victor lived with us for a couple of years. Henry became an army chaplain and later moved back to Fort Myers, where he married a lovely girl. Victor became a paramedic in the army and will soon become a nurse.

Adi and Vali lived with us for about six years. Adi lived with us until he married Diana. Because our apartment was available, they rented it and lived there as newlyweds. We often call the apartment the "Honeymoon Suite." They lived there a couple of years while Adi returned to school to become a physician's assistant. He now has his own walk-in medical clinic and is a youth pastor in a town about an hour away from us. Adi and Diana have a beautiful young son.

Vali, who lived with us until he graduated from high school, never did have the eye operation. By the time he arrived in the States, the doctor explained that the condition of his torn retina made it too risky to operate—he would only do so if his eye became worse. In 2018, he and Ana were married in Romania. Half our family was there for the joyous ceremony, and I was blessed to officiate at their wedding. Vali, now a restaurant manager, and Ana live in the States.

Karen graduated with honors and worked as an occupational therapist for Johns Hopkins All Children's Hospital for fifteen years before retiring in 2018. Her coworkers threw her a retirement party, which ended up being a testament to how good Karen was at her job, how kind she is, and how much people love her. Everyone remarked that it was the largest retirement party turnout they had seen. Karen routinely made friends with everyone, including the security people, who showed up, too!

CAN WE HELP STEFAN?

I have one more story about our family taking in someone in need. When our son Larry was in high school, contemplating becoming a veterinarian, he worked for a season at a vet's office, where he befriended Stefan from Bulgaria. Stefan was a veterinarian who secured a green card to come to the United States to learn about the business side of running a veterinary clinic. He would then return to his country.

An intelligent young man, Stefan quickly learned English and increased in knowledge and skills. Stefan was good at everything he did. Not only did he perform operations, but he took care of animals as needed (which, of course, for a veterinarian's office, is pretty much 24/7), cleaned the place, and did laundry as well. While his stipend included being able to live at the clinic, his living space was a cot in a closet. His monthly salary was one hundred dollars, which seemed like slave wages to me. Stefan saved up his money to purchase a used bike, which he pedaled to a Barnes & Noble bookstore, where he loved to read. The vet started complaining about Stefan leaving the premises. While a Christian and active in church, the vet wanted to ensure that Stefan didn't overstay his visa. His motives may have been all right, but his intentions and rigidness could sure have been softened with kindness and grace.

Not surprisingly, Stefan grew discouraged about America and planned to return to Bulgaria soon, even though he could remain longer. Larry, who felt bad that Stefan hadn't been treated kindly and wouldn't have any good memories of America, asked me, "Dad, can't we do something to help Stefan?"

So one night, Larry and I took Stefan to dinner and talked about his situation. Yes, we offered to Stefan that he could stay with us. I also suggested that he could take a breather from working so hard, while he took time to consider and research career options.

However, he quickly secured two jobs—construction during the day, and chopping vegetables for a Charthouse Restaurant at night. For his vocation, he decided that he wanted to become a pathologist. During the two years he stayed with us, Stefan saved up enough money to buy a used car and secured a full scholarship at the University of Illinois to pursue a pathology degree. While attending school in the Midwest and working part-time, he saved up twenty-three hundred dollars to take the national exam in California to become a board-certified pathologist. The exam is an intensive, grueling, three-day test and probably one reason there are fewer than fifteen hundred board-certified pathologists in the United States. Stefan passed the test and is doing well. He lives in California with his beautiful wife and two fine sons. We have been blessed to visit them, and it has been exciting to watch what he has done with his life and the opportunities given to him.

WILD RIDES

Yes, our family has experienced plenty of adventures! There are certainly many Christians who walk with God and live quiet lives, which is good. Mine has just not been a life like that. While Karen, our family, and I continued to share God's grace with people He brought our way, the Lord was continuing to work on me to cleanse and heal me, which would mean more wild rides.

Section Six

HEALING GRACE

Chapter 19

WHAT'S LOW WORTH GOT TO DO WITH IT?

My addictions, like so many other off-kilter and broken aspects of my life, originated with pain that I tried to fix and heal myself. Every time I have tried to do this, I become more broken. In my empty place, where I wanted to feel loved, my efforts to fix my problem brought me an addiction to pornography. It would take God's grace, power, and a series of miracles to rescue me from this lonely, shameful prison, which began so long ago.

Even as a young child, I remember feeling disconnected from my parents and peers, alone and worthless. I wanted to connect with someone and feel loved. In kindergarten, I discovered daydreaming. I daydreamed about Polly, a cute girl with pigtails, who sat two rows away, and felt a connection. Daydreaming became a favorite pastime. It didn't matter how many times my teacher made me stand in the corner, exasperatedly rebuking me, "Dale, you're daydreaming again!" No matter how sternly she corrected me, at the age of five, I was hooked on escaping pain and loneliness through fantasy. Sometimes I imagined kissing Polly. That particular daydream came to fruition at the end of my kindergarten year, when I quickly kissed Polly on the playground and ran.

In first grade, still daydreaming regularly about Polly, I talked my best friend, Jim, into helping me visit Polly at her house. I didn't have her address, just a general idea of where she lived—about five miles away. I didn't have a bicycle, but Jim did. He always let me ride on the handlebars, while he pedaled. Believe it or not, we managed to find her house. Her mother seemed a bit surprised when she answered the door but smiled when I said, "Hi, I'm Dale. Is Polly home?" Polly was in the backyard on her swing set, so I joined her on the swings, while Jim sat on the teeter-totter. After a bit, her mom brought us lemonade.

My infatuation with Polly gradually faded away, but my daydreaming habit continued.

REAL CONNECTION VERSUS ILLUSIONS

God created us with an intrinsic need for love and to experience deep personal connections. Because I lacked these amid the dysfunctional alcoholism and avoidance of reality at our house, I sought my own safe, loving connections—even if I had to make them up.

I didn't like who I believed I was, so I created an improved, fantasy version of myself. This Dale was loved, pursued, valued, and wonderful. I liked this Dale! Eventually I added smart, suave, and tall. For years, I wasn't happy about the height God gave me and, if given the option to request a divine alteration, I would have been first in line for a height change. Because I wanted to feel connected and significant—by loving someone and being loved by someone—I created fantasies in this regard as well.

When fantasies continue and grow, they bloom into lust and become addictions. Lust is an intense desire, an overmastering craving, and illicit urges. People can lust after all sorts of things: possessions, power, prestige, people, and sex.

As I grew, so did my childhood daydreams, thoughts, and desires. They turned into lust. I not only lusted, I wanted to be the object of someone else's love and lust. By the time I reached puberty, I was well on my way to addiction. I felt euphoria by drinking in images, creating fantasies, and later pursuing the objects of my fantasies. Swearing off these things never worked. Inevitably, I always succumbed to the intense cravings again. Add to that my participation in Mafia activities and nightclubs—where such habits are routine, bragged about, and flaunted—and it was like handing a gallon of gasoline and a box of matches to a pyromaniac.

There are lots of problems connected with finding substitutes other than God to alleviate hurt, pain, fear, and brokenness. It doesn't matter if it's a substance or habit. Substitutes block truth, reality, and intimacy, while they keep us from reaching out to God and others. They keep us from growing and produce guilt. All this is a never-ending loop. A trap that becomes more difficult to escape.

All my lust habits, aimed at fulfilling my needs and emptiness, created tremendous guilt, self-hatred, remorse, and more pain. This deadly combination drove me further inward, away from reality and love. I tried rationalizing that what I was doing wasn't hurting anyone, but that wasn't true. I was captive inside myself. Avoiding my brokenness kept me from my true desire: intimacy. I could never attain real connection with another because I was addicted to the unreal. Fantasy and lies prevented me from knowing real love.[34]

"We're as sick as our secrets" is a true saying. We are as sick as our pain, hurts, and shortcomings that we carry around and don't face or deal with because we don't know what to do with them or how to heal them. Instead, we shove them down, cover them over, run from them, fight against them, numb them, and deny them.

Fast-forward many years. Gravely sick with my secrets, I hated myself for my actions, addiction, and sin. However, I had no idea what to do about my problem and I certainly didn't want anyone to know, especially because I was a pastor and had been for several years. Still, I wanted healing and freedom, and desperately prayed: "Please, God, I need a miracle."

God brought me healing. It just wasn't the quick and easily fixed miracle that I had in mind. Nor was it the quiet, behind-the-scenes-so-no-one-has-to-know miracle. God's plan and miracles did, though, have His fingerprints and conspiracy of grace all over them.

Riverside Church was part of the plan. In fact, our church had been praying for some time for spiritual revival. We wanted God to awaken our hearts to desire Him more, help us live as He would have us live, and experience more of Him.

---

[34] These truths regarding lust in this section have been gleaned from "The White Book," which I will share more on shortly.

We asked Life Action Ministries to come minister to Riverside. Its mission then (and now) is to ignite God's revival, so that individual believers, homes, and churches can be healed and restored to new life and purpose and God's glory can be revealed.[35]

A team of several ministry people came from Life Action. They led church services, conducted special prayer times, held short retreats for our leadership, and encouraged us one-on-one. They ministered to us with specific applicable, biblical truth. For example, during a Sunday evening service, they discussed God's vital instructions that we are to forgive those who have hurt us. If we're seeking God and we remember that someone is angry with us, God tells us that we are to go to that person and make it right, then return to God (Matthew 5:23–24). At the close of the service, the team shared that if anyone was holding a grudge or hurt against others in the room, go to them, forgive them, and make amends. What a powerful, moving night! Relationships were mended with forgiveness, tears, and hugs. Love flowed throughout the room!

After this event, God seemed to set His sights on me.

IT'S DARKEST BEFORE THE DAWN

A couple of days after the powerful service, I had Friday off. I spent the morning at home by myself, when I became fixated on porn. It seemed that only minutes had passed, but when I looked at the clock, I was shocked. Several hours had passed! Spiritual and physical nausea came over me with waves of remorse, pain, conviction, and brokenness.

I saw myself as a helpless captive to this awful addiction and knew I needed help. Trying to battle the problem on my own had only dug me in deeper. I knew that I had to get honest about my struggle and sin, starting that day with Karen when she got home. I spent a loooooong day waiting for her.

---

[35] Life Action Ministries offers information on their website, LifeAction.org, and they publish a magazine titled *Revive*. Life Action's ministry reminds us of the great promised truth of Scripture, church history, and the history of nations—whenever God's people cry out to Him in humble honesty, seek Him, and surrender to Him, they are transformed and raised up anew to His glory (2 Chronicles 7:14).

When Karen arrived home, I trembled as I shared the truth of what I had been doing. This whole time, I thought I had been doing everything in secret, but she said she had known for a long time. I asked her how she knew. She replied that when I was meaner than normal, she recognized I had been actively pursuing my addiction and was then fighting guilt and shame. Before we finished, I told Karen that I was going to resign as pastor on Monday.

On Monday, crushed by shame and remorse, I shuffled into the building, quietly heading to my office, letter in hand. Before I could get there, Del from Life Action[36] saw me and recognized something was amiss. Following me into my office, he shut the door and inquired, "What's wrong, Dale?"

I confessed the whole thing—not just the previous Friday's episode, but what had been going on for a long time. I concluded with, "I'm going to resign as pastor." Del immediately said, "Let's stop and pray." After we prayed, Del asked me to explain what had brought me to my decision. I shared with him the long battles I had endured with alcohol and drugs and that, while I was happy to have gained victory over those addictions, I saw that pornography had become my drug of choice.

While I was expecting disapproval, a lecture, or some form of condemnation, Del expressed only kindness, grace, and truth. Though I still had to face the fact that my days of pastoring would soon be over, his kindness helped lessen my anxiety. As I went into the staff meeting that morning, Del was by my side.

After the meeting started, Del said that he had something to share. He related the earlier events and recommended that the staff prayerfully consider not accepting my resignation. Del emphasized that my confession must remain confidential—anyone sharing it would be sinning. He stressed the importance of the fact that I had come forward voluntarily to confess my sin and helped us recognize the ways the Holy Spirit was doing

---

36 Life Action Ministries' commitment to confidentiality and privacy is solid. Although he has since passed away, I want to acknowledge Del Fehsenfeld Sr. and his commitment to Jesus, truth, and grace. Del Jr. and the team at Life Action have given me permission to share their ministry and names.

a work in our church body. Then he recommended that they show me grace and that I be allowed to stay, with accountability and supervision.

Besides being ashamed, contrite, and gravely humbled, I was astonished and shocked that I was not fired. I'm still amazed at God's intervention and grace-filled miracles. As the days progressed, I grew more astounded at God's all-knowing sovereignty and timing. He had more plans already in place to help me.

Besides attending my regular AA meetings, I have attended (and still attend) other recovery meetings. During this time, I attended an Overcomers Outreach group at a church in Naples, when the group and hosting church held a weeklong seminar and Bible study for men who wanted to break free from sexual addiction. Christian counselor Mark Laaser led the event. [37] I marvel at God's sovereign provision and timing because the event had been scheduled many months prior to this. Not only that, but sexual addiction was just beginning to be addressed as an addiction and a mental-health topic.

I went to every meeting that Mark held and talked with him. With his encouragement and directives, I resumed my journey through the 12 Steps, focusing specifically on this addiction. Once again, I accepted my powerlessness and sought God's aid and power. (Riverside also scheduled Mark to minister to our congregation in several services.)

Then, with two other men, I started the first sexual-addiction 12 Step group in our county and chose a sponsor specifically to help me with this bondage. Especially in this addiction, we need the right sponsor to ask us specific, tough questions, so we can't hide, deny, or evade.

Our group read and discussed the book *Sexaholics Anonymous*, often called "The White Book." This book gives great guidance and brings to light the powerful truth and reminder that healing is found with the help

---

[37] Mark Laaser was given grace and assistance in his struggles from Patrick Carnes, the pioneer in the field of sexual addiction and recovery. When Laaser experienced healing, he began helping other men break free from this addiction and eventually opened a Christian counseling center, Faithful & True, in Eden Prairie, Minnesota. Laaser and Carnes have authored books together and separately.

of God's love and others.[38] I had a lot to learn regarding sexual addiction, including the fact that it is quite addictive because it involves physical, mental, emotional, relational, and spiritual aspects of our being. The addiction affects the entirety of the person, plus a good-feeling rush happens with this habit. Both God's help and power, and the help of others, are needed to find healing for the emotional and relational components. The road to freedom from sexual addiction is bumpy; however, the freedom and subsequent blessings are wonderful and more than worth our efforts.

KEY COMPONENTS

It is difficult to describe aspects of this addiction, the healing journey, and even love because they involve intangible ingredients, but I'll try.

Love itself includes elements of kindness, compassion, acceptance, connection, care, and significance. Love requires time and vulnerability, too. Well, there's a problem. We don't like being vulnerable. It's a Catch-22 kind of problem. If I want to be loved for me, I need to be genuine and honest. I must share the real me. However, as soon as I reveal something about myself, whatever it is—but particularly if it's a problem I have—you may disapprove, turn away, or not like me. Consequently, every time I uncover, disclose, and share something about myself with someone, I take a risk and am vulnerable.

Men seem to especially not like feeling vulnerable—physically or emotionally. Maybe this is why men struggle in revealing themselves. Maybe it's a reason pornography is so prevalent among them. This false world of pornography seemingly offers release, comfort, and escape—mentally, emotionally, and physically, and it appears safe.

Ah, but there is a great toll to be paid. When one is trapped in this addiction, we can't personally grow; neither can real relationships grow and develop. We lose out on closeness and intimacy—the very things we need and crave. Not only can we not experience love and intimacy, but we aren't able to give them to the very people we care about. Hiding

---

38 *Sexaholics Anonymous* ("The White Book") is a great resource, which can be purchased at http://sapub.handsservices.com. Hands Services, a family-owned company, handles and ships various product inventory.

ourselves and not sharing who we are (including hurts and fears) block intimacy.

We come to see how our denial and rationalizations were lies. I had certainly lied to myself. Like other married men trapped in pornography, I rationalized that I wasn't hurting anyone, and at least I wasn't having an affair. In fact, I was hurting myself and, sadly, I was a love cripple to Karen.

While these are some of the trouble spots surrounding sexual addiction, we can find what we were looking for: freedom, victory, healing, and connection with others.[39]

WHAT A REMEDY

For me, the invaluable remedy came through the help of a safe men's group. (I know, it sounds crazy.) A men's 12 Step group is where I keep learning to get honest, share, and experience bonds of trust and compassion. As I shared hurts, feelings, and struggles with the men who were safe and who accepted me, I experienced bonds of friendship and love that were amazing and life-changing.

The 12 Step groups work and help bring healing for several reasons.

1. They are safe places made up of a group of like-minded people, with similar struggles, who are all there to get well.
2. As others share their stories, sometimes crazy stories, we find people just like ourselves. We can relate to them (and their stories). What do you know? We're not so alone or different, after all!
3. We hear stories of victory as well, and find hope, strength, and new ways of living.
4. We begin to share what we have tried, so hard and for so long, to shove down or shoulder on our own.

---

[39] The following are a few more biblical considerations. People think pornography and lustful thoughts are "fine," but Jesus refuted this idea. He said that lust is like having sex with someone. Sex is a gift that God gives us for marriage, for a husband and wife to enjoy with each other, with great pleasure. It's not intended for us to take pleasure selfishly for our own interest, which is what sex outside of marriage is all about. Sex is to bring joy, intimacy, depth, and a unique bond to a husband and wife within the safety of a marriage relationship.

5. As we listen to others and begin getting honest about our emotional burdens and actions, we experience love and care.

Sharing the real-deal truth about ourselves and experiencing both care and connection with others are emotional gifts that are difficult to explain. It's an inadequate example but, when you share something with someone you care about—whether it's a cup of coffee, a meal, a fun or daring adventure, a secret, or a hurt—it creates a bond. The more personal the sharing, and the more understanding and help we receive, the greater the feeling of love that we experience with others.

As I grew and opened up with men, I tried this more with Karen, with baby steps. What do you know? As I continued to let myself be vulnerable and real with Karen, our relationship deepened and grew. I felt more loved and significant—not less.

The great need we each have is to feel loved, valued, and accepted. While we often try to put on a swaggering attitude to fulfill our need, this doesn't bring the deep life-giving bonds that God intended. As we come to God and the right people, with honesty, vulnerability, and humility, we find true meaningful connection and know what it means to be loved.

No longer do we feel that we will die if we don't have our addiction or habit. Instead, it feels wonderful to be free from it—free from the deadly trap, compulsion, shame, prison, and loneliness. It feels good to love and be loved. Healing and connection are real, possible, and far better than our old substitutes.

During this season, God helped me know more of His great love through these events. He drew my attention and heart to Paul's prayer for us in Ephesians.[40] We are to walk in, know, and be rooted in God's deep and expansive love through Jesus. While we focus on the Lord and His love, He does more than we can ask or imagine. In *The Message* version, the passage reads,

---

[40] For additional Scripture on "Being Fully Loved, Forgiven, Accepted & Complete in Christ," see Appendix E.

I ask [the Father] to strengthen you by his Spirit—not a brute strength but a glorious inner strength—that Christ will live in you as you open the door and invite him in. And I ask him that with both feet planted firmly on love, you'll be able to take in with all followers of Jesus the extravagant dimensions of Christ's love. Reach out and experience the breadth! Test its length! Plumb the depths! Rise to the heights! Live full lives, full in the fullness of God.

God can do anything, you know—far more than you could ever imagine or guess or request in your wildest dreams! He does it not by pushing us around but by working within us, his Spirit deeply and gently within us.

Glory to God in the church! Glory to God in the Messiah, in Jesus! Glory [forever and ever]! (Ephesians 3:16–21 MSG)

When we stop running after habits and substances to ease our pain and broken areas, and we pursue God instead, these are the places we can experience God and His love. He becomes more real to us. We experience the living, loving, true God!

MORE WONDERS

A few more surprising miracles happened during this journey.

As the men and I experienced amazing love and healing, somehow the changes in us couldn't be contained and kept secret. Word began to spread in our AA meetings. More men began coming to our SA group and to my door, seeking help. Churches started sending me men, sometimes pastors, who were hurting and struggling with this painful addiction. Our group and love grew!

There is another miracle that I marvel at every time I see it happen.

When I have counseled men with sexual addictions, I encourage them to attend SA meetings. I share with them what they can expect at the gatherings, and how each man introduces himself with his first name and then shares briefly. I explain to him that in the beginning, he doesn't have to speak—or even say his name. When the sharing comes around to him, he can just say, "I pass." Because I know they are scared beyond measure, many times I have accompanied men to SA meetings.

As the broken man sits there, he hears one man after another sharing, "Hi. My name is _____, and I'm a grateful recovering sex addict; I struggle with _____ [whatever the specific issue is]; and I have been enjoying freedom and sobriety for _____ [length of time]."

As he hears men honestly sharing their struggles and victories, he unknowingly experiences healing grace and truth. I sit there amazed as very often, even at the first meeting, the newcomer opens up and shares some pain or struggle. I know that the door to this man's prison just opened, and he too can find freedom and connection. Truly we need God and others for healing.

Chapter 20

JESUS, PRAYER MIRACLES & PEACE

God sometimes seems to drop gifts into our lives from out of the blue. Dr. Ed and his Transformation Prayer Ministry (which brought me great healing and peace) felt like such a gift.

Dr. Ed Smith and his family moved to Fort Myers and wanted to join Riverside Church, but he first requested a meeting with our pastoral staff to share about his counseling ministry. Those with whom he worked were experiencing miraculous breakthroughs; however, because it is somewhat unique, he knew the pastoral staff would want to review it. When we met with Dr. Ed, he shared his story about how he came to start the Transformation Prayer Ministry (TPM), which helps in understanding the process.[41]

Dr. Ed primarily counseled women who had been sexually abused as children. Consequently, many of them struggled with additional issues, including anxiety, panic attacks, depression, and eating disorders. He had been counseling for many years and was becoming discouraged and close to burnout because the women were not experiencing much in the way of lasting change. They were managing their pain, but they weren't experiencing true freedom. As a result, Dr. Ed wrestled with whether or not to

---

[41] Dr. Ed Smith granted me permission to share his story. It is also on his website at TransformationPrayer.org, along with free TPM materials. While originally incorporating a training period for TPM, the team now focuses on teaching the biblical principles of TPM and encouraging people to use them right away.

continue counseling. He sought God, praying, "Father, I don't know what to do anymore. Show me Your wisdom and what You want me to do."

He had been praying this way for some time. One day, while counseling a woman (we'll call Mary), it was the same story, with no progress or breakthroughs. Trembling and near tears, she again recalled her painful memories, and her feelings of shame, fear, and guilt.

"I know this is not true," Mary concluded, "but it feels that what happened was my fault. I feel so dirty and shameful."

Typically, this is when Dr. Ed would jump in and share truth with the woman—that it wasn't her fault. Not knowing what else to do, he asked Mary if she would be willing to try something different and if they could pray. She agreed. Dr. Ed took a breath and prayed, "Jesus, I do not know what to do. Is there something that You want her to know?"

Dr. Ed shared, "I did not have any expectations of what would happen. I was simply out of options. After a few moments, Mary stopped crying and calmed down. She sat up, opened her eyes and, with a bewildered, yet peaceful look, she declared, 'It's gone.'

"'What's gone?' I asked.

"'The shame and guilt all lifted off me,' Mary replied.

"'How is that?' I asked.

"Her countenance radiated joy, as she shared, 'He said I am not there anymore, and it was not my fault.'

"'I know; that is what I told you,' I responded.

"'Yes, but this time, He told me,' she declared.

"Hesitating briefly, I asked, 'Who told you?'

"'The Lord told me! He said it was not my fault,' she exclaimed.

"When she looked up through tear-filled eyes, her face was filled with peace and joy." Dr. Ed continued, "She had no traces of despair, shame, or fear. I had just witnessed a miracle! I could never have accomplished that myself, no matter how much I counseled her. The Lord transformed her by personally speaking His truth and perspective to her. She moved from hearing and believing the lies of Satan to experiencing and knowing God's truth and freedom."

Dr. Ed continued to develop the principles of Transformation Prayer

Ministry with Scripture, prayer, and God's help. Through TPM, many have come to experience God's miraculous freedom and peace. We found Dr. Ed Smith to be a humble, honest, God-fearing man. We reviewed his written materials and agreed that Transformation Prayer is godly and biblical.

POWERFUL PROMISES IN SCRIPTURE

Transformation Prayer brings God's healing to people because it is based on seeking God's assistance through prayer and on the promises of Scripture. Following are key Scripture promises that I think of regarding TPM.

> Again, truly I tell you that if two of you on earth agree about anything they ask for, it will be done for them by my Father in heaven. For where two or three gather in my name, there am I with them. (Matthew 18:19–20)

> Now may the Lord of peace himself give you his peace at all times and in every situation. The Lord be with you. (2 Thessalonians 3:16 NLT)

> Behold, you delight in truth in the inward being, and you teach me wisdom in the secret heart. (Psalm 51:6 ESV)

> Don't be like the people of this world, but let God change the way you think. Then you will know how to do everything that is good and pleasing to him. (Romans 12:2 CEV)

> So that you may live a life worthy of the Lord and please him in every way . . . growing in the knowledge of God, being strengthened with all power according to his glorious might. (Colossians 1:10–11)

BE WILLING

The entire staff was in wholehearted agreement that because I was the pastor for our Discovery and counseling ministry and, because everyone knows I am always in need of more healing, I should be the first to try Dr. Ed's Transformation Prayer. So, I scheduled an appointment.

The accounts that follow may make the healing process sound quick and simple. There are times that answers come quickly. In addition, we can learn to easily incorporate this way of praying into our lives. However, when someone is seeking breakthroughs for severe trauma and pain that may include PTSD components, each session can take up to two hours, and one often needs a number of prayer sessions. We must be willing to revisit painful wounds and memories, which we prefer to avoid. Patience, time, and active participation are needed to face these emotions in ourselves and take them to God for His healing and truth.

Next, I'll share a bit about shame, before I relate a few TPM stories.

SHAME & HEALING

Ever since I was sexually abused at five, shame is something that has plagued me. Shame is different from guilt. God's Spirit convicts us of guilt to help us turn from ungodly behavior. Shame is toxic because it turns the "I made a wrong and bad choice" message into "I am a defective person." Our shortcomings and deficiencies make us feel exposed and humiliated and that there is no help or hope for us.

Shame grows in the fertile soil of a dysfunctional childhood. It stems from beliefs and messages that parents and other significant people in our lives deliver. These beliefs and messages are fed by constant criticism, rejection, abandonment, guilt, and fear. Shame inflicts an almost indescribable pain. I felt inadequate, worthless, and a failure, unworthy of God's love. In addition, I felt tainted, dirty, and yucky—that I would never become clean.

This shame triggered the numerous behaviors that I have already shared. I tried to hide who I was, while at the same time trying desperately to prove my worth, no matter the cost. Early in life, I became an overachiever, which seemed to work in my career and business endeavors. Trying to prove that I mattered and was worth something is an understatement. Even in conversations, I sought to "one-up" others and always prove I was right. As you can imagine, this approach isn't helpful when it comes to forming healthy relationships and warm bonds.

Shame affected my moods. People frequently commented about my moodiness and how fast my moods changed. It was true. A fleeting thought or image could overwhelm me and instantly prompt a downward spiral of feeling tainted, dirty, and yucky. Definitely yucky.

As a Christian, I mentally knew God's love and cleansing power. Still, I experienced little deep peace. Mentally and spiritually, I said, *In Christ, I am fine*, but I often had this inner anguish. Because of the shame from the abuse, along with Mom's angry overreaction when I told her, I had never told another soul about the abuse. Not even Karen. However, when I was in my forties, something happened to change that.

Before students could graduate with a counseling degree from Liberty University and counsel others, they were required to complete an in-depth questionnaire and receive counseling themselves. I answered the questions honestly. Several counseling sessions followed. Finally, miraculously, I shared my pain, shame and struggles with someone, and he was a Christian counselor! The counselor shed light on many of my feelings and helped me understand that victims can hold more anger toward a parent or caregiver than toward the perpetrator. He also suggested that it would be helpful for me to join an abuse-support group and read a few books regarding pedophiles and sexual abuse. For some time after these sessions, I thought I had resolved and taken care of the issues regarding my abuse. What happened was a door to healing had cracked open and let light in. Although I didn't immediately go home and share with Karen, a day came when I began to put my story and feelings into words, with her first and later my sponsor.[42]

Now with TPM, I would face more of my shame.

---

[42] It amazes me how many times I think I'm fixed—only to discover I'm not—and that I need more of God's healing and help. Several years after my counseling at Liberty, God miraculously opened a door for me to participate in a support group. Our Discovery counseling center expanded and added counselor Peggy, who started a sexual-abuse support group. Hearing bits of my story, she encouraged me to attend. I resisted because it was all women. She kept encouraging me until I finally joined. It brought more healing, so that I helped lead nine groups, each of which was ten weeks in length. Besides the events of my life, God has also used the circumstances from Liberty and my abuse-group experiences many times over to help others.

IT'S A MIRACLE!

During one of my first prayer sessions, as I shared about my feelings surrounding the sexual abuse, my tears flowed. The prayer leader asked, "What do you feel?"

"Yucky and dirty," I replied.

"Does it feel true that you are yucky and dirty?" he inquired.

"Yes," I answered.

"Do you want to be free of these feelings and hear what Jesus desires to tell you?"

"Yes," I choked out.

"Jesus, what do you want Dale to know about his being yucky and dirty?" the leader asked.

As I sat there, I felt Jesus washing me with a cloth from the top of my head to my feet. Everywhere Jesus touched me and wiped, I was washed with brightness. I was clean and spotless. In His quiet, yet miracle-commanding voice, Jesus said, "I am cleaning you as white as snow." I felt a warm glow illuminate me everywhere He touched. It washed me and filled me. I was finally free from that lie and feeling! I felt loved, clean, and connected to Christ.

"Does it still feel true that you are yucky and dirty?" the leader asked me.

"No! I am clean!" I sat there a minute and took in this feeling. Not only did I know it, but now I felt accepted, loved, and forgiven in Jesus. I felt clean! What a wonderful feeling!

LIES & PAINFUL EMOTIONS FEEL TRUE

Transformation Prayer Ministry helps us confront the lies we believe. Our thoughts and beliefs that aren't based on truth influence us and produce our negative, painful emotions. These lies seem and feel like the truth, but anything standing in opposition to God's truth is a lie—a false belief or distorted message. Lies can feel true and be difficult to recognize and identify as lies.[43] (This is one reason the prayer leader asked if I still felt yucky and dirty.)

---

43 Scripture not only explains that Satan is the evil one and the father of lies and deception (John 8:44), but that, with Jesus's assistance, we are to learn to recognize and overcome Satan, his attacks, and tactics (Ephesians 6:11).

Those of us who grew up in dysfunctional homes may be fighting lies that have become deeply embedded and formed a stronghold within us because they've been reinforced over the years. At times, we mentally know a truth but struggle with an opposing feeling and belief. We mentally know that God loves us but are endeavoring to feel it in our hearts, where it can change us.

Transformation Prayer helps us mentally return to past events, hurts, and memories, and acknowledge the events, along with what we have come to feel, think, and believe about them. Then we seek God's healing, love, and truth regarding the events and our beliefs.

The following is one example about how a lie-based thought of mine developed. When I was young, Mom taught me to get myself ready for school, make my bed, and fix my own breakfast. She was also a perfectionist. Therefore, when I made my bed, she would often say to me, "Good job, Dale," while she remade the bed. She would tell me I did a good job of fixing my breakfast, yet follow it with, "Don't be so messy." When I got dressed, she would tell me how well I did, but add, "Those clothes are too wrinkled," or, "Your pants and shirt don't match."

Her actions spoke louder than her words did. I heard her say one thing, but meanwhile I took in all the negative messages—verbal and nonverbal. Whenever I heard, "Good job," I felt like a failure. The messages were continually reinforced: I wasn't good enough, and what I did wasn't good enough. I stopped believing compliments and doubted those who gave them to me.

KNOWING GOD'S TRUTH & PROTECTION

TPM helped me find healing in many different areas. One aspect I struggled with was feeling guilty from the abuse, as if it were my fault. I either brought it on or should have done something to stop it. Despite knowing I was innocent, I still felt guilty. In a prayer session on this, I heard Jesus tell me that I was only five and couldn't have run away. He reminded me how afraid I had been and that it wasn't my fault in any way. Jesus replaced guilt with truth, freedom, and peace.

Additionally, I struggled with feeling vulnerable and believed the lie that no one was protecting me. Feeling rejected and abandoned, I had to protect myself. As a Christian, I knew mentally that God cares for me and protects me—I could even recite verses about it—but I experienced little peace in this area. No matter how many times I told myself, "I'm safe in Christ," what I felt inside of me didn't match the truth I knew mentally. There were two specific types of circumstances in which these feelings overwhelmed me.

When I went out in public, my anxiety and apprehension were extremely high if people were behind me. If I was in a restaurant, I had to have my back against a wall or a booth. Family and a few close friends were aware that I struggled, but no one really knew the extreme panic and vulnerability I felt in these situations.

Additionally, I had a reflex reaction of hitting people who jumped out at me or accidentally startled me. My boys loved to persuade relatives or friends (when we ran out of relatives) to "tap Dad on the shoulder and see his funny reaction." It worked every time. My kids laughed hysterically whenever I hit someone.

I had several TPM sessions regarding these feelings. During one session about feeling the need to protect myself, I felt Jesus ask me, "Who do you think has kept you alive and protected you all these years?" Immediately, a memory flashed into my mind.

I was on a back porch of someone's house, where I shouldn't have been, when a man came charging at me with a pistol, shooting. I saw the fire explode from the muzzle as I turned, jumped over the railing, and lit out of there. While the guy kept firing until the chamber clicked empty, I wondered if I had been shot and just didn't know it yet. I kept running until I was far enough away that I could catch my breath and examine myself to see if there were any holes in me or blood. It surprised me to find that I was in one piece.

Jesus spoke again, saying, "I have protected you more than you know. I am with you and will never leave you or forsake you. I know you, and I have your life." As He spoke, peace filled me. I am safe and protected in Jesus, and I feel safe.

DARK NIGHTS & FRIENDS

Shortly after some of these sessions, Ed Smith and I were enjoying dinner together at a Bob Evans Restaurant. As I paid the bill, Ed wandered outside into the dark evening and hatched a crazy idea. He wanted to find out if Jesus really had healed me from my instantaneous overreactions.

As I came outside, I walked down the sidewalk, enjoying the nice night and looking for Ed. Suddenly, he jumped out from behind a bush and hollered, "Hah!"

This time instead of landing a quick knockout punch, I paused and looked at him, realized who he was, and smiled. Then we burst out laughing. We laughed like kids at ourselves and with joy at Jesus's healing. It's miraculous!

Today, I am free from so many lies, habits, and behaviors. I am free to sit with my back to windows, doors, and people. In fact, not only is my home office in the bedroom where we dropped off those first drunks so many years earlier, but my desk faces the door, putting my back to a window. How wonderful it is. With Jesus, we are to seek, pursue, and know healing and freedom!

It is just as God's Word and the familiar song share, "What a Friend We Have in Jesus." I keep experiencing Jesus as a friend—not because I have my life so perfectly together—but because He tells us to come to Him for every need. The more honest and real I am with my hurts and needs and the more I seek Him, the more of Him and His healing I experience.

This is also true with my friends. The more honest and real I am with those who follow Jesus, the more they can help me and intercede for me. Dr. Ed is one of those friends, who was even willing to risk being knocked out to ensure I found freedom.

It surprised me to discover yet another place of healing. Ever since I was fifteen, and my Mafia boss gave me a gun, I always carried one on me for protection. I carried one even after I became a pastor, until I began to think—*maybe a pastor shouldn't carry a gun*. Plus, it scared me to think that in a fit of rage I might use it. I decided to put my gun away, but continued to carry my knife (my security blanket). After many of these Transformation Prayer sessions, one morning before work I went to collect my wallet, keys, and knife from the spot where I kept them at night. When I saw the knife, I chuckled and thought—*I don't need that. I don't need to protect myself. Jesus kept me safe all those years—He has me now.*

Hallelujah! With the Lord, I am free!

HELP SHEDDING OUR GRAVE CLOTHES

The freedom we find through Jesus's grace, prayer, and the help of other Christians is pictured in a powerful way in the story of Jesus and his dear friend Lazarus (John 11:1–44). Jesus was traveling in another town when Lazarus died, was wrapped in grave clothes, and was buried in a tomb. Four days after his death, the Lord arrived back in town. Everyone rushed to Christ, telling Him the sad news (although He already knew, including what He was going to do). Standing before the tomb, Jesus declared, "Lazarus, come out!"

Lazarus came to life and walked out of the tomb, but he was still bound in the grave clothes wrapped around him. Jesus instructed their friends, "Free him, and let him go" (John 11:44 NHEB).[44]

Each of us is like Lazarus. When we receive Jesus, He gives us a new life, but we need help from God and others to be unwrapped from all sorts of thoughts, habits, and hurts from our old life of death. The ministry of the church and parachurch ministries (such as TPM and recovery groups) rely on the aid of God's caring family to administer His truth and healing to one another, unbinding heavy layers of bondage, shame, and hurt. We assist one another and lift up one another in prayer. This is the work we are called to do as Jesus's loved ones.

I love this story so much that on my office wall, I have a unique framed picture of Lazarus with his two friends, and Christ's instructions, "Free him, and let him go."

---

[44] The NIV says, "Take off the grave clothes and let him go." At least two translations read, "Unbind him."

HEALING FOR BROKEN, PAINFUL EMOTIONS

Unlike Lazarus, though—whose bondage was visible—identifying and being freed from the bondage of our hurts, painful emotions, and broken thoughts is often not quick or easy.

God gave us feelings and wants us to be emotionally rich and healthy people. We're to experience love, joy, sadness, fear, and even anger. Our feelings are meant to enhance our lives and let us know when something is wrong in our relationships or within ourselves. Hurt, sin, and brokenness affect our emotions, though. Frequently, we feel overrun by them. We try hard to "stuff" them down in our struggles to keep it together.

Part of our job is learning to identify, feel, and express in healthy ways the emotions that we experience. God wants us to learn how to handle our feelings in ways that honor Him. For example, we can be angry, but we are not to sin in our anger (Ephesians 4:26). We need to express our feelings in an honest, composed, forthright manner, instead of shutting down or blowing up.

This can be hard, especially if we are used to stuffing them and feel like a jumbled mess inside. As children, we may have received unhealthy messages about emotions. Some families experience only two of them: fine or angry (although, technically, fine isn't a feeling). Sometimes, just certain family members are allowed to be angry. Everyone else is supposed to be "fine" and "get with the program." How often I heard the words: "Suck it up, buttercup." This is what is known as an emotionally repressive family.

From a very early age, I found it necessary to deny and shut down my pain and discomfort and keep everything locked inside. Expressing fear, anger, wants, or needs brought another helping of rejection, anger, and punishment, followed with more inadequacy and shame. As I grew, I didn't know how to express pain, fear, anger, or needs, and fell into a pattern of compensating for repressed feelings by doing things to the extreme when it came to achievement, performance, and work. I also covered over and soothed my feelings with alcohol, drugs, sex, and food.

We must learn to identify and acknowledge our feelings; be able to sit with them and feel them for a time; and share them with others and Jesus. This can be extremely difficult; it's easier to run, ignore, or fight.

It can take a long time to get in touch with the many varied and layered emotions that we feel. As challenging as it can be, it helps us find powerful healing. I'll share two stories of helping people learn to identify their emotions.

FEAR & INSECURITY

One man, whom I will call Sam, experienced anger, but it took hours of working with him to help him uncover his emotions underneath that were driving his anger. In my office, he would look at the poster of emotions, get close to a feeling besides anger, and then go off on a tangent, talking about how mad other people made him. When I would ask him again what he was feeling, he would go off on another rabbit trail, describing how he was a good father, coach, and employer. We kept working; I kept probing.

Sam stumbled on the truth when he shared, "I feel like what I have to say is not important." Now, we had something we could work with! His anger was disguising fear and insecurity.

Another man, Dave, sought my assistance for struggles he had with family members. At one point, I shared with him that he needed to deal with his anger in a timely fashion.

Shocked, he looked at me and declared, "I don't get angry!"

"Okay, frustration," I replied.

"Oh, yeah, I get frustrated all the time," he admitted.

I explained that "frustration" is a polite word for anger. I shared how hurt, unmet expectations, fear, and frustration are all wrapped up in anger, resentment, bitterness, and even depression. Anger is usually a secondary emotion covering over fear, hurt, and unmet needs, which we must learn to honestly share with others and with God.

Many of us struggle, though, to realize that we have needs. It can be the hardest thing for people to recognize and acknowledge. By the time we have reached the age of two, we've been proclaiming every chance we get, "I can do it myself." (In fact, AA's first three Steps are about assisting individuals to accept that besides needing help, they require God's help.) It's a struggle to accept the fact that we lack anything because we keep proclaiming we're fine.

Except we're not.

God permits circumstances in our lives, even trials and tribulations, to reveal our needs to us, so that we might find a new relationship, life, and blessings in Him. He wants to expose the areas that are hindering our lives. This way, we find Jesus, freedom, healing, peace, and joy. [45] Sharing our thoughts, feelings, and needs with others and God is a good thing; it helps us draw closer and gives us richer, warmer, and more intimate relationships.

God desires for each of us to be a living example of His power and grace. It's not always about fixing our circumstances, but changing us in the midst of our difficulties. He wants us to be able to exclaim, "You won't believe what God did for me!" He wants other people to look at us and know that Jesus has transformed us.

There is, though, another aspect to facing our emotions. For sure, God wants to heal our emotions, but at times He calls us to do something, regardless of how we feel about it.

Sometimes, God makes a crazy, difficult request.

---

45 Scripture contains many promises regarding the Lord's desire and power to heal us. God's Word tells us: He is our healer (Exodus 15:26); He heals the brokenhearted and binds up their wounds (Psalm 147:3); He heals all manner of sickness and diseases (Psalm 103:1–5; Matthew 4:23); and He gives freedom to those bound and sets free those whom Satan oppresses (Isaiah 58:6, 61:1–2; Luke 4:18–19; Acts 10:38).We are also to know that God is an ever-present help (Psalm 46:1), available daily (Psalm 68:19), and His mercies are new every morning (Lamentations 3:21–26). Our tasks are to seek His assistance and presence and wait for Him (Psalm 33:20).

Chapter 21

GOD'S CRAZY, RELENTLESS INSTRUCTIONS

While there are plenty of times that I am happy doing what God wants me to do, I'm sad to say, there have been times when I have resisted His instructions. Sometimes, the Lord's directions don't make sense from my limited wisdom and viewpoint. Only when I am able to see things from His perspective do I understand. This is certainly one reason Scripture tells us to "trust in the LORD with all your heart and lean not on your own understanding; in all your ways submit to him, and he will make your paths straight" (Proverbs 3:5–6).

Scripture tells us that obeying (or following) God and His instructions is the best thing we can do—it's how we love Him, honor Him, and please Him. Doing what He says is better than any religious habit, act, observance, sacrifice, duty, or gift (1 Samuel 15:22). Instead of trying to choose our own way of doing what we think is "right," He wants us to seek and follow Him.

God promises us that whoever obeys Him will be blessed, honored, loved, protected, and treasured by Him; they will be considered a friend and family.[46] Jesus reiterated these truths, saying that those who love Him

---

[46] There is much in Scripture about the importance and blessings of following God and Christ in obedience. An easy online search could be made for a list. A few verses include Exodus 19:5, Luke 11:28, John 15:14, and James 1:25.

will obey His teaching; they will be blessed and He will make His home with them (John 14:15–24).

Whatever word or phrase we use—disobeying God, not following Him, or falling short of His glory and will—it is sin. It's missing His mark. It is displeasing to God and breaks our fellowship with Him. Throughout Scripture we see stories of painful consequences when people continually disobeyed God and stories of blessings when people followed and obeyed.

The New Testament expands further on this, explaining that, because of Jesus's perfect sacrifice on our behalf, and the fact that we no longer have to offer endless animal sacrifices (as the Israelites did), our lives are to be offered willingly back to God as our loving sacrifice. Scripture tells us:

> So then, my friends, because of God's great mercy to us I appeal to you: Offer yourselves as a living sacrifice to God, dedicated to his service and pleasing to him. This is the true worship that you should offer. (Romans 12:1 GNT)

This can be difficult. We can tend to wander off—intentionally or not—from either the instructions in His Word or the personal directions and nudges He gives us. Sometimes, I picture my altar marred with my footprints, skid marks, and smoke. Thankfully, God is faithful, even when I'm not. He lovingly brings me back and helps me to learn to follow Him. God keeps showing me that my desires, thoughts, and actions tend to be shortsighted and self-centered, whereas His ways are greater and more loving than mine are. While I keep discovering how much better God's ways are than mine, sometimes, regrettably, it takes me a while to get there, which is what happened in this next story.

"BUT I WAS JUST IN ROMANIA"

I made my first trip to Romania with two other Riverside pastors to visit Rich and the Muellers, our missionaries. We wanted to encourage them and meet the people they served and helped. When we visited Rich, we met his friends and the people at Alpha Omega Church in Bucharest.

I found myself making strong, God-given connections with Pastor Nicholas, church leaders, and members who were hungry to be discipled and wanted to learn more about the 12 Steps. Because they did not have a cultural bias toward the Steps (thinking of them as just a tool for addicts), they perceived them as powerful, well-rounded, biblical principles to help believers grow in their relationship with God and with others. In fact, they adopted the Steps as part of a yearlong program they were developing for their church. Potential leaders would be required to go through the program and work the 12 Steps with a sponsor who had worked them. (I ended up taking a number of trips to Romania to help the first leaders learn about and work the Steps.)

I had just made a trip several months previously when, one morning in my quiet time God told me, "Go to Romania."

This made no sense, so I responded, "But God, I was just in Romania."

In the days that followed, God kept repeating, "Go to Romania."

I shared my thoughts with God: "This is not a good idea, and it won't work. I have too much to do with Thanksgiving and Christmas coming. Plus, the church leadership will never approve the trip—I was just there. I'll go after the first of the year." I knew that the church leaders would not grant my request, and I had no interest in trying to convince them or in tangling with them over this issue.

To top it off, I had no idea why I was going and what I was supposed to do when I arrived. Fear has always been like a cancer, eating away at my life, leading me to try and hide behind fortresses that look secure to me. Forgetting the power and good purposes of God, I wanted to play it safe.

But God didn't let up. In fact, He became more insistent and specific in His directions and began saying, "Go back to Romania *now*."

He kept up this conversation over and over. I continued trying to tell Him, "God, I can't go right now; it's bad timing. I promise I'll go after the first of the year." The trip's timing and hurdles seemed impossible to me. Weariness was setting in from this conversation.

God was insistent. Relentless, actually. He ramped up the pressure and began waking me up at night. It sounded like a bad song stuck in my head day and night: "Go back to Romania—now!"

Great! I felt more miserable—I was tired and couldn't sleep!

After a few more days of this, when God woke me up yet again, I cried out in frustrated, sleepless anger, "Okay, God! I'll try."

Going to Pastor Ted, our missions pastor, I shared my story and how insistent God was in telling me to return to Romania. Ted confirmed that this would be a bad time to go. Somewhat relieved, I said, "Okay," and left his office.

Surely God would understand now and be satisfied. I tried, and Ted said no. I really didn't want to make a big deal about something I already knew wasn't going well. I had been sharing a little with the pastors and church staff about my God-Romania plight, but no one seemed supportive of my problem or my trip, or grasped how relentless God's instructions to me were that I needed to return. At least one pastor and a few elders doubted and questioned my God conversations. These elders dismissed the idea of God speaking directly to someone, saying they only heard from God while reading His Word or a Christian book. I sensed their response to be, "Why are you, with your background and issues, hearing from God like that? I don't hear God like that."

Can't say I blame them. I'm cautious, too, when people say they've heard from God. Plus, even I am surprised at the times and ways God speaks to me.

Talking with Ted and receiving the negative response didn't convince God of anything. A few more sleepless nights passed. God kept getting more aggressive about my going. Finally, one night when He woke me up, I cried out with frustration, "Okay, I'll go, God! But I don't think the church is going to be very happy about it."

Returning to Pastor Ted's office, I said, "Ted, I've got to get God off my back. I need some sleep, and I've got to go to Romania."

Thankfully, Ted believed me, took up my cause, and helped persuade church leaders to back my trip. Once I gained authorization, I contacted Pastor Nicholas and bought my plane ticket. After this, God was quiet and I slept like a baby.

Unfortunately, God was also quiet about reasons concerning this trip. Why was I going? What was I supposed to do when I got there? His silence whenever I asked, and my uncertainty about what I was to do, had me on edge. These uncertainties felt as unnerving as the leaders' opposition I faced about going. Everything added fuel to my anxious agitation.

Still, I got ready. Pastor Nicholas always wanted me to preach when I visited Romania, so I prepared my sermon. I have never felt gifted as a preacher, so I require time to carefully prepare my sermon and my notes. Then, I always have my notes with me when I preach.

THAT VOICE AGAIN

Finally, the time came and I flew to Romania. On Sunday morning, I was in church with everyone, sitting on the front row, with my Bible and my sermon notes. Because I still had no clue why I was there and what I was supposed to do, I also had, I'm sad to admit, my bad attitude. Then I heard the voice again.

God said, "Don't give the sermon you prepared."

What?!

Panic hit.

"What do You want me to preach on, God?"

There was no answer.

During the singing and praise time, I was pleading with God, but there was no response. There was only silence, along with a strong sense that I was not to deliver the sermon I had prepared. I tried to pray, as my mind raced and struggled to come up with something to preach on. Just then, I heard my name being called from the podium—first, by the Romanian pastor, and then by the interpreter.

Sweating and with my heart pounding, I rose to my feet and, with still no answer from God, I nervously left my sermon notes on the chair.

When I reached the front of the auditorium and the microphone, I could see all the people and my sermon notes on the chair. I'm begging and screaming silently to God, "Please help me—I don't know what to say!"

I stood there for what seemed like several minutes; finally, in total desperation, not knowing what else to do, I began to share my testimony. I shared about being beaten and verbally abused, and being sexually molested by my uncle as a little boy. All of these events brought painful feelings that grew within me. I felt abandoned, unprotected, unclean, dirty, and marred for life. I talked about my great hunger to feel connected to others and be loved; how I used alcohol in an effort to numb my pain and fill the void inside; and how I became addicted to pornography and battled feelings of shame. I shared how God had pursued me for years, and, when I finally surrendered and called on Him, Jesus saved me and began setting me free from my shame, sin, and addictions. He healed my brokenness and despair and helped me bring everything into the light, including my sexual addiction, especially with the help of my 12 Step groups. He then led me to start my area's first support group for sexual addiction. The more I was honest with others and the more I shared my hurts, pain, and problems—instead of keeping them secret—the more my feelings of unworthiness and loneliness were replaced with value and connection with Jesus and others. The Lord was healing me from every hurt and sin.

When I finished sharing my life and testimony, no one moved. Silence filled the room.

I left the podium and sat down. Emotionally drained, I wanted to crawl in a hole and be left alone. Then waves of shame, fear, and self-condemnation hit me and I began berating myself, asking, *Why did I tell all these people everything?* Lost in my thoughts, I had no idea that the pastor, speaking in Romanian, was sharing, "If anyone wants to talk to Pastor Dale, come to the front row."

I was startled as young Romanians, both men and women, came forward and began standing in front of me. They kept coming. Men and boys were weeping. An entire line of about fifty people, with heads down, stood hurting before me.

I watched this event unfold in amazement; it seemed like a dream. More feelings rolled over me in quick succession: relief for an instant, followed by a jolt of anxiety and the thoughts—*What do I do now? How can I possibly help all these people?* Plus, I knew that the church rented its building and needed to clear the premises in the next hour. I could not counsel fifty people about these deep issues in that short amount of time. Seemingly from out of nowhere, Maria, the pastor's wife, appeared with a pad of paper and quickly started taking names and assigning people appointment times to meet with me, beginning with later that afternoon.

With this, I breathed a sigh of relief and a calm came over me, followed by the thought, *I can simply tell these people what Jesus has done for me.* These thoughts and feelings were topped off with phrases from "Amazing Grace" playing in my head: *I once was blind . . . but now I see . . . and grace will lead me now.*

As the service ended, numerous individuals began thanking me for sharing my story. After everyone left, Nicholas, Maria, and I drove back to their house and were surprised to find some church members had already arrived, along with the interpreters. The small house quickly filled up. Despite so many people wanting to talk with me, Nicholas and Maria insisted that I eat lunch first, while they hurriedly converted a bedroom into a counseling office.

Before I began counseling, though, I needed do something. I went to my bedroom to be alone with God and pray regarding two aspects. First, I needed to ask the Lord for His forgiveness.

"Oh, God, I'm so sorry," I said, trying to blink back tears. "I'm so sorry I gave you such a hard time about coming. I'm so sorry I didn't understand." A wave of regret for my lack of wisdom, my arguments, resistance, and bad attitude about coming swept over me; I dissolved into tears and sobs. I prayed this many times after appointments when I heard people share their hurt and pain—many for the first time—and then witnessed God begin to heal them. His wisdom, grace, and timing are perfect, even when—from my puny perspective—His actions don't make sense. His ways are higher than mine (Isaiah 55:8–9).

The other aspect that I needed help with, before I counseled, was the attack of shame that came over me from sharing my whole story with a group of people. I couldn't shake the shame I felt. While still fairly new to transforming prayer, I asked Jesus what He wanted me to know regarding this shame. Suddenly, I flashed back to the room in which I had been sexually abused. Jesus sat next to me. He put His arm around me and talked to me. I felt a warm glow surround me as He spoke gently, "Dale, you don't understand how special you are to me. I have so many good thoughts about you. I made you for special purposes and have more good thoughts about you than there are stars in the heavens and grains of sand. You can't fathom the good purposes I have for you and my love for you."[47]

Though I had resisted God, as I repented, He forgave me. I felt His presence, forgiveness, comfort, peace, and strength. Now I was ready to share these gifts of grace with those who were waiting and wanted help.

MY WORK BEGINS

From that afternoon until eleven o'clock that night, I met with, counseled, ministered to, and prayed with hurting Romanians who wanted to be clean, set free, and healed. Every day that first week, I ministered from morning until night. It was exhausting and amazing. I continued to be humbled, sad, and remorseful for my resistance toward God's instruction that I go to Romania.

Some of the people shared events that had happened fairly recently, which helped me realize why God wanted me in Romania sooner rather than later. My perspective changed yet again! God didn't care about my busy calendar or the church's holiday schedule; He wanted people set free. His perspective and intentions are larger, more profound, and filled with greater love than mine are.

The needs were so great and pressing, and the painful problems were so moving, that I remained in Romania for a month while I used all the tools and truth that God had given me through the years. I called home and had more 12 Step materials shipped over. We started support groups for the abused and the country's first sexual-addiction group. As people began getting honest with themselves, one another, and God, they found grace, forgiveness, love, help, and healing.

In addition, I shared Transformation Prayer with them. As individuals shared their painful circumstances and feelings, I inquired if they wanted to know what Jesus desired to tell them, and then invited Him to

---

[47] The words Jesus spoke to me are addressed to each of us in Psalm 139:17–18. Numerous verses in Scripture (including Psalm 40:5 and Jeremiah 29:11) tell us that God's thoughts and plans for us are abundant, loving, and good.

speak. Jesus answered these prayers in amazing ways, breaking emotional chains and bringing peace and joy.

FREEDOM FROM CHAINS

Before I share some of these healing stories, some background information on Romania and the country's orphanages is helpful. Both have painful histories. Romania was a Communist nation from the early 1960s until 1989. The government had demanded that families have babies; however, when an economic crisis hit, the families couldn't care for the children. As a result, hundreds of thousands of children were housed in the communistic government-run orphanages, which became institutions of neglect and abuse. The orphanages lacked the basic necessities of electricity, heat, and food, and most also lacked love and kindness. Boys and girls were routinely victims of physical and sexual abuse. Violence was promoted to keep order and silence. One survivor described the orphanages as "slaughterhouses of souls."[48]

When Romania's borders were opened in 1989, Western media descended on the country. Documentaries were made, including ones that revealed the horrid conditions of the orphanages. Research followed, which detailed the effects on children who have been deprived of basic care, interaction, and love. They suffer mentally, developmentally, and emotionally. The ability for traumatized and love-starved children to attach to others is severely hindered, even when their circumstances change.

To top it off, when these children reached eighteen, the government simply released them. Now they struggled to fend for themselves, make a life, and connect with others. The struggle for survival was so great that many turned to begging, stealing, or prostituting themselves.

I met with Constantine, a young Christian man who was raised in one of these orphanages, had been chained to a bed, and been sexually abused. He was chained for so long that, as he grew, his leg became

---

[48] This quote from Daniel Rucareanu, an orphanage survivor, is taken from: https://www.pri.org/stories/2015-12-28/half-million-kids-survived-romanias-slaughterhouses-souls-now-they-want-justice. Estimates place the total number of orphans to be in the range of five hundred thousand. Some orphanages currently remain.

deformed, leaving him with a bad limp. When Constantine shared for the first time about the abuse and pain he endured, he sobbed like a child. It was gut-wrenching, even as I knew that healing for his grief, shame, and pain could begin. He was no longer holding on to these painful secrets that had kept him bound for years. The process of healing is amazing. As I've shared, instead of feeling that we will die if someone knows about our hurt and shame, as we get honest and bring everything into God's light, we find life.[49]

Constantine and I spent time in Transformation Prayer, and he experienced more healing. As we started support groups, Constantine and the other men could share openly and find help, grace, and healing from God and one another. They experienced the body of Christ as God intended for us to function—in close relationships with one another. These men and the church went on to pay for operations for Constantine's leg. The more healing, change, and freedom Jesus bestowed on Constantine, the stronger and more committed a follower he became. His testimony, joy, and deep love for Christ made him a powerful and strong witness for the Lord.

PAINFUL CONFESSIONS

Several days into these counseling sessions, a man admitted to me that he had sexually abused two brothers. He shared that he was close with the boys and their family; they considered him like an uncle. I told him that, although he shared these events with me in strict confidence, as a professional counselor I had taken an oath of ethics. My pledge bound me to report this to the proper authorities. Additionally, I told him that he must confess to the boys' mother and father. Under the conviction of the Holy Spirit, he did. I never heard such wailing from a human being as I heard from the boys' mother when she heard the news.

My heart broke for this family, especially as I knew their pain and grief was just beginning and would take time to process. When we are knocked to our knees with pain and grief, all we can do initially is hold on and cope as best we can. We will encounter waves of grief, shock, denial,

---

[49] For more on God's light bringing life and overcoming darkness, see Appendix F's endnote.

and anger. While it sometimes feels like more than we can bear, we try to roll with each as it comes. All I could do at that point was offer comfort, pray with them, and care for them as best I could.

Such circumstances are complicated to handle. When it comes to churches dealing with offenders, much depends on the situation, the victim, and the perpetrator's brokenness and willingness to face his issues and get help. Because church leaders want to protect the church, they often struggle in aiding the victims and their families. Families and relationships become strained and divided. In fact, some church leaders called me an "American troublemaker." Still, with God's help, I did all I could to assist them in considering the legal and spiritual aspects and seek God's truth, grace, and wisdom in these painful events.

TWO SISTERS: TWO MIRACLES

Additionally, two sisters in their late teens came to me for help. As with most of the people with whom I worked, it was with the assistance of interpreters. I worked with the girls separately, although they shared the same painful story. The girls' father was an abusive alcoholic. When they were about seven and eight, he drank himself into a drunken rage and locked them in their bedroom that had a window. He attacked their mother and, in horror and helplessness, they saw their father throw their mother off the seventh-floor balcony to her death.

Both girls suffered panic attacks for years. One sister, to stop her emotional pain, bit herself until she bled, and had numerous scars. The girls thought that they were responsible for their mother's death and that somehow they should have gotten out of the locked room and saved her. Numerous family members told them it was not their fault, that they could not have done anything. However, it didn't change the way they felt or the lie they believed.

I asked the girls in separate prayer sessions if they desired to know what Jesus wanted to tell them about their mother's death, and their pain, feelings, and beliefs. They said yes. Jesus told them that it was not their fault and that He saved their lives by locking them in that bedroom. The girls and their countenance changed in an instant! The lie was gone, replaced with comfort, peace, and freedom. Their pain was gone, as well as their panic attacks, self-mutilation, and depression. Every time I return to Romania, I ask how they're doing and check on them, including the sister's scars. They continue to be filled with peace and joy.

TEARS, PINK TOILET PAPER & GRACE

There were times I felt inadequate counseling in these serious and painful situations with these hurting people in another country with a different culture and language. Added to this, counseling isn't as common in Romania as it is in the United States.

Romanians, from years of hardscrabble existence, are stoic people; still, we cried together. We cried so much that we ran out of Kleenex tissues. Maria gave us rolls of toilet paper so we could blow our noses. It's not like the toilet paper I'm used to; it's rather rough and colored an odd grayish-shade of pink. Nevertheless, this old pastor blew his nose with pink-colored toilet paper, right along with them. I heard more than one person share in surprise, "This pastor cries with us!"

I'm amazed, blessed, and humbled at the loving work of grace and healing that God was doing in Romania and that He included me. Despite my stumbling ways, He forgives me, loves me, encourages me, and enables me to help others.

It also amazes me how God's good grace can truly change everything. God's grace changes us from the inside. Then, He wants to use us and our lives, along with His grace, to change others and give them hope and new life. He tops off the whole thing by blessing our feeble efforts, sometimes turning them into miracles.

When the time came to say good-bye, my friends and I traded more tears and hugs before I headed home.

Section Seven

RELENTLESS GRACE & MORE MIRACLES

Chapter 22

PEOPLE, BUMPS & BRUISES

Just because I traveled all the way to Romania, worked diligently, and even experienced deeply moving, miraculous events didn't mean that when I returned I would receive a hero's welcome, or that life would be easy, or even that I would have a bulletproof vest protecting me from difficulties. I could have used one. It felt as if I walked into a minefield.

As might be expected from the church leadership's resistance toward my trip to Romania, they were not happy that I stayed for a month, especially because it was fall and the staff was preparing for holiday events and services. I almost got fired, and would have been, without God's grace protecting me and keeping me where He wanted me. To be fair, though, some of the difficulties were probably due to things that I could have handled better. In fact, at least three aspects helped make it a perfect storm.

One was that I didn't ask for permission from the leadership to stay for a month. Actually, I was scared to ask because they might say no. Yet I knew I had to stay and do what God told me to do. Second, because I was overwhelmed with the magnitude of the problems in Romania and the counseling God set before me, there wasn't much time or energy to think about my work back home. Finally, I felt that I had a good assistant and good people helping me run the Discovery ministry, so I thought everything was fine.

Everything wasn't fine.

My assistant-intern sabotaged me. I kept him posted and shared the incredible events and miracles happening in Romania. Not only did he not share the good news with anyone, but he told everyone that he hadn't heard from me and didn't know what was going on. Consequently, the rumor mill went wild. All kinds of fantastic tales spread about me, with people questioning the reason I was over there for so long and what I could possibly be doing. This assistant was after my job, believing he could do it better. When we unraveled his scheme and the truth, yes, he was fired.

It saddens me to know that people in the church didn't know what God was doing in Romania, particularly because it was from their support! It was as if this misguided intern stole from them; they missed the opportunity to rejoice and pray. I wish, too, that I had called Pastor Tony and kept him posted about what God was doing in another country through Riverside's ministry.

It took time for ruffled feathers surrounding me and my ministry to get smoothed out again.

ONE OF THOSE PEOPLE

It's true that I have been more than blessed in my job as pastor and counselor, and yet there have been difficulties. I'll share a few stories, along with some helpful thoughts about bumps and bruises.

Pastors can be a magnet for all kinds of opinions, complaints, and odd comments about our jobs. I love the one that goes something like, "Your job sure is easy; you hardly have to work at all for your paycheck." I've also heard more than one person ask me or my fellow pastors, "What do you do all day?" People see a pastor standing in the pulpit once or twice a week (sometimes three), and forget about all the needed time for sermon preparation, Bible study, and prayer, as well as the time and care required for hospital visits, funerals, weddings, rehearsals, counseling, emergencies, and fielding all manner of interruptions and requests. A number of "crises" pastors deal with are serious, while a few come from folks who think their problems should take immediate priority over everything else because we're not doing much anyway.

As I've said before, working in recovery ministry added another layer to pastoring, even prompting Pastor Tony to sometimes exclaim, "Dale, it's like you're walking around with a target on your back." It certainly seemed true. There have been members, deacons, elders, and some pastors who have tried to take issue with me about my personal recovery, AA, and the 12 Steps.

Sometimes I found myself in the crosshairs of good, proper church folk who were uncomfortable being around recovery people or "those people," as they frequently called them. They didn't understand the time-consuming love, help, patience, and attention that addicts require. Other individuals were simply fearful of being considered "one of those people" if they attended too many classes or helped too much with the ministry.

Maybe there is another way to think about being "one of those people." We should consider ourselves blessed to recognize our needs and then to experience Jesus knowing us, loving us, and caring for us. Jesus spent time with, ate dinner with, healed, and cared for people in need. He sacrificed His life and paid the debt for our sins and shortcomings, so that each of us—whatever our sins, issues, and faults—can be reconciled to God and fellowship with Him. ("Perfect people with all the answers" were the ones the Lord rebuked.) May we be known as one of those people upon whom God is pouring His grace and help. May we be open to recognizing ways that we fall short of God's will for us, then spend time with Jesus, and be transformed by His grace.

WRESTLING WITH TRUTH

Reflecting on the difficulties of helping people in pain reminds me of a time I expected praise, but instead was reprimanded. I share it to maybe give you a laugh and impart some helpful thoughts for struggles we all face.

Our Discovery program seemed to be exploding with growth. All the groups that met during the week were averaging total weekly attendance of four hundred, as were our annual banquets that we held to celebrate what God was doing in our ministry. As part of our banquets, we asked a few people to share their testimony about finding freedom from addictions or hurts. To make the banquets a night of outreach and fun, we began bringing in well-known Christian comedians. At our last banquet, we focused on our Transformation Prayer Ministry.

During this time, Riverside had an interim pastor. Shortly after the banquet, he called me into his office, which wasn't an everyday occurrence now that our church had a few thousand members. I was thrilled, expecting an "attaboy" and words of encouragement for our amazing milestones and achievements. I even imagined the great conversation we would have.

Instead, almost as soon as I sat down, he reamed me out—and it was a good one. While generally supportive of Discovery, he had recently watched a Transformation Prayer session in which the person, overcome with pain, abruptly left the session in that state of mind. The pastor was not happy, and gave me some new "do's and don'ts" that he wanted put in place.

The pastor and I, though, are still friends today, and I understand his viewpoint. It is difficult to see and listen to people in pain. We want to help and fix others. It's difficult to let others wrestle with truth, but there are times when it is a necessary part of the journey toward helping them make new choices and find freedom and healing.

I believe in Christian counseling and Transformation Prayer, but I know from experience they don't always bring instant, warm-fuzzy miracles. They don't always go the way we hope because it's difficult to let people struggle with pain and truth. As difficult as it is to watch, there are times this hard part of the process is needed. Sometimes, the cliché is true: "No pain, no gain."

There have been many times when I have sadly watched individuals leave my office and have prayed for them, knowing that—except for God's miracle of grace—I would probably never see them again. People can have negative reactions to counseling and truth, no matter how nicely the truth is delivered or offered to them. Counseling and prayer sessions stir up feelings of hurt, anguish, and anger, which individuals need time to process, along with their thoughts and choices in light of the truth. Giving others a chance to face truth may be the most time-consuming and difficult aspect of counseling.

Even Jesus let people wrestle with truth. Reading the stories of His interactions with others can be perplexing because He didn't go around patting people gently just to make them feel better. He didn't run after them if they walked away or were antagonistic to His message. He gave them truth and grace and let them choose what they wanted, which also came with receiving the results and outcome of their choices.[50]

The person I mentioned previously, who had an initial painful response in the prayer session, did return for more prayer, and received healing and blessings!

LESSONS, PAIN & PEOPLE

If we're in a ministry that involves counseling, we need to carefully review what is being done and how it is working, sometimes adjusting our methods. Dr. Ed and I did review what happened, made changes as necessary, and grew from the events.

Because we don't all have the same gifts, not everyone is cut out for recovery work. However, we can seek to have a compassionate response toward those who suffer, as well as those who are in the trenches giving aid. As best we can, let's give one another grace and not beat up other Christian workers on the battlefield. Let's support our pastors and those who are on the frontlines of the battle.

Life and ministry are tough, giving us all bumps and bruises. We need God's help with our actions and reactions. We need God's forgiveness and God's help to forgive others. In fact, I would need a heaping helping of God's grace if I was ever to forgive, let go of my resentments, and love those closest to me—those who had hurt me so many years ago.

---

[50] These stories can be found in Matthew 10:14, 22–23; Luke 14:15–24; and John chapters 6–10, as well as throughout Matthew, Mark, Luke, John, and Acts.

Chapter 23

A LOVE THAT TRANSFORMS

God has much to tell us in Scripture about holding people accountable for wrongdoing. He also tells us we are to forgive others, so we certainly need His help and wisdom regarding these differing aspects. When it comes to letting go of our anger and forgiving someone who has abused us, the topic becomes even more difficult to consider.

Thankfully, we find great help from God in Ecclesiastes 3, which tells us poetically that there is a right time and season for everything.

A TIME FOR EVERYTHING

> For everything *that happens in life*—there is a season, a right time for everything under heaven:
> A time to be born, a time to die;
>   a time to plant, a time to collect the harvest;
> A time to kill, a time to heal;
>   a time to tear down, a time to build up;
> A time to cry, a time to laugh;
>   a time to mourn, a time to dance;
> A time to scatter stones, a time to pile them up;
>   a time for a *warm* embrace, a time for keeping your distance;
> A time to search, a time to give up as lost;
>   a time to keep, a time to throw out;

> A time to tear apart, a time to bind together;
>> a time to be quiet, a time to speak up;
> A time to love, a time to hate;
>> a time to go to war, a time to make peace.
> (Ecclesiastes 3:1–8 VOICE)

In addition, Scripture teaches a great deal about anger, including how to handle it in a righteous manner and correct ways to confront those who offend us. Our anger is important because it enables us to know something is wrong and it can drive us to speak up, set boundaries, protect ourselves, and seek help. It can even propel us to learn new ways of relating, so that we aren't allowing ourselves to continue being hurt. For example, if a loved one struggles with an addiction, we can seek wisdom from others, including support groups (like Al-Anon). We may even save ourselves some difficult times and from learning everything the hard way.[51]

However, there is a time to seek reconciliation and forgive. Staying with the heart of God's directives in Scripture and the Ecclesiastes 3 passage, when we have been hurt by others, we can say and ponder the following:

A TIME TO CONFRONT & A TIME TO FORGIVE

> There is a time to consider how God would have us handle offenses.
> There is a time to be angry, to speak up, to confront, and to set boundaries.
> There is a time to give another chance.
> There is a time to forgive, embrace, love, and seek peace.
> There is a time to rebuild and restore.
> There is a time to stand strong in our convictions and choose.
> There is a time to overlook an offense and be silent.
> There is a time to let go.
> There is a time to heal.
> Every day, in everything, it is always the right time—
>> to seek God and ask for His help, grace, wisdom, and strength.

---

51 Support groups for family members affected by alcohol include Al-Anon; Co-Dependents Anonymous (CoDA.org); and Adult Children of Alcoholics (AdultChildren.org).

JOYS & DIFFICULTIES OF MOUNTAIN CLIMBING

If we experienced any type of abuse as a child, we coped and adapted as best we could. However, children are damaged tremendously by abuse from those who should have protected them and instead inflicted or allowed such abuse. They are also damaged greatly by anger and rage displayed toward them. I know firsthand that it is weird to experience someone being violent and then acting as if nothing ever happened. It's hard to be hugged by a hitter. Add to this, when discipline is administered only punitively (simply for the purpose of anger), the one punished grows in resentment and anger toward the person in authority.

We coped as best we could, but a time may come as adults that we need to seek help and counseling. Whether we shut down internally or became outwardly angry, it helped us endure and put up boundaries. Sometimes, though, we continue relying on our coping mechanism when it no longer benefits us. While we don't want to feel that someone is getting away with an offense, and we want to protect ourselves from feeling more pain, a time comes when our anger may be working against our own physical, emotional, relational, and spiritual well-being.

Scripture proclaims several truths that direct and assist us in letting go of our animosity. A vital one is that Jesus and His sacrifice have enabled us to be forgiven and receive great mercy and grace, so we're called and commanded to forgive others.[52] Besides releasing people from their trespasses against us, we are to be kind to our enemies and those who mistreat us. We are told in Luke 6:27–28: "Love your enemies, do good to those who hate you, bless those who curse you, pray for those who mistreat you." Even if we don't feel loving, we are to act with kindness as we strive to have the right spirit.

Additonally it's important to know and remember that a day will come when God will judge and repay each and every person rightly; therefore, we must leave judgment of others to Him. We are called to give God the situation and our anger, trusting Him to bring justice and resolution.

Finally, Scripture goes on to reveal that anger, terse words, impatience, grudges, complaining, and bitterness are sin and hinder us from

---

[52] Scriptures about forgiving others include Matthew 5:21–24, 6:14–15; and Romans 12:17–21.

receiving forgiveness ourselves. Our anger and pride cause us to miss out on God's blessings, including knowing Him and His will and receiving answers to our prayers. Our broken attitude also blocks our ability to see and enjoy God's gifts, which means we miss out on thankfulness and joy.

While this topic of forgiveness can be easy to embrace and discuss in general terms, actually forgiving someone, acknowledging our pain, and trusting it to God can be a tough, grueling ordeal. It can feel like a personal Mount Everest. However, if we are willing and walk toward the summit, we can experience peace and freedom. No matter how old we are, and no matter how long we have carried our pain, we can forgive, grow, and heal.

BRICKS OF ANGER

I was well past childhood, and God had been patiently, persistently nudging me to dismantle my defensive brick wall and put down my bricks of anger. I remember when my friend and cosponsor Ron[53] and I were both so thrilled and proud simply because we hadn't hit anybody in a long time. Our happiness was short-lived when God opened our eyes to the fact that, while we had managed to overcome an outward manifestation of our anger, our inner attitudes had a ways to go. God has continued using those around me to help me deal with my troublesome temperament.

Ever since she was young, Brianna has been able to name my defects with simplicity, saying such things as, "You need to work on your anger

---

[53] Ron, whom I mentioned in chapter 15, was another great man in my life. I don't know why God chose to place so many spiritual leaders in my life, but He did, and all I can do is acknowledge them, their stories, and their influence for Jesus. Ron had a worse upbringing than mine and had family ties to the Mafia. When he landed in Fort Myers, he was what is known as a three-percenter—one of the three percent of alcoholics on skid row—destitute and homeless. Because of where he lived in downtown Fort Myers, he was part of what was called the "under-the-bridge gang." But with Christ's saving power and the biblical principles of the 12 Steps, he became a walking miracle. Eventually, he left Fort Myers and became the director of the Barnabas House in Wildwood, New Jersey (affiliated with the Atlantic City Rescue Mission). The men who came for help called him Chaplain Ron and looked up to him as a tough, firm, gentle father figure. Living and sharing God's grace and healing power, Ron helped so many down-and-out alcoholic men change their lives that he became a legend nationally in his recovery work at the Barnabas House.

because what you said wasn't very nice." Brianna's ability to speak up with childlike directness and boldness hasn't been enjoyable, but it has been helpful.

Bob, of course, helped. On one occasion, after observing me in a foul mood at my house, he asked, "Why are you still yelling with your family?" Without thinking, honest answers spilled out, "Because I can get away with it and I get what I want!" Well, there were a whole lot of hidden issues for me to work on! During this season, God worked with me on how I used anger to protect myself, to try to control others, and when I'm impatient. The Lord reminded me that He shows me grace and patience, and I need to give these gifts to others, as well.

FORGIVING DAD

A day came when God began guiding me to forgive my parents, beginning with my dad. The journey started when Bob admonished me, "I never hear you say anything good about your father. I want you to do a 4th Step on your dad and write down at least ten good things about him."

Until this point, I hadn't considered much about my father's good traits; I simply focused on the things that made me mad. Now I began to think about Dad differently. I made a list of his good gifts, especially the valuable skills he taught me, including carpentry, mechanics, and repairing just about anything. He taught me how to work hard, as well as how to observe and anticipate what's needed next (which has been beneficial for all sorts of tasks). Writing down these qualities and thinking about them began to change my thoughts and attitude.

Thankfully, my anger with Dad didn't run as deep as it did with Mom. While his drinking, rages, and beatings gave me plenty to be mad at him about, his positive traits helped temper my resentment. When he wasn't drinking, he was smart, industrious, conscientious, and generally happy and funny, so that I enjoyed being around him. Because I verbally stood up to him through the years, I didn't hold on to every anger-inducing episode. Plus, when I reached the age of fifteen and broke his nose, my fear of him and the dynamics of our relationship began to change.

Another pivotal point occurred as God enabled me to realize the times that Dad came to my rescue and did what he could to help me, including when he hired an attorney after my robbery arrest and the train-track incident. Though his love was almost overshadowed by his gruff exterior, I began to recognize his protective care for me.

It didn't happen overnight but, as I let myself consider and enjoy good thoughts about him and be thankful for his gifts, I slowly began forgiving Dad and grew in loving him. I was also blessed that before Dad died, he and I talked. I shared how I had been hurt by things he did, such as the time he threw my teddy bear into the fire. He shared that he was only trying to help me and teach me how to be "manly-tough"; he had never meant to hurt me. But he realized he had been wrong—an admission that helped heal some wounds.

FROM "HELL, NO" TO BEING WILLING

Forgiving Mom was more difficult and bumpier. A lot bumpier. On her side, she had lots of personal issues; on my side, I had many personal issues, including hurt, anger, and resentments that kept piling up. Much of my anger and resentment originated from the time I told her about her brother abusing me, and this person—who should have protected and comforted me—instead beat me and called me a liar. I was angrier at Mom than I was at my uncle. (This is often the case with abuse victims. They have more anger and hate toward the person who should have protected them than they do the perpetrator.) From that day on, I was determined to protect myself from Mom.

Besides this incident, Mom was adept at saying things that hurt me. With others, she was a people pleaser, so most people found her easy to get along with and loved her. But I had to limit the amount of time I spent with her. Any conversation could quickly turn into an argument or give me a knot in my stomach. If she thought she was losing an argument, she was quick to fight dirty, saying such things as, "You're just like your Dad, and you call yourself a pastor." There were times I thought I had forgiven Mom. However, it didn't take long being around her for the familiar hurt, pain, anger, and stomachache to return.

A number of years after my 4th Step regarding Dad, Dr. Ed helped direct me onto the road of forgiving Mom. His words had a familiar ring as he remarked, "I never hear you say anything good about your mom. Are you ready to work on this? Why don't you do a 4th Step on her, and write down ten good things about her?"

It took a while, but I worked on a 4th Step and listed her gifts. Mom's top gift? Her good cooking. After we moved to Florida, this gift meant a great deal, especially when Mom invited our family over for lunch every Sunday after church. I included a few more gifts on the list and a few fond memories when we did have a nice time together.

It was the right direction, but my progress stalled. Dr. Ed knew my anger was still brewing and one day confronted me, asking, "Dale, are you ready yet to give up your anger toward your Mom?"

Without thinking, I shot back, "Hell, no!"

"Well," he inquired, "how are your anger and resentments working for you?"

Ed was right. "Okay. Okay. I'll try," I grudgingly replied.

Once again I needed to work Steps 6 and 7. I needed to be willing, humble myself, and ask God for help in transforming my thoughts and character defects. As I prayed and journaled, God began showing me aspects concerning Mom and her life that helped ease my pain and anger. He showed me that Mom didn't have the easiest time as a child. Her mother (Grandma Keen) was hypercritical of everyone and everything, and seemed to be in a bad mood most of the time. She had zero tact. Whatever she thought came out of her mouth. She left a trail of unhappy and upset people wherever she went. As I mentioned earlier, despite being the pastor's wife, her lack of thoughtfulness before she spoke got her ousted from attending services for a time. By contrast, her father (Grandpa Keen) was a saint. God showed me how Mom lived with two opposing forces, which made her fear failure and constantly strive for perfection.

Mom attended church sporadically through the years, but it wasn't until she was older (I was twelve) when she received Jesus as her Savior. I was with Mom at that Rex Humbard service, which was being held in an old movie theater. A huge illuminated cross hung from the ceiling. When the invitation was extended, Mom went forward and stood with others beneath that cross. After that Sunday, Mom began to change, read her Bible, study it, and grow.

Mom and I enjoyed that church for a while, along with its Weatherford Quartet. Then she took me with her to visit a couple of churches before she settled on the Middleburg Heights Church of God. (This was actually our Daisy Avenue Church, now at a new location, with a new name, and a new pastor.) She became active in church, taught Sunday school, and kept growing. Previously she had a mouth like a drunken sailor; now she worked to improve her language and temper. There were other times she tended to be a doormat, especially with Dad, and she worked on this. She tried to deal with conflict in healthy ways, speaking up for herself calmly, although sometimes she went to the extreme. (When any of us works on an aspect in which we need to grow, we may initially swing between opposite sides of the spectrum as we attempt to identify and walk the new, narrow, better way.)

Reflecting on all she had been through and how she had changed, I found my heart softening toward her, but I wasn't free yet. In Dr. Ed's words, I was only miserably victorious.

MOM & A LADLE

When Dad passed away and we moved to Florida, Mom lived with us two different times a number of years apart. The first time, we added an apartment onto our house for her. I looked forward to having Mom live next door and harbored hopes of improving our relationship but, after a couple of months, I remembered a few more reasons why I left home at fifteen.

As I said, Dad did some things for me through the years that made me feel his love and protection. With Mom, I just felt betrayed and abandoned—feelings I couldn't shake on my own. While doing all I could to live at peace with her and forgive her, limits existed to what I could do in my flesh. Using my own strength, all I had was a knot in my stomach. Incapable of loving Mom by myself, I needed a miracle from God to love her. I kept praying as God continued to work.

Mom lived in the apartment for a couple of years when my cousin, whom I'll call April, moved in with her. It wasn't too long before April's boyfriend moved in as well. One day, our son Vali asked, "Why do you let April and her boyfriend live together when they aren't married? You would never let us get away with that. You would have told us that God says we are to be married, and we're not to have a sexual relationship outside of marriage."

Looking back, I should have handled the situation differently. Praying about it and sleeping on it overnight would have been helpful. But no, I had to march over there in my own wisdom, right then, and straighten things out with Mom. We stood in her small kitchen and, without much of a gentle conversation starter, I spouted, "April and her boyfriend can't live together without being married. April's boyfriend has to move out. He can live with us if he wants."

Mom blew her stack and snapped, "This is my house! You can't tell me what to do!" Grabbing a nearby ladle, she started hitting me. My glasses flew in one direction, and parts of my teeth landed in another. Quickly, I pushed her away and got out of there.

I couldn't believe what just happened! Mad, shocked, and with adrenaline pumping overtime, I ran back to my side of the house and spilled the story to Karen. A few minutes later, we heard a knock on our door. I opened it. There stood two deputies.

Mom called the cops on me!

As the deputies talked with each person, taking down their statements, my heart pounded as I flashed back to two deputies long ago. At this point, I looked guilty. Mom had a bruise on her face in the shape of my hand where I pushed her away. The deputies opened an investigation on me for possible violation of Florida's elder-abuse laws.

I did not hit Mom, although Karen and Vali both asked me if I had, which is a fair question, considering everything. Mom had bruised easily for years—something that was becoming worse with age.

First thing the next morning, I called to make an appointment for Transformation Prayer, and felt as if I practically ran into the first session. In addition, I shared with Pastor Tony the events and investigation on me. Thank goodness I shared because April and her boyfriend made an appointment with Pastor Tony to tell him what "Pastor Dale" had done. In the meantime, Mom was busy calling what seemed like every relative she could find to let them know what her son, the pastor, had done.

Mom and April, who were both mad at me, decided to buy a house. Soon they moved out and were gone from next door.

DESTINATION: TRANSFORMATION

While I was happy going to that particular TPM appointment and experienced some truth and comfort from Jesus, it was still a very difficult and emotional session. I really wasn't interested in making more appointments.

Thankfully, Dr. Ed became the pushy person (and lifesaver) in my life. He pursued me and encouraged me to keep seeking more healing for my battered emotions. He had sneaky ways. Unbeknownst to me, he would convince my secretary to clear my schedule; then, he would show up and tell me that he and I both had time for a session. He prodded and pushed me into a number of sessions, knowing the process wasn't easy. But, the sessions, time, effort, and tears were worth it.

Many of these prayers focused on when I told Mom that Uncle Al had molested me, and she beat me and called me a liar. What started as hurt and painful thoughts became deeply embedded lies that I believed. As Dr. Ed and I prayed and sought God, and as I journaled, God showed me many lies I believed about these events, beginning with feeling unprotected, unloved, unworthy, and alone. In fact, there were more than fifty lies on various themes that I believed! (Some lies pertaining to shame, guilt, and feeling dirty were healed in previous prayer times, which I shared in chapter 20: "Jesus, Prayer Miracles & Peace.")

God began showing me truth about Mom, including how she had been a damaged, hurt little girl because her mother had been such a hard person. God told me that in Mom's fragileness, she couldn't handle the pain and truth that her favorite brother had abused her child. The Lord helped me remember how much I had loved my brother, and Mom felt this way about her brother. As He gave me eyes to see Mom as a hurt child, my heart softened more toward her.

In one session, as Dr. Ed probed with questions to help me search my heart, I went back to the memory and the feelings. After he asked a number of times and in different ways, "How does the hurt feel?" I choked out in tears, "It hurts so bad, I hate her." My animosity surprised me, but that was the feeling I had as a hurting five-year-old, and I had never forgiven her. As I grew, I had minimized it down to "anger," tried to cover it over, and tried to make my moods palatable by using substances like alcohol; but God wanted me to root out my bitterness.

I would never have been able to have compassion for Mom if I hadn't discovered and identified the hate, become honest and confessed it, and asked God for His help. As we continued in the session and sought the Lord's help in prayer, He validated my feelings and told me that how Mom handled the situation was wrong and she should have done things differently. This was wonderful salve to my heart.

The Lord went further and shared that I was not to judge her, reminding me that I can't judge others because I don't know their experiences or their hearts. He told me, "Yes, she has faults, but you do too, and I love you and forgive you on a regular basis." God helped me feel His undeserved, yet overflowing love for me as He reminded me: His law declares that my sin deserves wrath, judgment, and separation from Him, but with love He has provided forgiveness and reconciliation for me in Jesus.

In this and other sessions, God spoke to me about love and forgiveness and brought several Scriptures to life. Just as He has loved me and been kind and merciful to me, I am to love even those difficult to love and show them kindness. I could choose to care for Mom, even if it seemed hard to do.[54] Otherwise, without goodwill in thoughts and deeds, all the words I speak to others about the Lord are simply worthless, annoying noises (1 Corinthians 13).

As I spent time with Jesus, with the assistance of a Transformation Prayer partner, my hurt and anger were replaced with love and compassion.

---

54 These truths on forgiveness can be found in Matthew 5:43–48; Luke 6:27–28; John 13:34; and Colossians 3:12–15.

CRAZY EVENTS

During this time, the authorities completed their investigation and, thankfully, dropped the charges on me. Mom had given three different accounts of what happened, which didn't help her case. I ended up feeling the investigation was a good thing and gave me a bit of validation.

As time passed, Mom was diagnosed with dementia and later with Alzheimer's. As her dementia progressed, April moved Mom into a nursing home and left.[55]

One day Mom called. After telling me where she was, she asked, ordered, and begged me to come get her. I shared with her that I couldn't come right away because I was headed to Romania, but I would get her when I returned. I told her that she could live with us in our extra bedroom because Adi and Diana, our newlyweds, were renting the apartment.

When I returned home, Nathan and I went to pick up Mom from the nursing home, which we discovered to be less than stellar. We almost fell over from the sickening smells. Mom was in a double room with a lady who hollered and moaned nonstop. The woman also suffered from incontinence, made worse by the staff failing to keep her clean. Mom was miserable and so were we, and we had just walked in.

Nathan pulled his truck up close to the building, and we loaded Mom's things, including her favorite chair. Then, we returned to get Mom. As we were wheeling her down the hall, a nurse stopped us and gruffly asked, "What are you doing?"

"We're taking Mom home," I replied.

"You can't take her out of here. You need a doctor's permission," the nurse snipped.

"Mom," I inquired, "do you want to leave this place?"

Mom mustered a hearty, "Yeah!"

"You aren't going to make her stay against her will, are you?" I asked the nurse, adding, "You need to step aside." Wheeling Mom around her, Nathan and I—rather gleefully—walked out with Mom, loaded her up in the truck, and drove away.

---

[55] As of the writing of this book, Karen and I are blessed to have restored our relationship with April.

GOD'S MIRACLE FOR ME!

This time, Mom lived with us about four years and God continued to heal me and soften my heart—so much so that Karen and I were both surprised at the change. We saw it in living color.

One day I took Mom to a dentist appointment, then we had lunch. After lunch I took her to a doctor's appointment, a couple of errands, and finally we went home. That night for dinner, I made Mom her favorite dish—potato pancakes. Usually, after we ate together, Mom would retire to her bedroom to watch her favorite TV show, *Lawrence Welk* and his famed Big Band. This night I suggested, "Hey, Mom, why don't you stay out here with us and we'll watch *Lawrence Welk* with you."

Karen caught me later in the kitchen and inquired, "Are you okay? What's going on with you?"

Wow! Until Karen asked that question, I hadn't realized the full implications of that day. Mom and I spent an entire day together—effortlessly and enjoyably! I didn't feel stressed out or have a knot in my stomach. As I was willing and sought God's help, He amazingly transformed my mind and heart. He replaced my anger, hurt, and pain with His truth and compassion. These are changes I could never have accomplished on my own![56]

Eventually, we needed to move Mom to an assisted-living facility and then to a memory-care ward for Alzheimer's patients. During this time, when Mom knew who I was, she was tender with me, and would take my hand and kiss it.

At the very end, just a few days before she passed away at the age of ninety-five, we needed to move Mom to a hospice home. As I helped Mom into her wheelchair, she took my hand, but this time she bit it hard and drew blood. It hurt, yet I found myself chuckling, thinking, well, this

---

[56] I am so thankful for Dr. Ed and his Transformation Prayer Ministry for several reasons in addition to my healing. TPM has provided me with numerous opportunities to pray with believers and participate in God's wonderful promise: when two or more believers pray together, seek Him, and intercede for one another, His loving, powerful, and healing presence is with them (Matthew 18:19-20). Additionally, TPM has helped me experience God in greater measures by reminding me to *anticipate* experiencing Him—*to be still* and *wait* for Him to share His truth and comfort.

adds to my story with Mom. Suddenly, I realized once again that I had no anger, but only love and compassion for her. What a miracle!

God wasn't just changing me, though. He had miracles in store for people I loved and for whom I had been praying.

Section Eight

ALWAYS MORE OF GOD

Chapter 24

GOOD TO GO!

In my chapter "Transitions & Family Memories," I shared about transitioning from teaching and joining my father-in-law, Eugene Michael Hardy, in business. If there's one word I would pick to describe Karen's father, it would be *chutzpah*, which is a Yiddish word that means bold and self-confident, spiced with brazen nerve.

Mike was six feet tall, strong, and ramrod tough. He came by his grit honestly, having grown up during the Great Depression on a small farm about thirty miles south of Cleveland. The son of a steel-mill worker, Mike worked as a plowboy during high school. However, he yearned to experience more adventure than, as he liked to say, "using the ass-end of a horse for a compass." Mike left school after the eleventh grade and bugged his mother to sign his underage papers allowing him to enlist in the US Navy. He joined on his seventeenth birthday. The year was 1940.

Mike would discover the excitement he sought. He was stationed for about a year at Ford Island, located at the entrance into Pearl Harbor. He loved standing on his ship, the USS *California*, and gazing out in amazement at "Battleship Row," a double line of massive gray battleships tied up side by side behind the *California*. One Sunday, while he took in the view, a bugler sounded general quarters—the call for all hands on board to immediately report to their battle stations. They all began running to their stations as they tried to assess if this was just another drill or a real signal of trouble. Mike ran as well, when suddenly everything exploded. Bombs blew apart machinery, metal, and men. It was December 7,

1941—the infamous day when the Japanese attacked Pearl Harbor, sparking our nation's entrance into World War II.

When commanders issued the orders to abandon ship, Mike and others jumped overboard into the sea and the expanding noxious film of burning fuel. Mike survived the attack on Pearl Harbor and his ship, as well as having two other naval ships sunk under him (the *Astoria* and *Santa Fe*) during World War II.[57]

Being a resourceful, hard worker, combined with the grit needed to survive the Great Depression and the war, shaped Mike into an official member of the "Greatest Generation."[58] After the war, he devoted all his efforts into making a success of himself in business.

From the start, given our respective hard-charging, get-it-done-or-get-out-of-the-way natures, Mike and I hit it off. He liked my boldness to say what was on my mind and my hardy work ethic to do what it took to accomplish any job. As I mentioned earlier, when I left teaching and we formed our partnership, we both put success in business ahead of everything else. One business grew into several successful businesses. We made a good team—until I asked Jesus into my life.

Mike, who grew up Catholic, was initially curious about the changes in me—but that quickly wore off. He didn't like my statements about each of us needing a personal, saving relationship with Christ. As a self-made man, Mike didn't need help from anybody and, as a "good person," he sure didn't need saving. He was good enough. To top it off, Mike told me that I was becoming too religious and fanatical. Long ago, I had stopped talking to Mike about Jesus. I did, though, keep praying for his salvation and relationship with Jesus.

A SAVIOR, AN INVITATION & A CHOICE

Not surprisingly, Mike was still running his business at the age of eighty-seven. It was still the most important aspect of his life when he fell ill and

---

57 Some of Mike's war story and that of other naval crew members are shared in author Steve Jackson's 2003 book, *Lucky Lady*.
58 Brokaw, *The Greatest Generation* (Random House, 1998).

was diagnosed with lung cancer. Karen flew to Ohio to take care of her dad. Within several weeks, he was hospitalized, and doctors told Mike and Karen that he had only a few days to live.[59]

All our children, their spouses, and their kids quickly threw things in suitcases and headed to Ohio to see Mike. Our daughter, Brianna; her husband, Nathan; their oldest daughter, Ainslee; and their twin girls, Ellie and Kayla, flew to Cleveland. So did our son Larry; his wife, Jessica; and their daughter, Jocelyn. Our son Nathan; his wife, Nana; and I loaded up our van and drove north.

By the time our standing-room-only contingent arrived, the medical team had inserted a breathing tube into Mike, so he was unable to talk. Instead, he wrote out what he wanted to say. I could tell Mike was glad to see me. When I asked if I could pray for him, he got angry and wrote down, "Why the hell would I need you to pray for me?" I smiled and gave him a hug.

Ellie and Kayla were eight. They wrote down words and phrases on index cards to help Mike communicate, such as, "Help me sit up," "Put some ice on my lips," "I need turning," and "Thank you."

When no one was looking, I slipped in a card that read, "This hurts like hell; would you pray for me?" When Mike saw the card, he showed it to Brianna. She started scolding her girls for writing that on a card. Mike thought it was funny and gave me a wink for that one.

We were all in the room when a very young priest arrived, explaining that he had come to administer Mike his last rites. Nervous and almost hesitant to enter, the priest dropped his prayer book as he walked over to Mike's bed. It appeared this was his first time delivering these solemn rites to a dying man. I felt bad for him. When it came time to offer the wafer and wine to Mike, the priest was totally at a loss for what to do because of Mike's breathing tube. I suggested he rub holy water on Mike's forehead and proceed, which he did. When the priest finished, he pronounced, "Eugene Mike Hardy, you are good to go," and quickly left the room.

---

59 All this was especially difficult because they had lost Karen's sister, Diane, to cancer about a month before Mike's illness. Karen's mother had passed away when Karen was twenty-five.

I felt so bad for this young priest that I hadn't noticed how displeased Larry was regarding the priest's statement. He began telling his grandfather that he was not good to go; he needed to invite Jesus into his life.

Larry had his iPad and in large print, he showed and read Mike the verse, Revelation 3:20:

> Here I am! I stand at the door and knock. If anyone hears my voice and opens the door, I will come in and eat with that person, and they with me.

Larry explained, "Grandpa, when an artist paints a picture of this promise, Jesus is knocking at the door, but there is no handle on the outside; only the person behind the door can open it and invite Jesus to enter. Only you can invite Jesus in. And we all need Jesus because no one is good enough on their own to enter God's kingdom. Look at Ephesians 2:8-9."

> For it is by grace you have been saved, through faith—and this is not from yourselves, it is the gift of God—not by works, so that no one can boast.

"Grandpa, it is God's grace that saves us, it's not due to *anything* we can do. It's a gift we cannot earn because then we would boast about how good we are. Jesus instead offers Himself as a free gift for us."

I was on pins and needles and scared to look at Mike, fearing that he might be so angry he would jump out of bed and maybe leave the room. When I finally looked, he was listening intently to his grandson, so Larry kept sharing. He showed Mike the third chapter of John and the story of Nicodemus and Jesus. Larry went on to say that, although Nicodemus was a very good man in the eyes of the community and spiritual leaders, he talked with Jesus about how someone could enter heaven—God's kingdom.

Jesus told Nicodemus that he needed to be born again. Nicodemus wasn't sure what Jesus meant and asked if he had to go back into his mother's womb. Jesus explained to him that people require a spiritual birth; they must be born again, spiritually, from God.

"Everyone needs a Savior," Larry urged, "including you, Grandpa."

Instead of anger, a tear trickled down Mike's cheek. Larry then asked Mike if he wanted to invite Jesus into his life, and Mike nodded his head slowly. Larry told his grandfather that if he desired to, he could pray and simply ask Jesus into his life. "I know you can't talk, so just think in your mind. I will pray aloud and if you want to, agree with the words as I say them."

Larry prayed something like the following:

"God, please come into my life. I haven't lived as You want me to. I have sinned and fall short of Your will, but You gave Your Son, Jesus, to die on the cross for me and pay the debt for my sins. Thank You for Your forgiveness. I want You to come into my life. I want the new and eternal life that You gave Jesus when You resurrected Him from the grave and that You promise to give to us. Help me to live for You. Thank You for Your gift and assurance that You are with me now in this life and that You will take me to be with You in the next."

Mike nodded his head in agreement. Just like that—he accepted Jesus! We all cried, hugged, and laughed. What a thrill and miracle!

My emotions overwhelmed me and tears ran down my cheeks. I was happy for Mike and proud of my son. I thought about all the times when I shared with Mike and he got angry, until I had to stop sharing. But I kept praying for his salvation for thirty-three years. I had to "let go and let God" do the impossible, which He did!

Amazingly, God was just getting started with Mike and would do more than any of us could imagine.

A MIRACLE FOR MIKE

The next day, Mike's lungs and breathing improved enough that the doctors removed the breathing tube. One of the first things he requested was for Larry to show him the Scriptures again.

After another day or so, the doctors told Mike that they had done all they could for him, and they released him to go home with hospice care. They also put him on an experimental cancer drug, which had the greatest effect with Asian women, but it was all they could offer him back then.

Karen stayed with Mike when he returned home. One day he asked her, "How long is this going to take?" She replied, "I don't know." They both thought, *one or two weeks,* although neither one spoke the words out loud.

But Mike continued getting stronger and improving. Finally, the doctors removed him from hospice care. Shortly after, he asked Karen to take a road trip with him to visit meaningful sites from his life: places he had lived, schools he had attended, job locations and farms where he had worked, and favorite locations where they had boated together as a family on Lake Erie. During this time, we kept asking Mike to come to Florida to live with Karen and me. Finally, he agreed if we would let him bring his ninety-year-old friend. We said yes.

Mike lived for a year after accepting Jesus as his Savior! Karen and I were blessed to not only have this time with Mike, but also to watch him discover the joys of knowing Jesus as his Savior and companion.

Mike and I had many great conversations about God and the Bible. Mike knew a little bit about the story of Moses, so I shared how God and Moses walked and talked together and knew each other as friends. Mike wanted to see the story. I showed him the story and a favorite verse of mine:

The LORD would speak to Moses face to face, as one speaks to a friend. (Exodus 33:11)

I shared that the more Moses knew God, the more Moses wanted to know Him and asked to see God's glory.

God said, "You cannot see my face, for no one may see me and live. . . . There is a place near me where you may stand on a rock. When my glory passes by, I will put you in a cleft in the rock and cover you with my hand until I have passed by. Then I will remove my hand and you will see my back; but my face must not be seen." (Exodus 33:20–23)

"God wants it to be like this for us," I told Mike. "We are to get a taste of God and want more of Him."

FRIENDS FOR LIFE

Mike wasn't the only close relative or friend whom I saw come to Christ. There was the delightfully named Laddie Jim, a close buddy, who became like a brother to me. We met when I was fifteen and worked as a stock boy at Woolworth's Five-and-Dime, the once-popular retail chain.[60]

While working at Woolworth's, I started dating Dolly, a Catholic girl who worked at the jewelry counter and whose family was very Italian. I called her mom "Aunty Ann." She always had a wonderful pot of spaghetti on the stove. When anyone came over, Aunty Ann would offer a boilermaker (a shot of whiskey followed by a beer) or a glass of wine before serving a plate of delicious spaghetti. I loved the smell and taste of her cooking and the warmth and acceptance I felt from her and her family.

One late winter night after the store closed, Dolly and I were waiting for her cousin, Laddie Jim, to give us a ride home. I was looking forward to a boilermaker and a hot dish of spaghetti and meatballs. This was my first time to meet Laddie Jim, who was home on leave from the navy. He showed up in a '57 red Ford convertible. We hit it off so well that, after eating dinner, I left Dolly at home and hit the bars with her cousin. Though underage, I had connections at a number of bars where I could drink.

Laddie Jim and I connected for a number of reasons, including the fact that we both felt alone in this world. He had become an orphan at twelve. His dad died first, and his mom remarried. He was living with his mom and stepfather when his mother died. Laddie Jim was living with a stepfather and a stepmother at twelve. Feeling abandoned, he joined the navy at the age of seventeen.

He was currently preparing to finish up his four-year hitch. Stationed in Spain, he had worked his way up to first-class boatswain's mate (pronounced "bo-sun mate"), the officer in charge of all the ship's rigging,

---

60 Part of my job entailed cleaning the bathrooms. Dad's lessons stuck with me because the first time I cleaned them, the manager came to me, amazed, and said he had never seen the bathrooms that clean!

anchors, cables, and deck crew. Before he returned to the navy, I asked Laddie Jim if he could find someone fitting my description and get his ID. He did. The next time he was home, we added my picture and gave it a glossy finish with the help of the laminating machine at Woolworth's. Now I had an official-looking ID that made me twenty-one—the legal drinking age in Ohio. Laddie Jim was with me during many of my escapades. He became like a brother to me, especially when my brother Larry died.

LADDIE JIM'S SALVATION

When I asked Jesus into my life, I was ragged and rough. While I knew I had changed inside, it took a long time for these changes to show on the outside. When life became tough and squeezed me, more junk than Jesus came out. I tried to share with Laddie Jim that each of us needs to ask Jesus into our life because we are never good enough to enter the kingdom of God on our own human merit. Not only did Laddie Jim resist everything I shared, but the poor condition of my life didn't present a good or believable testimony. Sharing Jesus wasn't going very well.

Later, Laddie Jim married an Irish-Catholic girl, whom I nicknamed the Wild Redhead. They were both kind and good-hearted people. I was attempting to share with both Laddie Jim and the Wild Redhead that they needed saving. What they saw was a former alcoholic with a bad temper, proclaiming to them that they must work on their faith. Needless to say, it didn't make much sense. Because my outward behavior didn't reflect my inner changes, we got into some heated arguments. Finally, I decided I didn't want to lose Laddie Jim as a friend, and I couldn't force him to become a follower, anyway. God would have to do the work within him. So I stopped telling them about my faith and prayed for them. Twenty years later, I was still praying.

One day, the phone rang. When I answered it, Laddie Jim excitedly shared with me that he and the Wild Redhead had just come from a Billy Graham crusade and asked Jesus into their hearts! To say their lives changed would be an understatement. They went from being "Chr-Easters" (people who just attend services on Christmas and Easter) to lively followers of Christ. They attended mass and a Bible study every week, became active in helping their church, and worked with the youth.

They have continued growing in their faith and walk with Jesus. Laddie Jim has since read through the Bible many times. While he is a wonderful student of God's Word and surpassed me, he still hungers to know God and the Scriptures more. I'm thrilled because now we are brothers in Christ.

A COMMON SALVATION STRUGGLE

God has given me the opportunity to talk with many people concerning salvation. There is a common struggle that I have encountered frequently, which I'll share as it may help someone.

Some people believe in Jesus and even remember accepting Christ into their lives, but they know they haven't been walking with Him and are rightly concerned about whether or not they are saved and will live forever in God's kingdom with Him when they die. As we talk, I ask them questions to confirm their beliefs, which go something like these:

> Do you believe that Jesus is God's Son?
> Do you believe that Jesus died for your sins so that you might be forgiven?
> Do you believe that He rose again?
> Have you prayed and invited Him into your life and heart?

For those who are still uncertain about their salvation, I urge them to settle it by nailing down a date with prayer and/or baptism. Some individuals have chosen to rededicate their lives, while others have chosen to be baptized or even be baptized again. Once they have decided and acted, I encourage them to move forward in their faith and relationship with Jesus and grow in knowing and following Him.

While establishing a date and even taking an action step are not miraculous in themselves, they are helpful. Scripture instructs us to creatively make and utilize spiritual memorials in our lives so that we remember the Lord's kindness, grace, and miracles He gives us, and we don't turn back. It's also beneficial because prayerfully asking Christ to come into our hearts and lives doesn't mean we immediately experience a dramatic spiritual or emotional event. Many people don't, and it doesn't mean anything is wrong with them, their decision, or God. Our walk with God is not based on our emotions, feelings, or circumstances; it is based on His truth, our faith, and action. We are called to investigate, decide, seek God, and follow Him, regardless of our feelings and circumstances.

WONDERFUL JOY

How amazing it is to experience God's grace, love, power, and miracles in my own life and to witness these gifts in the lives of others as well! There is one more thought that amazes me. God isn't done with me!

Chapter 25

GOD'S NOT DONE

If you're still breathing, God is not done with you. You may think you blew it or are maxed out. You may think because of some sin or problem you have, God can't use you. You may think you're too old, too young, too tired, not capable, or not spiritually qualified. You may want God to get someone else. None of this is God's truth or plan. He wants you.

When I retired after pastoring for twenty-five years, I was tired and burned out. I thought I was done. Boy, was I surprised! God wasn't finished with me.

My road to retirement was more like a roller-coaster ride, which came to a jarring stop. A number of years before I retired, our church, pastors, and leadership experienced an extended time of transition. First, our beloved music minister, Pastor Rick, left. Then, Pastor Tony, our senior pastor, left after twenty-three years to minister to a congregation in another state. This led to more changes and created a season of personal uneasiness and anxiety. Any day I expected to hear a knock on my door from someone in leadership, followed by a request that I pack my things and leave. Finally, I surrendered it all to God and said, "Okay, God, You put me here and, if You want me to leave, I'm all right with that."

I felt peace, and things smoothed out. Indeed, two more years passed. But then, stormy winds of change began to blow again. This time I knew that, one way or another, it was time to retire. Because I didn't expect it at this point, and it came through difficult circumstances, I struggled with disappointment and self-pity.

I did, though, have plans for my retirement, and they didn't include working hard. I had labored while teaching, in business, and serving twenty-five years in ministry. I was looking forward to taking it easy, being left alone, and not worrying when someone requiring my assistance might call or show up at our door. I would read, tend my flower garden, and take trips with Karen. For years, I had daydreamed about this kind of freedom and pressure-free life.

But God had other plans. Individuals kept calling and knocking on my door, seeking help. They still wanted and needed counsel from God's Word and Jesus. Although I kept ministering, my heart wasn't in it. I complained, protested, and regularly pitched fits to God, telling Him I didn't want to work hard and counsel. At my age, surely I deserved to take it easy. People kept coming.

One day I made a cardboard sign that read: "Go Away. I'm Not Your Pastor Anymore." Karen caught me headed to the front door. After reading my sign, she said, "No, you are not putting that on our door." While Karen and our kids kept telling me that I needed to do what God wanted me to do and counsel, I would mumble to myself, "That's easy for you to say." But, very slowly, I started to consider that maybe God did want me to keep counseling.

GRACE VISITS

One day my longtime close friend and church elder, Jim McNulty (whom I hadn't seen in some time), knocked on our front door. When I answered it, he gave me a big hug. A rush of words poured out: he missed me, I had been on his mind, and he was concerned about me.

I told him that I had been busy remodeling our kitchen, which was true. Tearing out the old and installing the new, I tried pounding out my troubles. My frustration hadn't budged. Jim asked to see the kitchen, which was close to being finished. During the next several weeks, Jim continued reaching out to me as only a friend who gives grace, understanding, and a listening ear can do.

As he listened and cared, Jim helped me come back to life. My hurt and anger began to heal as God worked His conspiracy of grace into me through Jim. I began accepting my circumstances. Though what had happened wasn't my plan or timing, it was God's.

Additionally, the Lord kept drawing me back to Jeremiah 29:11. Years ago, when Jay Strack preached verse-by-verse through Jeremiah, he had devoted an entire sermon to this passage. I had felt God speaking to me and claimed the promise, even using a marker to draw a big red frame around the verse in my Bible:

> "For I know the plans I have for you," declares the LORD, "plans to prosper you and not to harm you, plans to give you hope and a future." (Jeremiah 29:11)

I still use this Bible. Whenever I think of this verse, I picture it with the red frame. God's loving, faithful promise has carried me through many difficult times. It gave me hope during the business failure in Fort Myers and the fear during those fourteen long months, when I asked God so many times, "What is going on? What are You doing?" God brought His promise to my mind after I was ordained as pastor and felt so unsure of myself. Through the years and many ups and downs, the Lord has reminded me of it. He was reminding me once again that His plans for me are good.

I didn't comprehend the painful circumstances surrounding my retirement, but God had good plans and blessings in it. In fact, He had a better design for my retirement than I did. His plan came with good purposes. Finally, I surrendered and agreed, "Okay, God, I will counsel and do what You want."

Soon, Karen and our kids helped me turn our front bedroom into my counseling office. This is the bedroom where it all started years ago, when I dropped off those first drunks. This bedroom, with its door to the outside and next to our front door, is perfect. God still keeps surprising me with His amazing provisions for us in this house!

God surely isn't finished with me yet. Now in my early seventies, I'm counseling more than ever because I don't have church responsibilities. I still don't advertise or seek out clients, and yet a steady stream of people keeps showing up. Some days, it's as if the floodgates have opened, leaving me feeling that it's more than I can handle. At times, God brings people in groups, whether extended family members or from churches.[61] Once again, though, it's exciting to see who will show up or call. It's amazing to share God's grace and truth and watch Him work in their hearts and lives.

God isn't finished with me yet in so many ways. While working on this book, I chose to have weight-loss surgery. Yes, despite overcoming alcohol, drug use, and pornography, food was one more addiction I struggled with. I hope it's my last one.

Food was a place I could hide in, rebel with, and find comfort in apart from God. I was ignoring, burying, and trying to handle my emotions myself—stuffing my face, instead of facing my stuff. With my health deteriorating, I finally had to address my issues with eating and being overweight. Finally, I became willing to go to any lengths to get well in this area. "Going to any lengths" included having surgery, along with leaning on the help of an AA-like food sponsor and God.

As I travel this journey with Him, I am experiencing more of God and His conspiracy of grace. Now that I've had the surgery and can't use food to hide behind, I have experienced more intimate prayer times with God. To prepare for surgery, I was required to fast for five weeks. The first three weeks I was only allowed to take in a puny regimen of clear liquids and broth. This was followed by another two weeks of liquids and pureed foods. The first three days of the fast were miserably difficult for me and anyone around me. But then, after the cravings and hunger went away (and like others who fast), I began to experience a deeper spiritual awareness of God and, more intimate, tender prayer times with Him.

For example, one night I couldn't sleep. I felt I should get up and pray about a trip that I was contemplating taking. As I started praying, God told me he had a different topic He wanted to discuss my issues with food. Prayer is, after all, a two-way conversation that comprises talking and

---

61 To read an encouraging and insightful story regarding my work helping fallen pastors and their churches heal with grace, please visit https://www.ConspiracyofGrace.com.

listening to God. I was caught off guard. I didn't really want to go there, but God did.

Gently and lovingly, He told me that He grieved over my compulsive eating: "I created you. I want you to take care of the body that I gave you. It saddened me that you were abusing my creation that I love." As He said it, it was as if each word had power: "My. Creation. That. I. Love."

He showed me how I missed His mark (which is what sin is) and fell short in this area. My compulsive eating was a sin, and I confessed it. But God also told me that He wasn't condemning me; if I felt any condemnation, it was not from Him. He forgives me and desires that I know Him more intimately, including His power and love for me. He reminded me that in His love, He gave His life for me, paying an indescribable price. He still gives His life to me daily that I might be lifted up to know Him more. Truly, this is what the Bible calls "the gospel," which means the good news, glad and joyful tidings.[62]

DELIGHTFUL GIFTS

Besides this good news, we are to "taste and see that the Lord is good" (Psalm 34:8). He desires to give us good gifts and delightful surprises along the way. I want to share one that He gave to my kitchen remodeling confidant, Jim McNulty, and me.

Jim is a master craftsman of dulcimers and teaches classes on making dulcimers and guitars. A number of years ago, Jim encouraged me to build a guitar. It's close to being finished and, with God's grace and more time, I will complete it.

Jim and I both read and thoroughly loved the book, *Clapton's Guitar: Watching Wayne Henderson Build the Perfect Instrument*, written by Allen

---

62 While I briefly mention the gospel here and in chapter 6, "College Daze," it's a key, central topic of Scripture. The word *gospel* used in the New Testament literally means "good news." Luke 2:10 tells us that angels from heaven came and announced Jesus's birth to humble shepherds in a field, proclaiming it good news of great joy for all people. God, the great Creator, deeply desires for us to know Him through Christ, along with forgiveness, new life, and spiritual blessings.

St. John, a *New York Times* best-selling author.[63] Even the book's back cover copy, which is also the description on Amazon.com, is a delightful read. It shares how the author was searching for the best guitar and instead discovered the world's finest builder of guitars: a retired rural mail carrier, Wayne Henderson. With little more than a sharp whittling knife, in a room filled with sawdust, Henderson makes heirloom acoustic guitars that have a ten-year waiting list—even for legendary musician Eric Clapton. In his book, St. John artfully paints a story about exquisite craftsmanship and a world where "time is measured by old jokes, old-time music, and homemade lemon pies shared by good friends."

After Jim and I read the book, God provided some miracles that culminated in a most delightful meeting with Henderson. While eating lunch at a Bob Evans Restaurant, Jim and I overheard a couple talking about Henderson and struck up a conversation with them. They talked eagerly about a bluegrass-music event taking place at a small venue, where he would be playing with other musicians. We were all excited until they added, "It's a closed, private affair."

When we left, Jim disappointedly remarked, "Gosh, it's too bad we can't go." I piped up, "We're going. We just have to figure out how to get in." I proposed some ideas, although I had to explain to Jim what "case the joint" meant. He wasn't keen on that idea or my other one of climbing over a fence. I continued, "Well, God let us hear about this event—He must have a plan for us to go. We'll drive there and see what happens."

When we arrived, we were disheartened to see an extremely high fence. Jim, in his typical Eeyore fashion, exclaimed, "Well, I guess our idea won't work!" He was ready to turn around and go home, but just then—as I pulled near the gate—God miraculously opened it for us. Well, someone drove through it, so I quickly stepped on the gas, scooting in the gate behind the vehicle. Still, God brought it about. After this, God led us to the right building and the right people. Hearing our story, one man's heart softened. Actually he looked at us and at our unfinished

---

63 Allen St. John, *Clapton's Guitar: Watching Wayne Henderson Build the Perfect Instrument* (New York: Free Press, 2005).

handmade guitars and said to his friends, "It's just two old guys. They'll be all right to join us."

We didn't just join them; we sat in the second row from the stage! During intermission, Henderson was hanging around the stage, so Jim and I made a beeline down to him, taking our guitars with us. He excitedly talked with us during the whole intermission and even shared ideas for what we could do to make our guitars better.

What a night. Driving home, Jim kept saying, "Wow! God blessed our socks off!"

It's true and just like His promise: "Trust in the LORD and do good. . . . Take delight in the LORD, and he will give you the desires of your heart" (Psalm 37:3–4). For weeks afterward, I continued marveling at His instruction with a promise in this verse. This entire gift was from God. When we're in tune with God's will, He does give us delightful surprises. God is in charge of the universe, but He helped two old guys meet and talk with famed guitar builder Wayne Henderson.

UNIMAGINABLE GIFTS!

What an amazing life I have led, especially as I have walked with Jesus. This is even more remarkable given my past. Yes, my past is a part of my life, but with Jesus I'm no longer captive to it or defined by it. God has set me free! It is through my past and circumstances that I am able to know God's love and care for me.

God greatly desires to bless you and set you free, too. He does not want anything in your past or present to contaminate your life or defeat your future. Not only has the Lord given me a wonderful new life, but through the years He keeps revealing to me that I am to share His grace, power, and help with everyone I can.

One day while finishing my counseling degree at Liberty University, I was completing an assignment and on a Virginia mountain. I was to meditate on a verse that was meaningful to me and in which I felt God speak to me. My verse was this:

> But those who hope in the LORD
> will renew their strength.

> They will soar on wings like eagles;
> they will run and not grow weary,
> they will walk and not be faint. (Isaiah 40:31)

While I was thinking about God's incredible promise, an eagle flew into view and soared majestically. As I watched in wonder, the Lord spoke, "Dale, when you counsel and talk with people, point them to Me so I can set them free and they can fly."

God's intentions for us truly are good!

As I've shared my story, I have pointed you toward Jesus. I've shared how He wants to lift you up; help you with your burdens; set you free from your hurts, fears, and shortcomings; and, all the while, help you know and experience Him. He wants to walk with you and bless you, so that you might enjoy Him and love Him.

For the Lord to do these things, He needs you to respond to Him and talk with Him. If you have never invited God into your life, you can do that now. If you want to seek Jesus more, but you aren't sure what to do next, here are a few ideas:

- Do you need to find a friend who can encourage you, help you get honest, and live for God? Ask the Lord to guide you in this.
- When you pray and talk with God, keep praying even if you don't feel His presence. He is with you all the time. Also, because praying takes our thoughts, emotions, and being still, we may struggle for a time. Don't give up praying! Keep seeking God and continue listening for Him. Ask to know Him. Talk with Him now about your needs. Share with Him your feelings regarding my story. Grow in your time with Him.
- Find a way to read God's Word. Read the four Gospels (Matthew, Mark, Luke, and John) and the next book, Acts. Choose your favorite. Ask God to help you receive the truth and grace of His Word. Read one of the books again. For encouraging, faith-building passages read Psalms 34, 91, 103, 138, and 145.

- If you would like to find someone with whom to talk and share your story and hurt, we have included a list of resources in the appendix for you to consider. Ask God to lead you to the right person. Don't give up even if you need to try several options.
- Find an encouraging, uplifting Christian radio station. Ask God to help you take the words into your heart.
- Do you need to find a church home? Don't let it overwhelm you. Take one small step at a time. Select one church and visit it. Try another, if need be.
- Give this book to someone, ask if they'll read it and inquire if the two of you can meet together and discuss it. Read it again.

I wish that we didn't have to close but, as we do, I want to pray for you with promises from God's Word:

Father in heaven, I pray for this dear reader and ask that You fulfill Your great and marvelous promises for them. Grant them great grace and peace as they grow in knowledge of You and Jesus. It is Your marvelous glory and excellence that enable us to draw near to You and escape the world's corruption, wrong desires, and death. Then You bless us and empower us to participate in Your divine nature and to live a godly life.

In light of these truths, help this friend make every effort to respond to You and Your promises, and do all they can to build up their faith. We know that You are able to do immeasurably more than we can ask or imagine. I pray that through Your glorious riches and power, You will strengthen them so that Christ may dwell in their heart, and they will know Your deep, high, and powerful love and be able to share Your blessings and love with others.[64]

Friend, may you keep God's truths close to your heart, and be blessed in knowing His presence, peace, and joy!

---

[64] This prayer is adapted from the prayers in Ephesians 3:16–21 and 2 Peter 1:2–5 NLT.

Acknowledgments

My heart is overflowing with thankfulness for every family member and friend who has been a part of my life and loved me. If I start naming people, I am fearful that I will leave someone off. Please know that you mean the world to me.

I do, however, need to acknowledge a few people.

A wholehearted thanks is given to Dr. Ed Smith for his friendship, for his living example of a humble walk with God, and for his faithfulness to Jesus and Jesus's healing ministry through Transformation Prayer (which has brought me great healing).

A big thank-you is extended to Robbi Cary and her husband, Keith. Robbi has so believed in my story and the power of it to help many people that she has poured her heart, soul, and a good portion of her life into this book. She has been kind, patient, sacrificial, truthful, and encouraging, while providing a few necessary kicks in the seat of my backside to finish this book. Thank you for your unwavering, relentless, hard work.

A very warm and heartfelt thanks goes to our editor, Ken Walker, who, with editing skills bordering on superpowers and supersized portions of encouragement to keep us persevering, helped turn *Conspiracy of Grace* from a rough manuscript into a gem of a book! Thank you for keeping us on track and helping to polish this piece so it shines.

A generous thank-you also belongs to Marilyn A. Anderson for her sharp eye, strong assist with copyediting/proofreading skills, and deft touch.

This project has taken an entire creative team and I'm grateful for the amazing talents, inspiration, and guidance of these professionals: Katherine Lloyd (typesetting) at TheDESKonline.com; Yvonne Parks (cover design) at PearCreative.ca; Liz Smith (indexer) at InkSmith Editorial Services; Darcie Clemen, (proofreading and editorial work); and Michele Schiavone (proofreader).

APPENDIX

Appendix A

CLEVELAND & HOPPING TRAINS

I have always loved Cleveland's trains and terminals. As a young boy, I often rode the train with Grandma Keen to go into town. We went to shops like Higbee's and to the West Side Market, so she could buy fresh produce and a live chicken, which the vendors put in a flour sack with its head sticking out. On the train ride back, it was my job to hold the chicken. No, I wasn't happy about it. After arriving home, Grandma would kill, clean, and then cook the chicken, turning it into one of her delicious meals. Somehow, the chicken-holding train ride didn't seem quite so bad.

As I grew older, Larry and his friends let me go with them, when they would occasionally "hop a train" going to Pittsburgh, Pennsylvania. It was pretty much like what you see in the movies. We would hop into an empty train car, pass hobo camps, and sometimes ride in the same car with hoboes. Once in Pittsburgh, we headed to the well-known Primanti Brothers deli for lunch. We always ordered the famous "mile-high" sandwich—stacked with meat, coleslaw made with Italian dressing, and french fries on Italian bread![65] After lunch and some sightseeing, we hopped another train and headed home.

CLEVELAND & SETTING RECORDS

Cleveland is an old city founded in the 1700s. It sits on the southern end of Lake Erie and the mouth of the Cuyahoga River. The river runs

---

[65] Primanti's has practically been an institution since it opened in 1933. It now has several locations, including one in Ft. Lauderdale, Florida.

through the city, splitting it into east and west sides and driving many of the names, such as East Tech High School and west-side shops. The east side, originally the wealthy side, became the slums as the city grew. While we lived on the west side, I worked on the east side during my Mafia years and teaching in the inner-city schools.

Because of Cleveland's river location and its many canals, it was an ideal manufacturing hub that attracted four rail lines. The train terminal, with all the intersecting tracks, was downtown between the east and west sides; the train yard, where trains coupled and parked, was farther outside the city.

In the early 1900s, a new, larger Union Depot Station was designed and built after New York City's Grand Central Terminal and Tower. Cleveland's would be fifty-two stories high and the tallest building in North America outside of New York City until 1964. The boarding station would anchor the ground floor.

Excavation for the project started in 1922. More than 2,200 buildings were demolished, making it the second-largest excavation project in the world after the Panama Canal. The Tower was officially opened in 1930, later renamed Tower City Center, and added to the National Register of Historic Places in 1976.

Appendix B

THE 12 STEPS OF AA

1. We admitted we were powerless over alcohol—that our lives had become unmanageable.
2. Came to believe that a Power greater than ourselves could restore us to sanity.
3. Made a decision to turn our will and our lives over to the care of God as we understood Him.
4. Made a searching and fearless moral inventory of ourselves.
5. Admitted to God, to ourselves, and to another human being the exact nature of our wrongs.
6. Were entirely ready to have God remove all these defects of character.
7. Humbly asked Him to remove our shortcomings.
8. Made a list of persons we had harmed, and became willing to make amends to them all.
9. Made direct amends to such people wherever possible, except when to do so would injure them or others.
10. Continued to take personal inventory and when we were wrong, promptly admitted it.
11. Sought through prayer and meditation to improve our conscious contact with God as we understood Him, praying only for knowledge of His will for us and the power to carry that out.
12. Having had a spiritual awakening as the result of these steps, we tried to carry this message to alcoholics and to practice these principles in all our affairs.[66]

---

[66] Copyright © 1952, 1953, 1981 by Alcoholics Anonymous Publishing (now known as Alcoholics Anonymous World Services, Inc.). All rights reserved.

Appendix C
12 STEP & COUNSELING RESOURCES

Alcohol or Drug Addiction

https://www.aa.org (Alcoholics Anonymous)
https://www.na.org (Narcotics Anonymous)

Sexual Addiction

https://www.sa.org (Sexaholics Anonymous)
https://www.drpatrickcarnes.com
https://faithfulandtrue.com (Dr. Mark Laaser)

Suicide Prevention & Hotline

https://suicidepreventionlifeline.org   1-800-273-8255

Help for Families Affected by Alcohol or Dysfunction

https://adultchildren.org (Adult Children of Alcoholics, ACA, or Dysfunctional Families)
https://al-anon.org
https://al-anon.org/newcomers/teen-corner-alateen/ (For teenagers)
http://coda.org (Co-Dependents Anonymous)

Survivors of Abuse

https://www.sasaworldwide.org/12-steps (Sexual Assault Survivors Anonymous)
http://www.asca12step.org (Adult Survivors of Child Abuse Anonymous)

Note: You are not alone, if you were sexually abused as a child. Sadly, the statistics are staggering. As many as one in three women and one in seven men have been sexually abused by the time they reach eighteen. Ninety percent of child sexual abuse victims know their attacker (https://centerforfamilyjustice.org).

Christian 12 Step Recovery Programs

https://www.celebraterecovery.com

https://www.overcomersoutreach.org

Many churches and pastors provide excellent counseling that changes lives.

Transformation Prayer

https://www.transformationprayer.org

Southwest Florida Christian Counseling & 12 Step Recovery

http://www.egracechurch.com/recovery/

http://www.recoveryatsummit.com

https://www.riversidechurch.org/counseling/

http://fbcn.org/counseling/ (Naples area)

Appendix D

THOUGHTS ON ENJOYABLE LIVING & AA

While I know that enjoyable recovery is possible, and the 12 Steps work, many individuals have told me that AA didn't work for them or a family member. Just the other day, a woman—whom I'll call Sally—came to me requesting assistance because the court mandated her to attend 12 Step meetings. She shared that she had tried AA before, but it didn't help. Our conversation reflected many discussions that I've had with others. It went something like this:

Sally: "I need help. I've been to AA before, but it didn't work."
Dale: "I know what probably happened—you attended, but you never worked the program. Let me ask you some questions. Did you make ninety meetings?"
Sally: "Well, no, I didn't like them."
Dale: "Did you get a sponsor?"
Sally: "Yeah, but I didn't care for her."
Dale: "Did you work through at least the 5th Step?"
Sally: "No."

As Bob told me, and as I shared with Sally and many others, "You need to go to meetings until you like them; then, keep going. As soon as possible, you need to make it to ninety meetings, get a sponsor, work through the 5th Step with your sponsor's assistance, and begin calling on God daily for help. You have to actually *work* the Steps and not simply try to mentally figure them out or mentally work them. If you really want enjoyable recovery, and you do these things, you will succeed."

HELPFUL RECOVERY TRUTHS

Recovering from addiction isn't easy. Following are a number of truths that helped me as I worked toward healthy, happy sobriety:

- I had to accept that addiction is a disease, which is defined as primary, chronic, and progressive. Mine checked off all those boxes.
- Addiction is a disease affecting the whole person—physical, emotional, spiritual, and relational. Eventually each aspect needs to be addressed.
- Every disease requires a specific form of care. I had to learn about my disease, along with my issues, and the remedies (tools) available for recovery. Remedies for me have included: attending AA meetings regularly; leaning on God, a sponsor, and others; and working the Steps.
- I had to accept the fact that I would never be able to control my addictions. Trying to use reasonable methods would never work and neither would using my own effort, wisdom, or strength. We want to think that we're fine, we can handle it on our own, and we've got this. But we're not fine, and we can't fight this battle alone.
- In the beginning, my key focus was simply to become sober and stay sober. Trying to find out the reasons I used alcohol and drugs, or heal my pain before I was addiction-free, didn't work. I had to, first, get and live sober.
- I needed to be willing to go to any lengths to get well and find sobriety, peace, and joy. I went to great lengths to get high and numb the pain. Now, I had to go to the same lengths in another direction.
- Before and after we get sober, we will encounter problems that include cravings, denial, rationalization, and the desire for an easier way. We need to be prepared for these and lean on the

help of God and others. When the cravings and temptation kick in, our mind will try to rationalize giving in with these fine-sounding arguments: Just once more; Now I have this licked; I deserve this. We are especially vulnerable to cravings and temptation when we are sad, mad, glad, hurt, troubled, hungry, tired, or overly confident.
- Sobriety doesn't equal emotional health. Because our issues are more than our addictions—they are our thoughts and pain—it's important to understand the pain-shame-addiction cycle. When we don't face our hurt, pain, shame, and low self-esteem, we turn to our drug of choice. This behavior creates more consequences, shame, and emotional pain. The cycle keeps going and looks like this:

To break our pain-shame-addiction cycle, we need the help of God and others. We must stop denying, and running from, our suffering, sadness, anger, and fear, along with our issues, sin, and struggles. Up until now, our addictions have been all about using substances and habits to try to fix our pain and confusion. However, the minute we start working the 12 Steps (or seeking Transformation Prayer), it is about not escaping our feelings and actions. We face them, acknowledge them, sit with them, and deal with them—with the aid of God and others.

- Denial of our pain and issues negates our life and growth, freezes our emotions, results in lost energy, isolates us from God and others, and deepens and prolongs our pain. To stop denying and running from our pain and find healing, once again, we need the help of God and others.
- It's helpful to learn about healthy and unhealthy family patterns, and then, identify our family's unhealthy ways and

coping method.[67] We can learn a bit about codependency, which is an unhealthy coping strategy. Codependency is being extra caring and helpful with others, but being hard on ourselves. It's a pattern we unknowingly begin adopting when we're in a dysfunctional relationship. The book, *Codependent No More*, by Melody Beattie, is a great resource for helping us unglue ourselves from others.

- It's helpful to learn about the "ick." If we grew up in a dysfunctional home, or if we have been around an alcoholic long enough, we will have what some refer to as the ick, which includes low self-esteem and painfully broken thought patterns. Something as simple as a person's fleeting look, a tone of voice, a brief comment, mannerisms, or a passing thought of our own can quickly trigger our ick. We might go into a funk, engage in our addiction or habit, or immediately do something to pass our pain on to someone else.

- Most of us struggle with low self-esteem, revealed in thoughts like these: *I'm not good enough, smart enough; I'm not good-looking enough; I'm not as good as others; I don't feel loved; what I say isn't important.* There are various reasons we believe these lies, but none of them are from God. As soon as we start to feel one, we will do anything to fight it, run from it, or numb it. Remember, though, these choices negate our connection with God and our growth and send us through the pain-shame cycle again.

We should ponder, know, and accept that our true worth comes from God. Our value isn't based on performance or some flimsy, arbitrary

---

67 Healthy families seek to be kind, are mostly calm, and communicate well. Family members are able to discuss their experiences, thoughts, and emotions (including hurt, fear, and anger). They are affectionate, appreciative, and help one another. They seek to be positive and have fun together. Rules are simple and clear; conflicts get resolved. The family grows together, and each person grows as an individual. Healthy families have a strong faith and spiritual values, which they talk about. In times of difficulty, they seek to use positive coping skills (resting, eating well, seeking help if need be, and leaning on God and His good promises). For an expanded list of family patterns, please visit https://www.ConspiracyofGrace.com.

measure like possessions or talent. Our worth is derived from the Lord, who created us in His image and with His glory. Even when mankind fell into sin, God sent Jesus as a valuable sacrifice and gift for us, so that we might be saved and rescued, be given a whole new life, and experience a restored relationship with God. Truly, we are greatly valued and dearly loved.

We are to increase in understanding and personally experiencing God's love for us. Up until now, in our brokenness, we have swung between: I can do it myself; I can never do it well enough; or trying to prove our worth and that we're loved by achieving or doing. However, God tells us throughout Scripture that He has proved His love for us through His Son's life and sacrifice, and He has provided all we need spiritually. Our task is to know His love and live in His love. We really are to know and experience that we have someone who desires to help us daily, who is always with us, and who won't leave us. You and I have someone who loves us personally with a healing, guiding, and protective love!

WILLINGNESS & MIRACLES

Healing and growing are worth our efforts! I am living proof that enjoyable recovery is possible because there is a God who loves us, is good, powerful, and desires to bless us as we seek and follow Him!

Appendix E

SCRIPTURE ON BEING FULLY LOVED, FORGIVEN, ACCEPTED & COMPLETE IN CHRIST

(Referenced in Chapter 19: "What's Low Worth Got to Do with It?")

We are told throughout the pages of Scripture that *in Christ* we are immeasurably loved, totally forgiven, fully accepted, complete, and blessed.

This is also a paraphrase from Robert McGee, who unpacks these promises in his book, *The Search for Significance*.[68] Following are a few Scriptures that I have assembled on each truth.

We Are Loved:

> I pray that out of his glorious riches he may strengthen you with power through his Spirit in your inner being, so that Christ may dwell in your hearts through faith. And I pray that you, *being rooted and established in love*, may have power, together with all the Lord's holy people, *to grasp how wide and long and high and deep is the love of Christ, and to know this love* that surpasses knowledge—that *you may be filled* to the measure of all the fullness of God. (Ephesians 3:16–19, emphasis added)

We Are Forgiven:

> There is now no condemnation for those who are in Christ Jesus. (Romans 8:1)

---

[68] Robert S. McGee, *The Search for Significance: Seeing Your True Worth through God's Eyes* (Nashville: Thomas Nelson, 2003). McGee's website is OfficialMcGeePublishing.com. The quote above is offered for free on a "Truth Card" under the Resource tab.

For I will forgive their wickedness and will remember their sins no more. (Hebrews 8:12)

We Are Accepted:

Since we have been made right in God's sight by faith, we have peace with God because of what Jesus Christ our Lord has done for us. (Romans 5:1 NLT)

God loved us and chose us in Christ to be holy and without fault in his eyes. (Ephesians 1:4 NLT)

What shall we say about such wonderful things as these? If God is for us, who can ever be against us? (Romans 8:31 NLT)

For God so loved the world that he gave his one and only Son, that whoever believes in him shall not perish but have eternal life. For God did not send his Son into the world to condemn the world, but to save the world through him. Whoever believes in him is not condemned. (John 3:16–18)

We Are Complete:

His divine power has given us everything we need for a godly life through our knowledge of him who called us by his own glory and goodness. (2 Peter 1:3)

So you also are complete through your union with Christ, who is the head over every ruler and authority. (Colossians 2:10 NLT)

We Are Restored by God:

He restores my soul. He guides me in the paths of righteousness for his name's sake. (Psalm 23:3 NHEB)

We Are Blessed with Every Spiritual Blessing:

Praise be to the God and Father of our Lord Jesus Christ, who has blessed us in the heavenly realms with every spiritual blessing in Christ. (Ephesians 1:3; there is much in Ephesians 1 and Scripture about our spiritual blessings in Christ.)

Appendix F

SCRIPTURE ON THE BLESSINGS OF BEING HUMBLE & CONFESSING

(Referenced in Chapter 14: "Steps on the Road of Grace")

Humility & Blessings (emphasis added):

"God opposes the proud but *shows favor to the humble.*" Submit yourselves, then, to God. . . . Come near to God and he will come near to you. (James 4:6–8)

Humble yourselves before the Lord, and he will lift you up in honor. (James 4:10 NLT)

For the Lord takes delight in his people; *he crowns the humble with victory.* (Psalm 149:4)

He *guides the humble* in what is right and teaches them his way. (Psalm 25:9)

He mocks proud mockers but *shows favor to the humble and oppressed.* (Proverbs 3:34)

Confession & Blessings:

Therefore confess your sins to each other and pray for each other so that you may be healed. (James 5:16)

You will never succeed in life if you try to hide your sins. Confess them and give them up; then God will show mercy to you. (Proverbs 28:13 GNT)

Repent, then, and turn to God, so that your sins may be wiped out, that times of refreshing may come from the Lord. (Acts 3:19)

Blessed is the one whose transgressions are forgiven, whose sins are covered. Blessed is the one whose sin the Lord does not count against them and in whose spirit is no deceit. When I kept silent, my bones wasted away through my groaning all day long. For day and night your hand was heavy on me; my strength was sapped as in the heat of summer. Then I acknowledged my sin to you and did not cover up my iniquity. I said, "I will confess my transgressions to the Lord." And you forgave the guilt of my sin. (Psalm 32:1–5)

• • •

Note: The topics above (confession and humility) are connected with coming into God's light and leaving darkness. These themes are discussed often in Scripture, beginning in Genesis, chapter 1. Sin, wrongful deeds, lies, and deception are all kept hidden by darkness, but God and Christ are the light of the world and overcome darkness. God's light brings life (John 8:12 and 1 John 1:5). Because one day everything hidden will be disclosed (Luke 8:17), and justice will be rendered, now is when we are able to come into the light, and be made clean, reconciled to God, and healed.

Appendix G

SCRIPTURE ON BEING CONFORMED TO & TRANSFORMED BY JESUS

(Referenced in Chapter 13: "Grace Gifts Everywhere")

Emphasis added to Scriptures.

> Then God said, "*Let us make mankind in our image, in our likeness,* so that they may rule over the fish in the sea and the birds in the sky, over the livestock and all the wild animals, and over all the creatures that move along the ground." *So God created mankind in his own image, in the image of God he created them*; male and female he created them. (Genesis 1:26–27)

> God knew what he was doing from the very beginning. He decided from the outset *to shape the lives of those who love him along the same lines as the life of his Son. The Son stands first in the line of humanity he restored. We see the original and intended shape of our lives there in him.* After God made that decision of what his children should be like, he followed it up by calling people by name. After he called them by name, he set them on a solid basis with himself. And then, after getting them established, he stayed with them to the end, gloriously completing what he had begun. (Romans 8:29–30 MSG)

> And just as we have borne the image of the earthly man, *so shall we bear the image of the heavenly man.* (1 Corinthians 15:49; see also 1 John 3:2)

SCRIPTURE ON BEING TRANSFORMED BY JESUS

So all of us who have had that veil removed can see and *reflect the glory of the Lord*. And the Lord—who is the Spirit—makes us more and more like him as we are changed into his glorious image. (2 Corinthians 3:18 NLT)

Throw off your old sinful nature and your former way of life, which is corrupted by lust and deception. Instead, let the Spirit renew your thoughts and attitudes. *Put on your new nature, created to be like God—truly righteous and holy.* (Ephesians 4:22–24 NLT; see also Romans 12:2)

Put on your new nature, and be renewed as you learn to know your Creator *and become like him.* (Colossians 3:10 NLT)

Through these he has given us his very great and precious promises, *so that through them you may participate in the divine nature,* having escaped the corruption in the world caused by evil desires. (2 Peter 1:4; see also 2 Peter 1:2–11)

Appendix H

SCRIPTURE ON GOD'S PROOF & EVIDENCE

(Referenced in Chapter 4: "The Wrong Crowd")

God provides proof and evidence for us regarding Himself, creation, salvation, and all that He wants to share with us. He gives us evidence to strengthen us, answer our questions, and give us hope. These verses can encourage us to know and trust God's love, power, and plan.[69]

Amos 4:13 promises us, "He who forms the mountains . . . reveals his thoughts to mankind."

Proof Concerning God's Word:

I am God, the only God you've had or ever will have—incomparable, irreplaceable—from the very beginning telling you what the ending will be, all along letting you in on what is going to happen, assuring you, "I'm in this for the long haul, I'll do exactly what I set out to do." . . . I've planned it, so it's as good as done. (Isaiah 46:10–11 MSG)

Do not treat prophecies with contempt but test them all.
(1 Thessalonians 5:20–21)

Proof Concerning Jesus:

But the angel said to them, "Do not be afraid. I bring you good news that will cause great joy for all the people. Today in the town of David a Savior has been born to you; he is the Messiah, the Lord. This will

---

[69] Adapted from the gift book, *No Matter What, It's a Good Day When: Finding Blessings in Difficult Days,* by Robbi Cary (Fort Myers, FL: Hilltop House Publishing, 2013), 43–47. Used by permission.

be a sign to you: You will find a baby wrapped in cloths and lying in a manger." (Luke 2:10–12)

Just believe that I am in the Father and the Father is in me. Or at least believe because of the work you have seen me do. (John 14:11 NLT)

God also testified to it [this great salvation] by signs, wonders and various miracles, and by gifts of the Holy Spirit distributed according to his will. (Hebrews 2:4)

For he has set a day when he will judge the world with justice by the man he has appointed. He has given proof of this to everyone by raising him from the dead. (Acts 17:31)

Appendix I

SCRIPTURE ON END TIMES & GOOD THINGS TO COME

These Scripture verses are just a few of many regarding these topics.

Good News:

No eye has seen, no ear has heard, and no mind has imagined what God has prepared for those who love him. (1 Corinthians 2:9 NLT)

Difficult News:

But mark this: There will be terrible times in the last days. (2 Timothy 3:1)

Stand firm, and you will win life. (Luke 21:19)

Good News to Come:

The saying is trustworthy, for: If we have died with him, we will also live with him; if we endure, we will also reign with him; if we deny him, he also will deny us. (2 Timothy 2:11-12 ESV)

See, I will create new heavens and a new earth. (Isaiah 65:17)

There are many rooms in my Father's house. I wouldn't tell you this, unless it was true. I am going there to prepare a place for each of you. After I have done this, I will come back and take you with me. Then we will be together. (John 14:2-3 CEV)

His master said to him, "Well done, good and faithful servant. You have been faithful over a little; I will set you over much. Enter into the joy of your master." (Matthew 25:21 ESV)

I heard a loud shout from the throne, saying, "Look, God's home is now among his people! He will live with them, and they will be his people. God himself will be with them. He will wipe every tear from their eyes, and there will be no more death or sorrow or crying or pain. All these things are gone forever." (Revelation 21:3–4 NLT)

Topical Index

12 Steps, the
    alignment with Scripture, 100–101, 190, 194, 213n52
    explanation of, 108–118, 253–254
    list of, 250–251
    sexual-addiction groups and, 173
    uses of, 215, 217
12 Step meetings, Alcoholics Anonymous (AA), 31, 78–81, 91, 92, 94, 118, 137, 159, 197, 199, 251–254

A
accepted and complete in Christ, 31, 258
addiction, 56, 67–69, 82, 106, 109, 159–160, 168, 239–240, 254–257
addiction, effect on family members, 154–155. *See also* codependency
admit, 30, 69, 74, 109, 111–115. *See also* honesty
admitting guilt. *See* confession of sin
Al-Anon, 56, 212, 251. *See also* 12 Step meetings
Alcoholics Anonymous (AA), 29–30, 56, 77–81, 92, 95, 111, 137, 142, 190, 253–257. *See also* 12 Step meetings, Alcoholics Anonymous (AA)
alcoholism, 17–18, 56, 61–62, 71, 76, 104–105, 214n53. *See also* addiction
anger, 86–87, 115, 212, 213, 214–215, 221
assurance of salvation, 85, 234–235

B
baptism, 96–97
blame-shifting, 68, 71, 84, 110, 113
blessings of God, 88, 133–164, 240–243, 258–261

C
codependency, 154–155, 255–256
confession of sin, 20, 103, 113–115, 172, 260–261
conformed to Christ. *See* transformation into image of Christ
conviction, 39, 51

D
daily spiritual review, 102–103
daydreaming and fantasies, 168–169
dealing with repentant offenders, 201–202
denial, 17–18, 30, 31, 56, 68–69, 72, 79, 255
Discovery meetings, 159, 183n42, 206–210

E
emotions, too many to list

F
family patterns, healthy, unhealthy, 255–256
forgive, forgiven, forgiving, too many to list

G
going around the desert, 92, 94, 141
gospel, the, 36–37, 240
grace of God
    definition of, 98
    extended through Christians, 99–100
    gifts of God and, 105–107, 145–146

mercy of God and, 92–93,
102–104, 106, 199, 239
providence of God and, 39–41, 50,
58, 71, 102, 104–105, 107, 173
sanctification and, 43, 129–130,
136, 203
as shown in Scripture, 100–101
trials as means of, 69
guilt, 38, 73, 106, 170, 172, 180, 182,
185, 220, 260–261. *See also* shame

H
healing, 184, 189–190, 191, 199, 201,
223–224, 230–231. *See also* renewal
honesty, 82–83, 91, 94, 103, 171–172
hospitality, 156–165
humble, humility, 79, 90, 217, 260–261

I
ick, the, 255

J
Jesus
revealed, 21, 74, 100–102, 142,
149–150, 176–177, 191, 257–258
love and salvation 37, 208–209,
229–231, 234, 240n62
too many more to list
judging others, 51, 90–91, 93, 208, 213,
221
judgment, God's, 213, 221

L
lies, 31, 170, 175, 180, 184–185, 187,
220, 261
Life Action Ministries, 171, 172
light of God (over darkness and sin),
201, 261
listening to God, 150–152, 180–181,
240. *See also* prayer
love of God, 59, 106, 147, 152, 221,
240, 257, 258
loving God, 147–153

low self-esteem, 82, 168–178, 181–182,
197, 220, 254, 256–257. *See also*
pornography, addiction to
lust, 169–170

M
making amends, 116–117

N
new birth. *See* salvation
new life. *See* renewal

O
obedience to God, 192–199
one day at a time, 81

P
pain-shame-addiction cycle, 255
pastors, role of, 207–208
peace of God. *See also* healing
amid troubles, 39
Christian's general experience of,
93, 115, 145, 200, 253
as a result of obedience, 73, 88, 97,
113, 117, 199, 214, 236
in salvation, 74, 104
Transformation Prayer Ministry
and, 179–191, 203
Perfect Christian Behavior, 90–91, 93
performance-based Christianity, 91,
93, 95
pornography, addiction to, 168–178
prayer. *See also* Transformation Prayer
Ministry (TPM)
12 Steps and, 250
Christian habits of, 80, 99
commands in Scripture, 260
confession and, 113–114, 198
desperation and, 20
fasting and, 239–240
formed from Scripture, 142
hearing from God and, 139, 148,
150–152, 194–196, 217, 220–221.

See also listening to God
help, 58
invitation and response, 38, 72, 105, 230, 234–235
as regular practice of Christians, 102, 111
results of, 100, 135, 160–162, 170, 199–200
salvation, 63, 227, 230, 233
sin, hinders, 213
for wisdom and help, 58, 83, 85, 117, 129, 135, 138, 145, 172
pride, 72, 73, 97, 110, 114–115, 150, 214
proof and evidence of God, 20, 264–265
protection of God, 88, 185–186

R
rationalization. *See* denial
rebellion, 66–67, 69
rededicate, 234–235
renewal
baptism and, 96
as effect of salvation, 105
promises in Scripture of, 259
salvation and, 73, 118, 188
sanctification and, 103–104, 109–110, 184, 191, 223–224
restoration. *See* renewal

S
salvation, 73, 85, 105, 110, 217, 229–230, 233–234
salvation prayer, 230
sanctification. *See* renewal; transformation into image of Christ
self-examination. *See* honesty
self-worth, 23, 31–32, 114–115, 168–178, 181–182, 197, 220, 256–257, 258–259. *See also* accepted and complete in Christ; low self-esteem

sex addiction (SA). *See* Sexaholics Anonymous
Sexaholics Anonymous groups 173, 177–178, 197, 199, 251–257. *See also* pornography, addiction to Sexaholics Anonymous "The White Book," 170n34, 173–174
shame, 20, 25, 31, 38, 43, 91, 94, 182–183, 201, 255
spiritual birth, 229
spiritual warfare, 75, 88, 184–185
surrendering to God, 38, 66–75, 95, 97, 102, 110, 112, 144, 195, 238

T
thoughts, too many to list
tithing, 131–132
transformation into image of Christ, 101–102, 191, 208, 223–224, 262–263. *See also* healing; renewal
Transformation Prayer Ministry (TPM), 179–191, 199, 201, 202–203, 209–210, 219–221, 223n56
truth of God, 184–186
truth sandwich, 86, 153
truthfulness. *See* honesty
Twelve Steps, the. *See* 12 Steps, the
Twelve Step meetings. *See* 12 Step meetings, Alcoholics Anonymous (AA)

U
unworthiness. *See* low self-esteem

W
White Book, The. *See* Sexaholics Anonymous "The White Book"
will of God, 101, 117–118, 138–139
wisdom of God, 112, 135–136, 180, 199–200
worry, 151–152
worth, our, 255–257
worthlessness. See low self-esteem

We pray that you have been touched by
Conspiracy of Grace: A Wild Tale of Transformation.
We would love for you to help us and others by
sharing a good review on Amazon,
telling your friends and family, and
tweeting and posting on social media.
Spread the word that *Conspiracy of Grace*
can be purchased at Amazon.com
or any favorite bookstore.

• • •

For more helpful, inspirational articles from Dale,
please visit **ConspiracyofGrace.com**.
In particular, check out:
"Grace for Broken Pastors & Their Churches,"
"Family Patterns—Healthy versus Unhealthy Patterns," and
"Encouraging Ideas for Growing in God's Grace."

www.ingramcontent.com/pod-product-compliance
Lightning Source LLC
Chambersburg PA
CBHW052014290426
44112CB00014B/2241